WHAT PEOPLE ARE SAYING ABOUT *PREACHING THAT CHANGES LIVES*:

"This volume is must reading for expositors who would both explain the text and apply the text."—***Dr. Richard Mayhue***, *Senior VP and Dean of the Master's Seminary and Senior VP and Provost of the Master's College*

"This book will be a powerful tool in the hands of any person called to communicate the Word of God to this generation. I highly recommend it." —***Greg Laurie***, *Pastor of the Harvest Christian Fellowship in Riverside, California*

"In a day when reaching people and building the church has become far too horizontal, Mike Fabarez call us back to our calling—Preach the Word! Here's a book that reminds us not just what and why we preach, but how to do it effectively."—***Dr. James MacDonald***, *Pastor of the Harvest Bible Chapel in Rolling Meadows, Illinois, and host of "Walk in the Word" radio program*

"In *Preaching That Changes Lives*, Pastor Mike Fabarez provides a powerful antidote to the instant gratification and incessant novelty that characterize much of the preaching in today's fast-food culture."—***Hank Hanegraaff***, *host of the "Bible Answer Man" radio program and president of the Christian Research Institute*

"A form of preaching that distorts it by overemphasizing biblical theology at the expense of application permeates many seminaries. *Preaching That Changes Lives* is a needed remedy. Moreover, it is just the kind of helpful step-by-step guide that many preachers are looking for (and others ought to be!) I highly recommend it. Get it, study it, follow it!"—***Jay Adams***, *author of* Preaching with Purpose *and 60 other books; former pastor and former professor of homiletics and counseling at Westminster Theological Seminary in Philadelphia*

"Men and women caught on the barbed wire of life today are eager to hear a sure word from God. *Preaching That Changes Lives* is a welcomed help for this important task."—***Dr. Haddon Robinson***, *Harold John Ockenga Distinguished Professor of Preaching at Gordon-Conwell Theological Seminary*

"Mike Fabarez understands that in order for our preaching to be instrumental in changing lives, we must be both didactic and practical. The book is loaded with helpful advice on how to achieve and maintain the equilibrium." —***John MacArthur***, *in his Foreword to the book*

Preaching That Changes Lives

Michael Fabarez

THOMAS NELSON PUBLISHERS

Nashville

Published in Nashville, Tennessee, by Thomas Nelson, Inc.

Book design and composition by Bob Bubnis, Booksetters, White House, Tennessee

Library of Congress Cataloging-in-Publication Data

Fabarez, Michael, 1964–
    Preaching that changes lives / Michael Fabarez.
        p. cm.
    Includes bibliographical references.
    ISBN 0-7852-4914-1
    1. Preaching. I. Title.

BV4211.3 .F33 2002   2002026428
252—dc21

Printed in the United States of America

1 2 3 4 5 6 7 — 06 05 04 03 02

Contents

FOREWORD

TRUE BIBLICAL PREACHING OUGHT TO BE A LIFE-CHANGING ENDEAVOR. THE conscientious preacher does not merely seek to impart abstract doctrine or plain facts to his people; he also pleads with them for heartfelt and earnest obedience. After all, to be hearers of the Word without being doers is to be dangerously deceived (James 1:22). And one sure way for preachers to cultivate hearers-only is to deliver nothing more than dry, didactic lectures—dull performances for the intellectually curious. That is not biblical preaching, no matter how sound the teaching may be on an academic level.

Understand, I am not suggesting that sound doctrine and careful teaching are of secondary importance. Aptness to teach and doctrinal skill are basic requirements for every elder (1 Timothy 3:2; Titus 1:9). At the heart of the Great Commission is this imperative: "Go ye therefore, and *teach* all nations" (Matthew 28:19). Make disciples. Cultivate learners. We cannot do that without the skilled and careful teaching of sound doctrine.

But the ultimate goal of our teaching ministry is not merely to fill people's heads with information; it is to press on their hearts the duty of obedience. Notice the rest of the Great Commission: "Teaching them *to observe all things whatsoever I have commanded you*" (v. 20, emphasis added).

All sound doctrine, when correctly understood and properly taught, is practical. The modern hard-line distinction between doctrinal and practical truth is artificial and unbiblical. Sound doctrine is the necessary foundation for godly living. Orthodoxy is essential to orthopraxy.

We have imposed an artificial meaning on the word *doctrine*. We've made it something abstract and threatening, unrelated to daily living. That has given rise to the disastrous idea that "doctrinal" truth and "practical" truth are polar opposites. They are not. Notice that when the apostle Paul reminded Titus to speak the things that are proper for sound doctrine, he then enumerated several points of "doctrine" that many would class as "practical" issues:

. . . that the older men be sober, reverent, temperate, sound in faith, in love, in patience; the older women likewise, that they be reverent in behavior, not slanderers, not given to much wine, teachers of good things; that they admonish the young women to love their husbands, to love their children, to be discreet, chaste, homemakers, good, obedient to their own husbands, that the word of God may not be blasphemed. Likewise exhort the young men to be sober-minded, in all things showing yourself to be a pattern of good works; in doctrine showing integrity, reverence, incorruptibility, sound speech that cannot be condemned, that one who is an opponent may be ashamed, having nothing evil to say of you (Titus 2:2–8).

In fact, at the outset of his epistle to Titus, Paul characterized the Christian message as "the truth which accords with godliness" (1:1). He certainly stressed and defended the objective facts of the gospel and sound doctrine (3:3–7). But he placed equal stress on the truth that "those who have believed in God should be careful to maintain good works" (v. 8).

This was always Paul's approach. His epistle to the Romans, for example, begins with eleven chapters of systematic theology—abstract doctrine. He scales incredible heights of truth, dealing with such doctrines as human depravity, justification by faith, sin, righteousness, sanctification, and the security of the believer—all culminating in 11:33–36, where he says, "Oh, the depth of the riches both of the wisdom and knowledge of God! How unsearchable are His judgments and His ways past finding out! 'For who has known the mind of the LORD? Or who has become His counselor?' 'Or who has first given to Him And it shall be repaid to him?' For of Him and through Him and to Him are all things, to whom be glory forever. Amen."

But the epistle doesn't stop with that benediction. Paul doesn't leave the discussion in the realm of the abstract. Beginning in chapter 12, he turns immediately to the practical consequences of the doctrine of the first eleven chapters. No passage in Scripture captures the Christian's responsibility in the face of truth more clearly than Romans 12:1-2. Resting on eleven chapters of profound doctrine, Paul calls each believer to a supreme act of spiritual worship—giving oneself as a living sacrifice. Doctrine gives rise to dedication to Christ, the greatest practical act. And the remainder of the Book of Romans goes on to exhort the Romans to apply practically the truth he has dealt with in the early chapters.

Paul follows the same pattern in Galatians, Ephesians, Philippians, Colossians, and 1 Thessalonians. The doctrinal message comes first. Upon that foundation he builds the practical application, making the logical connection with the word *therefore* (Romans 12:1; Galatians 5:1; Ephesians 4:1; Philippians 2:1) or *then* (Colossians 3:1; 1 Thessalonians 4:1).

Here's a principle all preachers would do well to remember: After you have studied and taught a doctrine, there is always a *therefore*. A major part of the preacher's task is to highlight the *therefore* and press on his hearers their duty to obey.

In other words, truly biblical preaching must be *both* didactic and practical. The two things are not opposed to one another. They are, however, notoriously difficult to keep in balance. Those who stress sound doctrine sometimes neglect the passion and pleading that are necessary parts of biblical preaching (cf. 2 Corinthians 5:11, 20; Luke 14:23). And those who stress practical matters too often neglect to build the foundation of sound doctrine.

To be lopsided in either direction is a serious mistake. Practical insights, gimmicks, and illustrations mean little if they're not attached to divine principle. There's no basis for godly behavior apart from the truth of God's Word. Before the preacher asks anyone to perform a certain duty, he must first deal with doctrine. He must develop his message around theological themes and draw out the principles of the texts. Then the truth can be applied.

Similarly, doctrine without exhortation is lame, being deprived of the whole point. The preacher who delivers a theological lecture or an academic analysis of some passage of Scripture and then sits down without pressing the practical ramifications of the truth on his hearers has not finished his task.

I'm thankful for the careful way in which Mike Fabarez has sought to maintain the balance in this book. He understands that in order for our preaching to be instrumental in changing lives, we must be *both* didactic and practical. The book is loaded with helpful advice on how to achieve and maintain the equilibrium. This is a wonderful resource for all pastors and teachers, regardless of their stage in ministry. My prayer is that it will be taken to heart by all who read it.

—*John MacArthur*

INTRODUCTION

THIS WEEKEND PREACHERS ALL OVER THE WORLD WILL STAND BEFORE PEOPLE congregated in churches large and small and attempt to fulfill Christ's call to His undershepherds to "preach the word" (2 Tim. 4:2). Their sermons will be delivered, their stories told, their cross-references referenced, and their illustrations carefully drawn. Despite their monumental efforts, much of their preaching will never be heard—at least not in a biblical sense.

When Jesus spoke of "hearing the word," He made a radical distinction between delivering the sermon to His audience's ears and delivering the sermon to affect their lives. In reference to His own preaching, Jesus often said, "He who has ears to hear, let him hear!"[1] Obviously He meant something far more than people having an auditory experience, or even a mere learning experience. Jesus' goal in preaching was to produce a "life-changing" experience.

At the conclusion of His longest recorded sermon, Jesus made His expectations crystal clear when He said:

> Therefore whoever hears these sayings of Mine, and does them, I will liken him to a wise man who built his house on the rock: and the rain descended, the floods came, and the winds blew and beat on that house; and it did not fall, for it was founded on the rock. But everyone who hears these sayings of Mine, and does not do them, will be like a foolish man who built his house on the sand: and the rain descended, the floods came, and the winds blew and beat on that house; and it fell. And great was its fall (Matt. 7:24–27).[2]

To Jesus, successful preaching was not simply to disseminate truth. Successful preaching was not bringing the congregation to an understanding of the truth. To Jesus, an effective sermon resulted in people grasping truth *and putting it into action!*

Biblical preaching always aims to change lives. If this is not the conscious goal of the preacher, then the preacher will miss the very point of his calling. And don't underestimate how easy that is to miss. After all, many responses can send the preacher home "warmed and filled." A heartfelt "I get it," or "That made sense," or "That was the best sermon I ever heard" can leave the average preacher feeling quite content. He tells himself that at least on this day he has hit the bull's-eye and accomplished his goal. In reality, the New Testament warns us that this type of feedback may cloud the real issue. Yes, we may have been understood and our sermon may have been enthusiastically embraced. But unless our preaching has changed the lives of the people in our pews, then everyone involved has been deceived. In his typically stinging style, A. W. Tozer forcefully makes the point:

> Bible teaching without moral application could be worse than no teaching at all and could result in positive injury to the hearers. What is generally overlooked is that truth as set forth in the Christian Scriptures is a moral thing; it is not addressed to the intellect only, but to the will also. It addresses itself to the total man, and its obligations cannot be discharged by grasping it mentally. Truth engages the citadel of the human heart and is not satisfied until it has conquered everything there.[3]

This concern is not a new one. James warns the earliest church against the self-deception of simply cogitating on a biblical message without consistently putting it into practice:

> But be doers of the word, and not hearers only, deceiving yourselves. For if anyone is a hearer of the word and not a doer, he is like a man observing his natural face in a mirror; for he observes himself, goes away, and immediately forgets what kind of man he was. But he who looks into the perfect law of liberty and continues in it, and is not a forgetful hearer but a doer of the work, this one will be blessed in what he does (James 1:22–25).

Unfortunately, "hearing only," is the pinnacle of responsiveness reached by too many people week after week. Some of the blame for this failure in preaching can be rightly attributed to the hardness of the pew-warmers' hearts. On the other hand, those of us who fail to deliver biblical messages with the clarity and urgency of Jesus and James must shoulder a great deal of the blame.

Impotent Preaching

Debating who is at greater fault for this failure, the congregant or the preacher, may lead to a split decision. However, the fact that today's preaching fails to change lives should be obvious to everyone, and not only is it failing, it is failing at an alarming rate. The percentage of people attending church these days is holding steady.[4] That means that millions of people sit under the teaching of hundreds of thousands of pastors, who collectively preach countless sermons to them every year. Assuming that most of these people are exposed to the word, it appears from the evidence that they are "putting it into action" less than ever before. A recent Barna Group report claimed that "among born-again Christians, 27 percent are currently or have previously been divorced, compared to 24 percent among adults who are not born-again."[5] In an article on high-profile Christian infidelity, *Focus on the Family* reported, "recent data from several leading demographic agencies indicate that no region of the nation has a higher divorce rate than the Bible Belt."[6] Planned Parenthood's Alan Guttmacher Institute reports that one in five women having abortions is a professing born-again or evangelical Christian.[7] According to a Zogby poll,[8] Internet pornography sites have been visited by nearly 18 percent of surveyed born-again Christians—just two percent below the national average. If preaching is intended to change lives, then it is missing its mark in the modern church.

What This Book Is All About

While some of the failure of modern preaching is traceable to those who are listening to it, much is not. In Jesus' parable regarding the four kinds of listeners (hard, shallow, thorny, and good), the constant factor assumed in every case is a potent and properly cast seed. Even to the unfruitful soils, the powerful, life-changing message is rightly presented. While assumed in the parable of the soils, its proper presentation certainly cannot be assumed today.

In an effort to produce the fruit of righteousness, the apostle Paul goes to great lengths to train his pastoral protégés to make sure they do their part. He anticipates that some people will not "endure sound doctrine" and will prefer to "have their ears tickled," so he warns his disciples to "be watchful in all things" (2 Tim. 4:3–5). He wants them to "fulfill [their] ministry" so no fruitless seed can ever be traced to their hand.

To be faithful and effective preachers, we must ensure that we are doing all that *we* can in every sermon to assist our people in becoming "doers of the word." We must be sure that we are not just presenting biblical information or simply lecturing about the Bible. Rather, we must verify that we are actually *preaching*. We must unabashedly do what all great preachers have always done—we must cause our people to gaze face to face in the mirror of James 1:23 and commit themselves to change in the area which God's Word is addressing to them each week.

Tacking on a few scant applicational thoughts at the end of a sermon certainly will not accomplish this goal. The transformational call of texts we preach must saturate our sermons. Application must be strategically thought out as we master the passage to be preached, and we must pray them through on the floor of our studies. It must be skillfully presented in every element of each point, and it must continue as our urgent concern in our pastoral care. Real biblical preaching brings about changes that conform a person to the image of Christ.

Truth without application is inadequate. As J. I. Packer put it, "Preaching is essentially teaching plus application . . . where the *plus* is lacking something less than preaching takes place."[9] Broadus concurs, "The application in a sermon is not merely an appendage to the discussion or a subordinate part of it, but is the main thing."[10] Spurgeon poignantly adds, "Where the application begins, there the sermon begins."[11] Packer aptly summarizes the concern:

> Far too many pulpit discourses have been put together on wrong principles. . . . Some have expounded biblical doctrine without applying it, thus qualifying as lectures rather than preachments (for lecturing aims only to clear the head, while preaching seeks to change the life); some have been no more than addresses focusing the present self-awareness of the listeners, but not at any stage confronting them with the Word of God. . . . Such discourses are less than preaching . . . but because they were announced as sermons they are treated as preaching and people's idea of preaching gets formed in terms of them, so that the true conception of preaching is forgotten.[12]

This book is intended to be a reminder—a humble yet forthright plea to regain what has been so widely forgotten. Regaining ground in effective application is critically important, not only for our hearers' sake, but more importantly for Christ's sake. As Bryan Chapell states:

> Preaching without application may serve the mind, but preaching with application requires service to Christ. Application makes Jesus the center of a sermon's exhortation as well as the focus of its explanation.[13]

Please don't read this book in search of a homiletics text, or as a guide to exegesis and sermon construction. Nor should this book be the first you have ever read on the topic of preaching. I assume you already possess a general knowledge of the principles of sermon preparation.[14] Rather, my goal is to challenge you to reevaluate and consider your current practice of preaching through the matrix of application.

It is my contention that there is a great need for this kind of reevaluation. And I am not alone. Haddon Robinson laments, "Many homileticians have not given application the attention it deserves."[15] William Klein adds:

> Despite the importance of application, few modern evangelical scholars have focused on this topic. In fact, most hermeneutic textbooks give it only brief coverage, and many major commentary series only mention application with passing remarks to help readers bridge the gap from the biblical world to the modern world. Perhaps many assume that sound application is more "caught than taught." This is probably true, but sound application often seems hard to find, much less to catch![16]

It is my prayer that this book assists you in presenting sermons that are not only accurate but also life-changing. I trust that you will assess your preaching honestly as you read this book and adjust any part of your procedure in an effort to make your congregants not just hearers, but doers of the word. To do so, you will need to give attention to life-changing application in three primary areas of your ministry: your preparation, your preaching, and your follow-through. Eventually, it will lead you to develop a new pattern of *preparing* to change lives, *preaching* to change lives, *and following through* to change lives.

PART ONE

RETHINK YOUR TASK

CHAPTER ONE

Understand the Life-changing Power of Preaching

THE MOST IMPORTANT LESSON I LEARNED DURING MY TIME IN BIBLE COLLEGE WAS not learned on campus, and it was not learned from a faculty member. During a summer break from college I was asked to help teach a group study in my home church. I was to alternately team-teach with a pickup-driving construction worker who had no formal Bible education. I was certain my theological training equipped me to plunge that Bible study class to new depths of understanding in God's Word.

My partner taught the first week, and after class I was happy to offer my "helpful" critique. I freely and generously shared my newfound theological and doctrinal insights on the passage with him, since he obviously lacked the time and the resources to elucidate these truths to our eager audience.

The next week I was ready. I jammed as much information as a fast-talking college student could into my fifty minutes of air time. With quiet confidence I assured myself that I had given the group the best expositional message on that passage they had ever heard.

Now it was time for my partner to evaluate my message and share his feedback on my seamless teaching technique. His painfully simple critique has reverberated in my mind ever since. He asked, in a slightly confused tone, "So what was it that God wanted us to *do* as a result of that message?"

I had no answer.

All delusions of grandeur regarding my sermon instantly drained from my heart. He had succinctly nailed the problem, and it was no small imperfection. It was a fatal flaw. Whatever I did in that hour of ministry, it fell far short of what God intended preaching to do. I realized in that instant, and have not since forgotten, that all the theological knowledge in the world is no match for a pickup-driving construction worker with just one biblical truth and the passion to see his audience transformed.

A TRENDY MISTAKE

Someone has always been ready to tell the church to keep quiet. The world has never wanted to hear the implications of God's truth, boldly and authoritatively proclaimed by His spokesmen. Unfortunately, in our day, the pressure is not just from outside the church. In too many places the disdain for preaching pervades the pew just as it does our post-modern society. Though the church still tolerates a man behind the pulpit, she has become quite concerned as to what he says, how he says it, and how much of her time he takes to say it!

It hasn't always been this way. A retooling of the modern church service has been hammered out in America's seminaries over the past few decades. Up-and-coming churchmen—many with a God-given passion and an untapped gift to preach—are taught to keep their Bible lecture (*if* retained as part of the Sunday service) positive, palatable, trendy, and above all, short. One author read by seminarians exhorts the preacher to "limit [his] sermons to 20 minutes . . . and don't forget to keep [the] messages light and informal, liberally sprinkling them with humor and personal anecdotes."[1]

A popular mantra rings, "If we are to win our generation we must redefine how church is done." Best-selling titles by liberals and conservatives warn us that it is time for the church to "change or die!" No longer is church the place where God confronts and comforts His people by means of weekly exposition and application of His timeless Word. It is now a gathering driven and shaped by the latest marketing techniques, based on focus groups and polling data.

These Sunday morning changes have been dramatic. Admittedly, the initial reaction of many has been favorable. Church is more fun. The music is better. The skits break up monotony. The multimedia looks really cool. Best of all, the sermons are definitely more tolerable. Church has changed, but has it changed churchgoers? As our culture continues its downward spiral, we have little data to demonstrate that our people in the pews are any holier today than their unchurched counterparts!

J. I. Packer unloads his bold commentary on our modern experiment when he writes, "I suspect that the widespread perplexity today as to the relevance of the New Testament gospel should be seen as God's judgment on

4

two generations of inadequate preaching by inadequate preachers."[2] Note this stinging indictment does not point to a deficiency in music or marketing. It is aimed at the heart of what has been sacrificed in our pulpits in recent years. As D. A. Carson declares, "A want of biblical preaching is an announcement of death" for the church.[3]

We are certainly not the first generation to lose sight of this precious provision of God. In Jeremiah's day, plenty of those who claimed to speak for God were willing to adjust their message and methods to accommodate their hearers' tastes and preferences. Their savvy philosophy of preaching would have qualified them as experts to lead the latest "How to Grow Your Congregation in a Modern Jewish Society" seminars. Yet God made it clear He would not tolerate the pawning of solid biblical preaching for "ministerial relevance." So disdainful was He of this practice that God commanded His people, "Do not listen to the words of the prophets who prophesy to you. . . . For who has stood in the counsel of the LORD, and has perceived and heard His word?" (Jer. 23:16, 18).

The Bible does not call pastor-teachers to be entertainers, movie directors, or psychologists. God calls His shepherds to be preachers. He calls them to stand in the gap and skillfully proclaim His Word. In 2 Timothy 4:1–5, God explicitly calls them to preach the Word, in season and out of season. He calls them to convince, rebuke, and exhort—carefully instructing the church with great patience. He calls them to continue to do so even when a generation refuses to put up with sound doctrine. He calls them to endure hardship that may be incurred by their faithful exposition of His Word. He calls them to faithfully discharge their ministry even when congregants flock to other teachers who will say what their itching ears want to hear.

Over a century ago Edwin Dargan summarized the historic problem and offered hope.

> The decline of spiritual life and activity in the churches is commonly accompanied by a lifeless, formal, unfruitful preaching, and this is partly as cause, partly as effect. On the other hand, the great revivals of Christian history can most usually be traced to the work of the pulpit, and in their progress they have developed and rendered possible a high order of preaching.[4]

Though the church may be enhanced by a few creative, well-placed amenities, be assured she cannot survive without the consistent, accurate, and authoritative preaching that intends, in every instance, to transform its hearers. Every preacher must be fully assured that his calling to preach is essential to the health of the church, and is unmitigated by modern culture or trends in society.

GOD'S POWERFUL TOOL

If we need to be reminded of the power of biblical preaching, all we need to do is reacquaint ourselves with the explosive impact of preaching in the early church. Jesus gave only one tool to His band of former fishermen and tax-collectors, and by this preaching in the power of the Holy Spirit they subsequently turned the ancient world upside down.[5] Not surprisingly, this tool has continued to transform entire cultures whenever it has been faithfully and persistently wielded. William Sangster writes:

> Confidence in preaching is not so very hard to maintain. . . . If he treasures up the proofs which God gives him of the power of preaching, and if he remembers clearly what someone's preaching did for him, he will not slide into supposing that it is a useless and parasitic occupation. When he thinks on all that God has done by preaching through the years—Gregory of Nazianzus, Chrysostom, Ambrose, Bernard of Clairvaux, Wycliffe, Edwards, Spurgeon, Hugh Price Hughes, and tens of thousands of lesser known men—he will not wave it aside as "sound and fury, signifying nothing."[6]

We must take Sangster's counsel. Recall the effects of powerful preaching on your own life. Have you forgotten the life-changing impact of sermons you have heard? Do you continue to be challenged and changed by the preaching of your peers and the great preachers of the past?

Like many of you, it was through the means of a sermon that I first repented of my sin and put my trust in Christ. As a result of a sermon I laid aside my secular ambitions. As a result of a sermon I determined to follow Christ into professional ministry. By means of dozens of subsequent sermons God has continued to realign, refocus, and redirect my life. Who could not attest to similar experiences as the result of powerful, God-ordained, life-changing preaching? Sangster concludes:

> Preaching is a constant agent of the divine power by which the greatest miracle God ever works is wrought and wrought again. God uses it *to change lives.* It is hard for any mortal to tell, either of himself or of others, what forces have worked upon him to issue in some dramatic change of life, but many affirm that the occasion, and no small part of the cause, was *one* sermon.[7]

We must never underestimate, or by our tone or manner antiquate, the timeless power of biblical preaching. By it God transforms His people, so He calls all preachers everywhere to heed that first-century commission:

> In the presence of God and of Christ Jesus, who will judge the living and the dead, and in view of his appearing and his kingdom,

I give you this charge: Preach the Word; be prepared in season and out of season; correct, rebuke and encourage—with great patience and careful instruction. (2 Timothy 4:1–2 NIV)

GOD'S POWERFUL DESCRIPTION

Even a cursory overview of the words used by the Holy Spirit to describe our task reflects the power God has vested in preaching. There are several Greek words in the New Testament that represent the "preaching" task of the preacher.[8] The most common word to translate into English "preach" or "preaching" is the word used in 2 Timothy 4:2 where Paul commands Timothy to "preach (*kerysso*) the word."

Kerysso

When Timothy and other second-generation preachers were exhorted by the apostles to *kerysso*[9] the word, they understood that a clearly mandated divine power accompanied the command. To *kerysso* the word of God was to proclaim it or herald it as an ambassador or royal representative.[10] The importance and relevance of the message is bound up in the use of *kerysso*. The word conjures the image of a crowd of citizens gathering in a distant ancient village to hear from the king through the proclamation of his royal spokesman. Seen in this light, preaching must *never* be relegated to a secondary role in the church service. *Kerysso* depicts an act that is always relevant, always important, and always powerful. When the ambassador proclaims the message of the king, the royal citizens cannot be passive. They are compelled by the nature of the communiqué to respond!

The Angello Family of Words

The cognate words *euangelizo, katangello,* and *anangello* are important New Testament words depicting the power, the importance, and the urgency of our preaching task. *Euangelizo*[11] is found in Acts 15:35, where we are told, "Paul and Barnabas also remained in Antioch, teaching and preaching (*euangelizo*) the word of the Lord, with many others also." Its first cousin, *katangello,*[12] is used by Paul in Colossians 1:28 as he tells the young church that he and Timothy were called to "preach" (*katangello*) Christ, "warning every man and teaching every man in all wisdom, that we may present every man perfect in Christ Jesus." The third cognate is found in Acts 20:20. Here Paul recounts his ministry in Ephesus by saying, "I kept nothing back that was helpful, but proclaimed (*anangello*) it to you, and taught you publicly and from house to house."[13]

All three words naturally draw our linguistic minds toward the root word transliterated "angel"—a heavenly messenger dispatched by God to take to mankind a message from the King of kings. All three connote a supremely important announcement. *Euangelizo* adds the idea of a "good" announcement, reminding us (most often in an evangelistic context) that the message proclaimed is good, and brings a good result when one properly responds to it.

Didasko

The word *didasko,* commonly translated "to teach," is often found in connection with *kerysso* and the *angello* cognates. *Didasko* means more than just the transmission of information. In a biblical context, the word has in view an intended impact on the recipient's behavior. Note its reference in the commission of Christ at the end of Matthew's Gospel:

> Go therefore and make disciples of all nations, baptizing them in the name of the Father and of the Son and of the Holy Spirit, teaching (*didasko*) them to observe all things that I have commanded you; and lo, I am with you always, even to the end of the age (Matt. 28:19–20).

Clearly, what Jesus had in mind was much more than a dry recitation of biblical facts. He wanted them to proclaim a life-changing message—a message that would move His followers to live a life in accordance with the imperatives He had entrusted to them.

Some have categorized *teaching* as preaching to Christians, and *preaching* as gospel preaching to non-Christians. Others label *teaching* a non-emotional lecture that speaks to the mind, and *preaching* as a polished and passionate proclamation that speaks to the heart. Though there may be stylistic distinctions between modern evangelistic preaching, Sunday school lectures, and the pastor's sermon, the *biblical differences are inconsequential.* The words *kerysso, euangelizo, katangello, anangello* and *didasko,* along with a host of other New Testament words,[14] all add to our understanding of the powerful, authoritative, and life-changing oration the preacher is called to deliver to God's people.

PAUL'S HOMILETICS CLASS

Paul was careful to point out to his students that preaching the Word should stimulate the listener to act. His instruction regarding preaching was surrounded with verbs that never let the young preacher lose sight of this goal. In 2 Timothy 4:2, Paul crystallizes Timothy's command to "preach the word" with the clarifying verbs *convince, rebuke,* and *exhort.*

The Greek word *elencho,* translated "convince" or "reprove," is used by Jesus in Matthew 18:15 to explain how to point out a brother's sin and move him to change his behavior. Jesus said to "go and tell him his fault (*elencho*)," that is, "go to show him his sin and summon him to repentance."[15] James equates exposure to preaching with a stark reflection of ourselves in a mirror (James 1:22–24). In His Word, God calls for our preaching to not only affirm what is honorable, but also expose the imperfections of our audience. We must boldly point out what needs *to be* changed, and then help them *to* change.

The second clarifying word Paul uses is the word *epitimao*, translated "rebuke." This word also focuses on the change of behavior Timothy should expect in the lives of his hearers. Lexicographers define the word as speaking or warning "in order to prevent an action or bring one to an end."[16] It is the word used to describe Christ's command to the wind and the waves to *cease their activity* (Matt. 8:26; Mark 4:39; Luke 8:24).

Paul employs a third word, *parakaleo,* to describe the preaching event often translated "exhort," "urge," or "beseech." Though the use of this word is broad in the New Testament, in this context it complements the previous two verbs while conveying an intensity not communicated by them. This is implied in Paul's use of the word in 1 Timothy 1:3 when he "urges" (*parakaleo*) Timothy to remain in Ephesus and teach, in Ephesians 4:1 when he "beseeches" (*parakaleo*) Christians in Ephesus to live a life worthy of their calling, and in Romans 12:1 when Paul "beseeches" (*parakaleo*) the Roman Christians to offer themselves to God as living sacrifices. In each case it's obvious that Paul expects the act of preaching to make a distinct difference in the lives of those who hear.

OUR CHALLENGE

A good sermon is one that bears fruit—a message from God that transforms believers' lives. A good sermon, once ingested by the hearer and molded by the Holy Spirit, will prompt its audience to abandon a sinful thought, value, or behavior. Likewise, it will embolden the hearers to walk down paths of righteousness previously untraveled.

We, as pastor-teachers, need to focus on our call to preach messages that *change lives*. Our members need to know we are going to be faithful to that call whether they like it or not—and if they cooperate with the Holy Spirit, *lives will change*.

Throwing down this gauntlet means we can no longer evaluate our sermons solely on the basis of theological or exegetical soundness. It isn't enough to drive home from church basking in self-congratulation because our outline was memorable, or because we were fluent and articulate. We must resist the temptation of instant gratification based on soundness of delivery, or even content. *Instead, we must purpose to evaluate every sermon we preach in light of the biblical change it brings about in the lives of our congregants!*

Look back again. Recall the sermons you judged as flops—even *you* couldn't wait until the clock struck twelve! Yet in time you came to find how God used those sermons to significantly touch lives. Evaluating a sermon on technical merit is important, to be sure, but long after we've dissected our grammar we should witness real change in the lives of the people God has placed in our hands.

A FAMINE IN THE LAND

Amos warned Israel of a coming famine—the kind of famine that would emaciate the human spirit, not the human frame. It was the kind of famine many churches are experiencing today. He warned:

> Behold, the days are coming, says the Lord God,
> That I will send a famine on the land,
> Not a famine of bread,
> Nor a thirst for water,
> But of hearing the words of the Lord.
> They shall wander from sea to sea,
> And from north to east;
> They shall run to and fro, seeking the word of the Lord,
> But shall not find it (Amos 8:11–12).

Sad to say, people are still searching for the words of the Lord. How can that be? Pastors are better trained, church budgets are bigger, and worship technology is on the cutting edge. Yet many Christians move from church to church in search of sermons that do more than affirm what they already know and stroke them for what they are already doing. Remarkably, they don't even realize the reason for their wanderings. God's people are hungry for His Word. The church has subsisted on the junk food of hollow platitudes for so long that it should not surprise us to see people come running at the sound of a dinner bell that calls them to a real biblical meal! If we want to meet the need of the hungry, we must feed them with God-breathed sermons that call for change.

I used to scratch my head when I saw churches growing *without* following the principles of contemporary church-growth recipes. How could a pastor preach for an hour every Sunday *and* unapologetically call his people to repentance? Wasn't it too much for him to expect his people to conform to the high standards of New Testament Christianity and expect the church to grow in numbers, too? Conventional church wisdom dooms such strategies to failure. A bold pulpit ministry, after all, is deemed a kiss of death. Yet week after week, inexplicably, their numbers grew.

There I was fresh out of seminary, standing at the crossroads of ministerial philosophy. I had inherited the leadership of a church that had long since seen its heyday. By now I had read all the hot books telling me how I could keep a dying church alive. In the midst of implementing these conventional CPR techniques, I faced a critical point in my own preaching ministry. I was struggling to follow a template that suppressed the very thing my own heart was longing for: God's Word, clearly taught and properly applied. I was trying to make the church relevant by following the trends and employing the gadgets, yet inside I ached to transfer to my people the life-changing relevance I found in my own daily study of God's Word.

With that realization, I had turned a corner in my own philosophy of ministry. I abandoned contemporary wisdom for an ancient call. I began to preach with the expectation of transformation. I began to present the Bible in the same way the Holy Spirit presented it to me each day—with the clarion call to understand and do what was expected of me.

Preaching with an expectation that people "do it" was a risky endeavor. At first, I thought this strategy could surely empty our little church completely! Yet I knew it was biblical. I told myself that, at worst, I'd go down satisfying the hearts of a few who would benefit from a biblical call to action.

How wrong I was—not about the strategy, but about its results! I soon realized there were more than a few thirsty hearts. I watched our people grow and mature. I watched new people flock to the church. I watched non-Christians putting their trust in Christ as a result of sermons that were neither sensitive to their eavesdropping nor aimed at the capriciousness of their felt needs. I watched my own mediocre preaching gifts being voraciously consumed, first by hundreds, then by thousands of people who were hungry—really hungry!

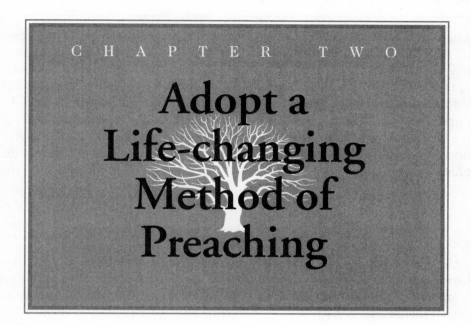

CHAPTER TWO

Adopt a Life-changing Method of Preaching

KARL MARX, WINSTON CHURCHILL, ABRAHAM LINCOLN, AND ADOLF HITLER collectively moved millions with their powerful and persuasive orations. Those who heard these men walked away with altered thoughts, beliefs, and behaviors after being exposed to such awesome arguments and skillful rhetoric.

There was a method underlying their delivery. These men, famous and infamous alike, spoke to align their audiences' minds and lives with their own thoughts, theories, and agendas. Their points of reference were varied and, of course, subjective; their speeches were fermentations of their own experiences, experiments, and all too often, of their own imaginations. Drawing from these, they spoke skillfully to effect change in people, culture, and society.

Those of us who preach the word of God likewise have the potential to effect change in people, culture, and society. The drastic difference is that we are called to do so from a singular, *divinely objective* point of reference. We are distinct from the world's orators in that we have a clearly delineated and divinely prescribed template. In 2 Timothy 4:2, Paul puts it as succinctly as possible: "Preach the Word."

As preachers, we are called to proclaim the word that God has already spoken—*nothing less, and certainly nothing more.* We are not commissioned to proclaim truth that is novel or unique. A particular truth may be one heard infrequently in our own corner of the church world, and it undoubtedly will revolutionize those who embrace it, but our calling is not to deliver the unique or even the profound. Preaching is, as D. A. Carson put it, "the clear, human utterance of *God's* message."[1] That is what we have been called to proclaim. As John Calvin wrote, "The office of teaching is committed to pastors for no other purpose than that God alone may be heard there."[2] Dietrich Bonhoeffer adds, "The sermon is not a discourse in which I develop my own thoughts; it is not my word but God's own word."[3] Considering the wellspring of truth in God's Word, we must choose to minimize our own experiences and opinions and relegate them at least to the periphery. In other words, earthly static must be eliminated from our message in order to give God's voice the preeminence it is due.

A PLEA FOR EXPOSITORY PREACHING

Almost every pastor has had some frustrating experiences with a church sound system. They tend to hum, hiss, squawk, or pop at the most inopportune times. My friend Ted told me about one of the worst sound system disasters ever.

His cordless microphone seemed to be working just fine, and the sermon was just kicking into high gear, when the crackling voice of a jaded truck driver began coming in trough the system. It was faint at first, so the pastor tried to drown out the intrusion by speaking louder. But as the trucker got nearer and nearer the church, the driver's voice over his powerful CB radio continued to get clearer and louder.

The parishioners began to chuckle, then laugh, and then blush. Apparently this lovesick truck driver had radioed "his lady" at a vulnerable moment in his life. Before the soundboard operator figured out what was happening and could shut the whole system down, the point of the sermon was long gone. The church members still think of it as a memorable occasion, but not because of anything the pastor said.

The goal of a church sound system is to provide a singular clarity for one voice during the weekly sermon. While most pastors would object to static and other interference on Sunday mornings, we should realize that God feels that way too. Like the sound system, our work each Sunday should provide a singular and crystal clarity for God's voice—not ours. That, in a nutshell, is what expository preaching is all about.

When we preach God's Word, it effects God's changes. When we allow some other point of reference to commingle with or replace God's message in our preaching, we risk effecting change of another sort. We may impact lives, as have great orators of the past, but we will fall far short of our highest call: being used by God to *transform* lives.

To make sure we produce God-ordained changes through our speaking, we must be resolute about our *source and method* of preaching.

14

Contemporary preachers may propose many popular methodological options, but we must adopt a form that will produce sermons that deliver nothing short of the "human utterance of God's message."

Expository preaching provides our best hope of attaining His desired results. Though a fair amount of confusion and debate surround the label "expository preaching,"[4] it is fair to sum up the essence of expository preaching in this way and with these primary components:[5]

(1) it clearly derives its content from the Bible;

(2) it accurately explains what the Bible is saying; and

(3) it effects the change God intends for the Bible to effect.

Being faithful to these components means I first exegete the biblical passage (the first component), then attempt to set forth or explain what God is saying (the second component). Of course, all of my preaching presupposes that God wants His Word to make a difference in the lives of those who hear it (the third component). While it is a concern for this third and oft-lost component that constitutes the reason for this book, it *must* rest firmly on the foundation of the first two components in order to effect eternal change. Although other elements of expository preaching merit discussion, they lie beyond the scope of this book. Rather, let me reiterate the importance of the first two components of expository preaching so that we may eventually camp on the third.

PREACH THE BIBLE

Because true expository preaching derives its content from the only concrete information source given by God, it qualifies as the foremost method of Bible teaching we can practice. As Sidney Greidanus writes, "[The Bible] is the *only* normative source for contemporary preaching . . . because it alone provides the normative *proclamation* of God's redemption and the response he requires. The Bible itself, therefore, can be seen as preaching."[6] The Bible is what we are attempting to communicate. We should look to it for the source of our message, the substance of our message, and the structure for our message. *It* is powerful to change lives in accordance with God's will. *It* is the seed that brings about the initial transformation of man's conversion:

> For you have been born again, not of perishable seed, but of imperishable, through the living and enduring word of God. For, "All men are like grass, and all their glory is like the flowers of the field; the grass withers and the flowers fall, but the word of the Lord stands forever." And this is the word that was preached to you (1 Pet. 1:23–25 NIV).

15

It is also the sword that is wielded by the Spirit to cause the daily progress of one's sanctification:

> For the word of God is living and powerful, and sharper than any two-edged sword, piercing even to the division of soul and spirit, and of joints and marrow, and is a discerner of the thoughts and intents of the heart (Heb. 4:12).

> All Scripture is God-breathed and is useful for teaching, rebuking, correcting and training in righteousness, so that the man of God may be thoroughly equipped for every good work (2 Tim. 3:16–17 NIV).

With this appropriately high view of the value and power of Scripture, we can rest in doing our job: to preach expositorially, while trusting God to do His: to change lives. We must resist the urge to merely incorporate Bible verses into our messages to support our own opinions and agenda. To preach expositorially is to actually *preach* Bible verses. To truly derive our messages from the Bible means that we are going *to the Bible* to find out what we will say. In the end the preacher does not use the Bible to preach his own message; *instead, it is the Bible that uses the preacher to preach its message.* Because the Bible's message is God's message, when we preach expositorially we engage ourselves in the incredible task of "giving human utterance to God's message."

There are two ways we can safely accomplish this task. We can preach from a single passage of Scripture, or we can preach from a number of biblical passages. Preaching from one text (as short as a single verse or as long as a chapter or more) challenges us to faithfully represent that text with every aspect of our sermon. Preaching from a number of biblical texts presents us with the arduous task of constructing a sermon that, as a whole, accurately reflects the sum of its parts.

Those who try to preach from multiple texts in the same sermon often end up using the Scriptures to preach their own message. Most preachers will find it safer to make a regular practice of seeking to convey the message of God in one passage per sermon. While other passages may be mentioned to reinforce the meaning of the text at hand, one primary passage should drive each sermon.

If we occasionally venture to preach a sermon that gives a voice to multiple texts at one time, we must do so with the utmost care. To do this, we must grasp how each part appropriately complements the others, resulting in a message that is truly biblical. This is admittedly the harder of the two options. Mastery of both systematic and biblical theology is required to preach multiple texts without violating the integrity of each one.

Preaching Consecutive Texts

Though some decide to exposit a text from one part of the Bible one week and from an entirely different part the next, most expository preachers find it difficult to give adequate attention to the study of such varied contexts week after week. To satisfactorily prepare a message from Matthew 16 for this weekend, from 2 Peter for the next, and 1 Samuel the next makes accurate exposition extremely difficult, because it requires one to analyze three entirely different contexts. I suggest moving from one portion of Scripture to the following portion, because so much of the contextual flow already has been established and mastered the previous week.[7]

There are those who object to preaching through consecutive passages of a book of the Bible simply because they see no precedent for it in the preaching of the apostles. As Jay Adams rightly points out,

> We must recognize that the apostles were the recipients and the earthly source of special revelation; indeed, they themselves were writing Scripture! We are not. That makes quite a difference. Moreover, we have no record of an apostolic address given in a Christian assembly. But we do see Jesus, "as was his custom," entering the synagogue and preaching from the biblical portion assigned for the day (Luke 4:16–32).[8]

Others object to the preaching of consecutive texts through a book because they do not sense that messages thus derived will be "relevant" to their audience. Instead they prefer to offer a series of messages molded to meet their own perception of the needs of their congregation. As we shall see, we ought not be concerned that the Book of Colossians or the Book of Jude will ever be irrelevant to the needs of your congregation. Both Colossians and Jude, along with the other sixty-four books of the Bible, are "living and powerful." They cannot fail to penetrate the lives of an audience and effect significant changes *if the preacher is willing to give those passages a voice.*

Still others object to passage-by-passage preaching because they do not believe that the Bible adequately addresses the needs of the modern congregant. To adequately minister to contemporary believers, they feel they must touch on a variety of "front-burner" subjects not found in Scripture. The widespread popularity of this opinion should not dissuade us from true expository preaching, Indeed, the Scripture itself flatly rejects this false assumption of the majority. Note again the superlatives and the unapologetic emphasis on the sufficiency of Scripture:

> All Scripture is given by inspiration of God, and is profitable for doctrine, for reproof, for correction, for instruction in righteousness,

that the man of God may be *complete, thoroughly* equipped for *every* good work (2 Tim. 3:16–17, emphasis added).

. . . as His divine power has given to us *all things* that pertain to life and godliness, through the knowledge of Him who called us by glory and virtue, by which have been given to us exceedingly great and precious promises, that through these you may be partakers of the divine nature, having escaped the corruption that is in the world through lust (2 Pet. 1:3–4, emphasis added).

The Bible does not directly address subjects that confront the modern Christians such as genetic engineering or euthanasia, but do not naively assume that Scripture does not speak to these issues. When one proclaims the whole counsel of God with intelligent and accurate application, the modern church will be empowered to hammer out her business ethics as well as her bioethics. Contrary to popular belief, if taught well, contemporary Christians can, like previous generations, be "thoroughly equipped for every good work" (2 Tim. 3:17).

PREACH THE BIBLE ACCURATELY

To ensure that the changes our sermons effect are biblical changes, we must take care that our expository preaching accurately "exposits" the text we are preaching. Though many intend to base a sermon on a text of Scripture, incompetent handling of the text can lead the preacher to reach unbiblical conclusions and thus waylay his congregants. God commissions teachers to use the utmost care in the handling of His Word. As 2 Timothy 2:15 reminds us, "Be diligent to present yourself approved to God, a worker who does not need to be ashamed, rightly dividing the word of truth." To do so is to make the biblical passage perfectly clear while maintaining perfect accuracy. This has been the goal of biblical interpretation from the beginning: "They read from the Book of the Law of God, making it clear and giving the meaning so that the people could understand what was being read" (Neh. 8:8 NIV).

To "correctly handle the word" requires a commitment to expend a great deal of energy and hard work. We must labor to understand our passage in its historical, grammatical, and literary context.[9] We cannot compromise this step on any level. We must commit to achieve a thorough understanding of what God and the biblical author intended to say to God's people. This will also require a monetary investment in quality Bible study tools such as reliable lexicons, theological dictionaries, concordances, grammatical aids, Bible encyclopedias, and atlases.[10]

18

Once we understand the meaning of the text, we must tread within the boundaries of that meaning as we construct our sermon. We must purpose to explain the passage in a way that would evoke from God and the biblical author a comment like, "That's right—that's what we were talking about!"

It is wise for us to continually sharpen our skills in the exegetical facet of expository preaching by gleaning from the many books on the subject.[11] We must become proficient in this aspect of sermon preparation before we ever attempt to preach a life-changing sermon. Pastor Joseph Parker of London has encouraged generations of pastor-teachers with this timeless admonition:

> That is what we need: a man to tell us the meaning of hard words and difficult things and mysteries which press too heavily upon our staggering faith. The interpretation comes to us as a lamp, we instantly feel the comfort and the liberty of illumination. . . . So we need the interpreter. We shall always need him. . . . We want men who can turn foreign words, difficult languages, into our mother tongue; then how simple they are and how beautiful, and that which was a difficulty before becomes a gate opening upon a wide liberty. We need a man who can interpret to us the meaning of confused and confusing and bewildering events; some man with a key from heaven, some man with divine insight, the vision that sees the poetry and the reality of things, and a man with a clear, simple, strong, penetrating voice.[12]

Much has been written on the first two components of expository preaching—the facets of drawing our message solely from the well of Scripture, and presenting that information to our hearers. It is the third component, however, which is all too often neglected, that has driven me to write this book.

PREACH GOD'S CHANGES

Much preaching passes for expository preaching because its content is truly derived from the Bible and its material accurately explains what God is saying in the Bible. But if it stops there—if it fails to boldly call people to respond to the Bible—it is not true expository preaching. The expositional preaching process is not completed, as Timothy Warren writes, "until God's people think and act differently for having heard the Word expounded, . . . for its goal is to manifest or reveal God's truth by living it out."[13]

God's Word *always* demands a human response. As Scripture itself testifies, when a congregation merely hears the word, even with a profound level of understanding, and yet fails to "do it," the whole event is a deceptive enterprise (James 1:22). We can easily send our listeners home feeling godlier because of something they have learned, but that is only part of our task. While we are to aid their growth by expanding their knowledge, we must also move them to act upon that which they now know! When we preach expositorially we should *expect* people to respond to truth.

We are responsible as preachers to be crystal clear in demonstrating the relevance of every portion of God's Word, convinced that "every passage seeks a response from the audience."[14] Unfortunately, our historic Christian heritage and our personal training have likely worked together against this essential component becoming an integral part of our preaching ministry. Before we can expect change in our congregants, we need to take an honest look at what has shaped our methodologies and dulled our expectations.

Overcoming the Vestiges of Scholasticism

All modern Christian preachers bob in the wake of church history's legacy of medieval scholasticism.[15] The influence of scholasticism has survived through the periods of the Reformation and Puritanism and finds its way into most sermons preached in Christian pulpits today. From the sixth century through the sixteenth, the church was marked by increased corruption of Christian life and doctrine. This growing corruption was at best a reason for, and at worst to blame for, a style of preaching devoid of significant applicational thrust. Words were parsed, truths were analyzed, concepts were expounded, but most often parishioners left their Sunday Bible lectures with little compelling reason to do anything about what they had heard. Preaching, by and large, had become a cerebral event characterized by a "sophisticated dialectical method."[16] The heroes of the church became those who "knew" the truth instead of those who "did" the truth. Dargan summarizes the problem:

> The metaphysical subtleties, hairsplitting distinctions, attenuated reasonings, the dogmas, fancies, speculations about things of no particular consequence then or now, all became in some measure the possession of the pulpit.[17]

Though there is something to be gleaned from our scholastic heritage in the fields of hermeneutics, apologetics, and our understanding of the relationship between faith and reason, for the most part, the influence of scholasticism on preaching has been enormously detrimental and lasting.[18] Its continuing impact on modern preaching explains why we are now concerned that our sermons deliver information to minds instead of transform lives.

The term scholasticism shares etymological roots with words like "school" and "scholar." The word itself conjures images of classrooms, chalkboards, professors, and syllabi. It is also reminiscent of the setting in which most preachers were trained to do ministry. Unlike the first-century preachers, most of us learned exegesis, hermeneutics, theology, and even homiletics in the classroom environment. Detailed outlines, classroom lectures, and one-hundred-question exams were means by which we absorbed biblical truths. While these methods clearly helped us *master the truth*, this approach has left most Bible schools and seminaries ineffective, or at best inefficient, in helping us *live the truth*. We generally were not "preached to;" we were "lectured at." We were expected to *know* more, but we generally were not expected to *be* more!

Most of our biblical education was filled with enlightening and even exhilarating experiences of discovery. Sitting at the feet of a capable theologian who could unfold the deep truths of Romans 8 was a memorable encounter for our budding ministerial minds. Time and again we were struck with new insights as we listened to our professors speak. Our assigned reading repeated the same sort of didactic experience for us night after night, semester after semester.

After years of this "training" we were unleashed to "preach" to our unsuspecting congregations. When we preached from Romans, we so wanted our hearers to have the same kind of illuminating experience we had when we first were hit with the power of that epistle in the classroom. Yet for far too many of us, consciously or unconsciously, we turned our pulpits into lecterns and our churches into classrooms. Though we may have been taught that preaching is to be distinctly different from the method of instruction we received, in practice we ended up following the didactic model. Hence, we found it difficult to make truth more than merely mind-changing. Rarely did our words touch the hands, feet, and mouth as well!

We must not settle for a style of preaching that replicates the schoolroom experience. Preaching should be loftier than that. It should be designed to do much more than fill or even tantalize the mind. We must not simply set our sights on conquering the intellects of our congregants, essential as that may be. Preaching is designed by God to make an impact on their entire lives.

PART TWO

PREPARE TO CHANGE LIVES

CHAPTER THREE

Make Sure Your Life Is Changing

THE PERSONAL LIFE OF THE PREACHER IS THE FOUNDATION UPON WHICH HIS EVERY sermon stands. He certainly cannot expect to be used of God to change lives if his own life is stagnant. The New Testament's emphasis on the character requirements of those entrusted with teaching responsibilities should be ample proof of this (1 Tim. 3; Titus 1), yet it is far from the only proof.

If you are to preach life-changing sermons, you must be able to say with 1 Corinthians 11:1, "Imitate me, just as I also imitate Christ." That is why Paul tells the young preacher to "watch your life and doctrine closely" (1 Tim. 4:16 NIV). While many of those interested in effective preaching enthusiastically and rigorously hone their doctrine and theology, considerably less attention seems to be paid to the personal holiness of the preacher's life. As Calvin Miller observes, "Not too much is said in most current books on preaching about the pastor's life in Christ. Still, the spiritual life of the pastor far supersedes sermon know-how."[1] If God is to speak through human personality, then let us remember the urgent need for that human vessel to be clean. Only in that state may we in the pulpit be "a vessel for honor, sanctified and useful for the Master" (2 Tim. 2:21).

CHRIST'S JUDGMENT ON HYPOCRITICAL PREACHERS

Jesus pointed to several condemnable traits in the lives of the ancient Pharisaical preachers, traits that modern preachers would be wise to note, and wiser to avoid.

The Failure to Heed Your Own Sermons

All through high school and college I worked on the sales floor of two prominent shoe store chains. Both companies had a dress code for their employees that didn't bother me much, but what got me was their relentless insistence that the shoes on our feet be a cut above. They maintained the simple idea that people don't want to buy fine dress shoes from a guy in sneakers.

This, of course, is how most businesses work. Walk into the men's clothing store at the mall and you're unlikely to find dated lapels or poorly fitting coats on the salesmen. You'll also have a hard time finding obese people working at the weight loss clinic, or ninety-eight pound weaklings working at the gym. One naturally expects the product advocate to model the goods.

This was in the forefront of my mind recently when I went to have my eyes lasered. After years of poor eyesight, the advertisements were intriguing. But I had to be sold. It is hard not to have your defenses up when walking into a place that hopes to tinker with your eyeballs. With each employee I met in their facility, I immediately checked to see if they were wearing glasses! I wanted to make sure they were taking their own medicine. Had I found half the office staff wearing glasses or contacts I would have been out the door.

The vulnerability I felt regarding that kind of surgery made integrity priority one. When I found it, I took the plunge.

Surely many people feel the same when dealing with us as preachers. The defenses are bound to be up when we are perceived to be "tinkering with one's soul." We must never forget that preaching involves a kind of heart surgery that calls for the ultimate display of integrity on our part. They have every right to expect to find in us the lifestyle and relationship to God we are preaching about.

Jesus showed little tolerance for the teacher who failed to do what he was telling others to do. Modern preachers would do well to revisit regularly the sobering words of Matthew 23, where Jesus unleashes scathing words of disapproval upon the hypocritical teachers of his day. He acknowledges the Pharisees are dispensing truth (v. 3), but he quickly points out that their lives do not match their words of truth. They were eager to "bind heavy burdens on men's shoulders," but as instructors they were not willing to "move them with one of their fingers" (v. 4). Paul spells out this most blatant form of hypocrisy when he asks:

> You, therefore, who teach another, do you not teach yourself? You who preach that a man should not steal, do you steal? You who say, "Do not commit adultery," do you commit adultery? You who abhor idols, do you rob temples? You who make your boast

in the law, do you dishonor God through breaking the law? For "The name of God is blasphemed among the Gentiles because of you," as it is written. (Rom. 2:21–24)

The importance of submitting yourself to the principles you teach cannot be overstated. An effective teaching ministry cannot be realized until the teacher is committed to practice the lessons he attempts to teach. Do you ever find yourself preaching principles you yourself have not even attempted to put into practice? Have you taught the importance of spiritual growth through personal Bible study, knowing that most of your Bible study is obligatory preparation for your next sermon? Have you preached a sermon on experiencing joy in trials after grumbling and complaining all week about your own ecclesiastical headaches?

We must not miss the fundamental importance of integrity in the pulpit. Notice the commitment to obedience sandwiched in the middle of this description of Ezra's commitments as Israel's teacher: "For Ezra had prepared his heart to seek the law of the LORD, and *to do it*, and to teach statutes and ordinances in Israel" (Ezra 7:10, emphasis added). Study and teaching without observance is a formula that will incur the opposition of Christ in your preaching ministry. We must strive every day, by the Holy Spirit's empowerment, to truly practice what we preach.

No point of our preaching is so small that it warrants neglect. If it is right to preach, then it is right for the preacher to live it out. If we are unfaithful in the small things, it is only a matter of time until we are unfaithful in areas that will result in catastrophe. Scripture notes that the stakes are high—the name and reputation of God! His name has been "blasphemed among the Gentiles" because of hypocritical preachers who failed to heed their own preaching. The pages of our country's newspapers abound with stories of "workmen" who have shamed God and disgraced the church. Let us resolve to heed even the smallest application delivered to our audiences each week. As Richard Baxter writes in his convicting exhortation to preachers:

> Be careful . . . . that you preach to yourselves the sermons which you study, before you preach them to others. If you did this for your own sakes, it would not be lost labor; but I am speaking to you upon the public account, that you would do it for the sake of the Church.[2]

As Matthew unfolds Jesus' encounter with the Pharisees in chapter 23, Jesus reveals what may be the single most important insight into why some preachers don't practice what they preach. It is pride. Though an altogether worthy point to note in any context, it is necessary to recognize how pride often lies at the heart of our hypocrisy. It is much like the doctor who zealously and forcefully prescribes a healthy diet for a patient while feeling that he himself is above the need to follow his own prescription. This mentality creeps into the mind of the preacher who starts to believe that he is his congregation's spiritual expert and, as such, exempts himself from following his own counsel. This dangerous and self-defeating tendency can easily grip the minds of preachers who have made legitimate progress in their spiritual lives. We must seek to avoid thinking that we are in some way above the crowd and thus above the principles and application that we set forth in our sermons.

A Thirst for the Spotlight

The Pharisee's prideful quest for recognition and applause is vehemently condemned by Jesus in Matthew 23:5–12. Much like today's preachers, they worked hard to attain their teaching posts. They spent countless hours in schools and took great pains in their studies. They paid their dues at the feet of their professors and labored under the tutelage of demanding instructors. Certainly it's appropriate for people to recognize their achievements. What was the harm in enjoying the plaudits given them, or seeking what was rightly theirs?

According to Jesus, everything was wrong with it!

Why? Because the love of man's approval quickly degenerates into something far worse, fueling the teacher's hypocrisy on every level. Like the Pharisees, we can easily develop an insatiable appetite for praise, which can lead us to do things in our ministry just to be noticed and exalted. If we look at ourselves honestly, we may have to admit that some elements of our messages are more about our reputation than our congregation's transformation. To the extent that this is true, we have exchanged the glory of exalting Christ and impacting people for the base goal of exalting ourselves.

Self-promotion, without a doubt, will lead God to remove His hand from our preaching ministry. He promised to oppose the proud (James 4:6; 1 Pet. 5:5; Prov. 3:34) and He will. He unequivocally vowed to keep His glory from being claimed by His servants (1 Cor. 1:26–31) and He will. When we face the temptation to touch His glory we must recall Jesus' words to the Pharisees: "Whoever exalts himself will be abased, and whoever humbles himself will be exalted" (v. 12).

Every generation of preachers needs such a reminder. Our belief in humility must be more than theoretical, and we must thirst to see the humility of Christ fleshed out in our ministries. As Andrew Murray wrote:

> If humility is the root of the tree, its nature must be seen in every branch, leaf, and fruit. If humility is the first, the all-inclusive grace of the life of Jesus, the secret of His atonement—then the health and strength of our own spiritual life will entirely depend

upon our putting this grace first, too. We must make humility the chief thing we admire in Him, the chief thing we ask of Him, the one thing for which we sacrifice all else.[3]

Unconverted Preachers

To the teachers of the Bible, Jesus raises the ultimate question regarding the extent of one's hypocrisy: are you truly saved? So severe was the breech between their words and their lives that Jesus charged the Pharisees hadn't even appropriated their teaching's most basic and urgent tenet. They were not on their way to the kingdom of heaven, but rather they were excluded from it. And though much of their teaching was accurate and could lead their hearers on the right path (v. 2), their pattern of behavior, if replicated, would lead others to destruction.

It would seem inappropriate, almost disrespectful, to question the salvation of those who proclaim the gospel, but the New Testament writers didn't hesitate to do so. They not only urged the "professing" churchgoers to reexamine the reality of their relationship to Christ (2 Cor. 13:5; Heb. 12:15; 2 Pet. 1:10–11), but even inferred that preachers should regularly examine the genuineness of their faith and fruit (cf. 1 Tim. 4:13). A thoughtful reading of Jesus' words in Matthew 7:21–23 will provoke the same kind of soul-searching among preachers. Is it too much to ask for all preachers to soberly consider their own salvation? Have we not heard and read the testimonies of many who have preached to others while they themselves were lost? After all, who are those before the throne of Christ who ask, "Did we not prophesy in your name?" Are they not those to whom Jesus responds, "I never knew you"?

Considering the fundamental importance of the question, it is always appropriate to question the reality of the preacher's relationship with God. Richard Baxter probes the matter in the opening chapter of his insightful classic on the pastor's life:

> See that the work of saving grace be thoroughly wrought in your own souls. Take heed to yourselves, lest you be void of that saving grace of God which you offer to others, and be strangers to the effectual working of that gospel which you preach; and lest, while you proclaim to the world the necessity of a Savior, your own hearts should neglect him, and you should miss of an interest in him and his saving benefits. Take heed to yourselves, lest you perish, while you call upon others to take heed of perishing.[4]

Scripture Abuse

The fourth problem we note in Jesus' commentary on the Pharisees' hypocrisy was their tendency to slip through applicational loopholes in their theological constructs (Matthew 23:16–24). By manipulating God's Word, they circumvented what they deemed inconvenient or distasteful. They refused to be ruled by Scripture, and they proceeded to use Scripture in a manner that would make allowances for their own selfish agendas.

We can assume such abuse of Scripture began subtly among the Pharisees, just as it does among us. Soon we find ourselves twisting Scripture, ever so slightly, in order to justify an area that someone has questioned in our lives or our sermons. We use our superior knowledge of Scripture to quickly retort the constructively critical comment or e-mail. We console ourselves as we rationalize subtle areas of sin and compromise, enlisting Scripture as our defense. The Bible soon becomes a tool to get *our* point across, or to establish *our* preferences. Instead of allowing it to be a "living and powerful, two-edged sword" that does its authoritative work on the totality of our lives (Heb. 4:12), we wield it to suit ourselves. It will only be a matter of time before we are judged as the Pharisees were.

The Reputation-Character Gap

Jesus sums up the problem of hypocritical teachers by demonstrating the chasm that existed between the Pharisees' reputation and the quality of their character (Matt. 23:25–26). The Pharisees were consumed with their reputations, yet content with the sin in their hearts. They relished their role as spiritual guides, yet harbored evil thoughts in their minds. Peter described the bold and powerful preachers who had secretly crept into the early church as having "eyes full of adultery" and "hearts trained in covetous practices" (2 Pet. 2:14). Their sins may not have been readily apparent to the young church, but their hypocrisy was malignant. Peter assures these false teachers that their "destruction does not slumber" (2 Pet. 2:3).

God is patient in waiting for people to repent, but the Bible warns us that He does not strive with man forever (Gen. 6:3). Amos says "for three sins . . . even for four, I will not turn back my wrath" (Amos 1:3, 6, 9, 11, 13 NIV). Christ is jealous for the purity of His church, and His concern begins with His spokesmen. If you preach His Word, He insists that both your reputation and your character be in order. As He makes clear in verse 26, restoration begins "inside the cup," then others will note the outside is truly clean. If we do not bridge the gap between our reputation and our character, Christ will, as He promised the Pharisees, send "wise men and teachers" to replace us (v. 34 NIV).

Recognizing Christ's opinion of hypocritical teachers should motivate us to carefully and honestly reevaluate our qualifications for this great work. Doing so will guide us to an acute awareness of our need to abide in Christ. It should make us vigilant in our walk of faith. It ought to lead to ardent repentance when we stumble. It will undoubtedly keep our feet firmly grounded when tempted to embrace the accolades of men. B. B. Warfield reflects the humble dependence on Christ that results from consistently and conscientiously examining our own lives—a trait present in any vessel that is used greatly in the pulpit:

> O that I may begin to be in earnest. Every week I cry out—my leanness! My leanness! Surely I am a worthless worm! I do not deserve even the rank of a common soldier in Christ's army.[5]

We must plead with God to lead us to regular and honest appraisal of our need for holiness. May He safeguard us from engaging in a ministry of preaching to others while we ourselves are disqualified from gaining the prize (1 Cor. 9:27).

A WILLINGNESS TO BE BENCHED

Disqualification is a sobering word for preachers of God's Word, but one that needs to be sincerely considered. If we do not periodically evaluate our fitness for this task, or have others do so, we risk forcing upon Christ and His church a teacher who could easily prove more harmful than helpful. James warned that not many in the body should "presume to be teachers," explaining that as such we "shall receive a stricter judgment" (James 3:1). This would seem to be the perfect verse for thinning the ranks of "wannabe" preachers, but it may also be just the warning needed to lead some existing preachers to remove themselves from the pulpit.

A willingness to be benched from the preaching ministry may be the scariest proposition the preacher could ever consider, especially one who has found great joy and fulfillment in the proclamation of God's Word. Certainly the personal, financial and career implications are huge. But if we aren't open to handing in our "license to preach," then we are clutching too tightly to a calling God never deemed irrevocable. The Lord retains the right to amend our calling and redirect our paths at any time. Who has not confessed this basic truth and uttered it in prayer to God at one point or another? Since He is the Lord of our ministry, there must be a willingness to apply this truth to it at any juncture, regardless of the consequences.

A candid review of one's life using the template of virtues listed in 1 Timothy 3 and Titus 1 may bring any honest preacher to say with Warfield, "I am a worthless worm," yet it is important to note that *feeling unworthy* and *being disqualified* are two very different things. Seeing sin and hating it for what it is should be constants in the preacher's changing life. But if the preacher detects a pattern of sin in his own life that renders him other

31

than "above reproach"— someone who no longer sets the pace for his flock in pursuing holiness, albeit imperfectly—then he must voluntarily step out of the pulpit. If there is any question or doubt, we should seek wise and godly counsel, and the sin in question must be brought before the appropriate spiritual authorities for objective review.

An overreaction? Too dramatic? A threat to the stability of the church? What tragedy and disgrace would be spared the name of Christ if all of us who proclaim God's Word would humbly submit ourselves to the possibility that we should not be ministers of His Word? What amount of cancer would be removed from the church if there were a marked return to the sober and vigilant reevaluation of our calling? And in the end, what grace would God bestow upon the man who would resign his pulpit for the benefit of his congregants! God's consistently gracious response toward repentant sinners ought to shield our hearts against anxiety as we lay our preaching ministries before His tribunal.

THE IMPORTANCE OF SPIRITUAL DISCIPLINES

If we are to remain useful tools for changing lives, we must continue to follow even the most elementary disciplines taught to the newest of Christians. We are quick to coach from the pulpit and the counseling office that biblical faith can only flourish if consistently nourished. We reiterate that spiritual growth requires our determined cooperation with the sanctifying work of God's Spirit. We can point new converts to passages like Hebrews 5:13–14 to underscore the importance of Christians indulging in Scripture's "solid food" so that "by constant use" they can be "trained . . . to distinguish good from evil" (NIV). Yet, knowing all this, it is easy for the average preacher himself to suffer from spiritual malnutrition. This sad state is not due to a lack of time in the Word each week. Rather it develops because he has neglected the Word as the source of spiritual vibrancy for his own soul.

For many of us, this tendency begins in seminary or Bible school, where the intimacy of spiritual "devotions" or "quiet times" is replaced by studying for the next Old Testament exam. At first we hardly feel the effects of this transition because our minds are stimulated by daily discoveries in the classroom. Eventually, though, we are bound to feel the ministerial impotence caused by the deprivation of our intimate time with Christ. Meager snatches of personal prayer and Bible study simply cannot sustain an effective ministry. Every pastor who has attempted to preach with his spiritual reservoirs running dry realizes that "only a robust devotional life, a pulsating piety, could possibly meet the needs of such an exacting office or provide the qualities of life it demands."[6]

Biblical Intake for the Preacher's Heart

Many modes of biblical intake exist, and a preacher can pursue them for a variety of reasons. Bible reading, Bible study, and Scripture memory all can be regular features of the preacher's life. If we "plan it right," every encounter with biblical truth in a given week also can provide strategic preparation for something on our ministry schedule. All biblical intake is good and essential, but "sermon prep time" alone certainly is not sufficient to meet the high personal demands of preaching that changes lives.

Therefore, a clear distinction must be made between the spiritual dividends yielded from Bible study pursued in preparation for teaching and Bible study pursued for personal enrichment. I do not suggest that biblical preparation for a sermon or a counseling appointment cannot be personally enriching—it often is. Cramming for a seminary exam may produce a good grade, but because the focus is on the grade, the truth and application of the text may never penetrate the student's life. Sermon preparation can be much the same. If you only consider Sunday's text in light of your audience and its spiritual needs, you may be edified, but only in areas of common need. Scripture will impact your life, but only at the point best described as the "lowest common spiritual denominator" existing between you and your congregation. Thus, you are bound to miss a number of key implications that would specifically address your particular challenges, temptations, and fears.

Biblical intake of the second type could be viewed as self-profiting. It is the kind of Bible study that gives no thought to how the passage can or should be taught. In these encounters, the preacher specifically looks to God to deepen, enhance, stretch, and shape his heart. Certainly all other modes of study will abound, but this kind of study must *never* be squeezed out of our schedules.

Intimate Prayer Encounters

Engaging in regular times of undistracted communion with God through prayer is perhaps the most difficult spiritual discipline of all. In our world of endless distractions, few things are harder than kneeling to talk with our Maker for even thirty minutes each day. But talk we must. To "pour out our hearts before Him" (Ps. 62:8) is the privilege and responsibility of those who would speak on His behalf here on earth. The ambassador must be intimately engaged with the One who sent him, or the distance between the two will soon become evident to all. Since the empowerment gained from time spent in prayer cannot be successfully manufactured, any pretense of intimacy will come across as artificial.

33

Jesus modeled this critical feature of Christian leadership in spite of a harried and demanding ministry load none of us will ever know! He didn't *find* the time for intimate prayer encounters with the Father; He *made* the time. According to Mark 1:35, Jesus rearranged His sleep schedule to incorporate this kind of focused prayer time into His life:

> Now in the morning, having risen a long while before daylight, He went out and departed to a solitary place; and there He prayed. And Simon and those who were with Him searched for Him. When they found Him, they said to Him, "Everyone is looking for You" (Mark 1:35–37).

At the end of another busy day of ministry, Matthew writes:

> And when He had sent the multitudes away, He went up on a mountain by Himself to pray. And when evening had come, He was alone there (Matt. 14:23).

Whether early in the morning or late in the evening, Jesus sustained a habitual pattern of prayer in the course of the demanding pace of His preaching ministry. And he did it without the benefit of a Day Timer™ or Palm Pilot™! Time with His Father was the priority of *every* day. Likewise, today's preacher must creatively steal away substantial blocks of time in quiet and lonely places if he is to speak on behalf of the Father.

That idea that your personal time of prayer is important is not a news flash, yet we all can use a fresh reminder to engage in it. Surely the Spirit calls us throughout our day to meet in quiet communion and conversation with the Father. Let us not underestimate its paramount importance, as Richard Newton fittingly testifies:

> The principal cause of my leanness and unfruitfulness is owing to an unaccountable backwardness to pray. I can write or read or converse or hear with a ready heart; but prayer is more spiritual and inward than any of these, and the more spiritual any duty is the more my carnal heart is apt to start from it. Prayer and patience and faith are never disappointed. I have long since learned that if ever I was to be a minister, faith and prayer must make me one. When I can find my heart in frame and liberty for prayer, everything else is comparatively easy.[7]

If meaningful times of Bible study and prayer were faithfully maintained and ruthlessly guarded, even when your life becomes busy and hectic, your vital connection to Christ's empowering Spirit would *never* fail to carry you strongly through the challenges associated with a preaching ministry that transforms lives.

34

PARTNERSHIPS OVER PRIVACY

A holy and useful life that is grounded in habitual life-giving spiritual disciplines rarely exists in isolation. You will rarely encounter a person who lives above reproach and walks closely with Christ who has not learned that two journey better than one (Eccl. 4:9). Unfortunately, when it comes to personal progress in Christ, preachers are perhaps the most isolated people on earth. Pastors and Bible teachers have an unhealthy and potentially devastating tendency to attempt to scale the hurdles of spiritual growth on their own. *Recognize that this is a choice, not an occupational hazard, and a poor choice at that!*

We must vigorously fight the temptation to privatize our spiritual quest. Pride, fear, and exhaustion from living in the fishbowl should not become an excuse for spiritual seclusion. Attempting to live your life without accountability to another godly Christian is a sure way to increase the odds of future disqualification from ministry.

When Paul wrote to Timothy on living as "a vessel for honor, sanctified and useful for the Master," he was quick to follow up with the specific exhortation for Timothy to "Flee also youthful lusts; but pursue righteousness, faith, love, peace *with those who call on the Lord out of a pure heart*" (2 Tim. 2:21–22, emphasis added). Paul's instruction was personally directed to Timothy, and it was Timothy's responsibility to flee evil desires and live righteously, yet note Timothy was to do so along "with those who call on the Lord out of a pure heart." Timothy's goals of holiness and usefulness were to be pursued alongside those with like passions—alongside brothers and sisters who knew his heart as he knew theirs.

Spirituality is not a solo flight. Call to your side one, two, or even three godly men who really know *your* heart—men who have been invited each week to explore it thoroughly. Far from an intrusion, it will provide invaluable protection and indispensable objectivity in your quest for spirituality. To be effective, you must allow these men absolute freedom to ask the hard questions. Commit yourself to be brutally honest about your struggles with power, greed, and lust. These men must become familiar with the workings of your sanctification. They must know your spiritual Achilles' heel and commit to stand with you to defend it when attacked. Their weekly feedback regarding your words, actions, and attitudes—both public and private—will soon become the valued and faithful wounds of a friend (Prov. 27:6) without which we dare not attempt to live, minister, or preach.

THE POWER OF A HOLY LIFE

Robert Murray McCheyne, the influential Scottish minister known for his self-discipline, devotion to prayer, and life-changing sermons, reminds

35

us that "it is not great talents God blesses so much as great likeness to Jesus. A holy minister is an awful weapon in the hands of a holy God."[8] McCheyne should know. He watched God transform an entire generation as preachers like himself faithfully proclaimed the word from a foundation of personal holiness. McCheyne and others like him were not perfect, but their lives were constantly changing as they fully submitted themselves to the Word of God and the transforming work of the Holy Spirit.

As we consider our calling to preach and our need for personal piety, let us never forget this timeless invitation extended to all who long to be used in His kingdom, "For the eyes of the Lord run to and fro throughout the whole earth, to show Himself strong on behalf of those whose heart is loyal to Him" (2 Chron. 16:9).

May He find in our day a generation of preachers who have spurned hypocrisy and shown diligence in cultivating hearts tenaciously loyal to Him!

AMEN!

CHAPTER FOUR

Study Your Passage and Your Audience with Life-change in Mind

TRYING TO FOLLOW A SET OF COMPLICATED WRITTEN DIRECTIONS TO A SECLUDED golf course once led me to a different destination—frustration! Certain I had spied our verdant destination just across the way, I boldly announced to my golf partner that a "shortcut" over the bridge would have us on the tee in no time. As you might have guessed, my deviation from the printed directions led to disaster! As we crossed the bridge, we were ushered onto a freeway on-ramp—and the next exit was over ten miles down the road.

My twenty-mile "shortcut" didn't score any points with my golfing partner, yet it reaffirmed a lesson we all have a hard time learning—shortcuts are rarely what they seem!

When it comes to sermon preparation you can be sure this is true. After hours of hard work deciphering a text's meaning, we may grow frustrated that we are still not yet ready to birth the sermon itself. Regardless of the temptation to prematurely move on, we dare not neglect the important work of carefully determining the text's ancient and contemporary significance. This work is costly and at times complicated, but take heart—you and your congregation will be rewarded in the resulting sermon.

Godly pastors, trained to decipher a text's meaning, must follow that task by facing the equal challenge of discovering how God means to use the passage to impact lives.[1] The critical distinction, so often missed in one's study, lies between the "meaning" of a text and its "significance."[2] Meaning is discovered as I rightly understand the truth presented in a passage of

Scripture; significance is discovered as I rightly determine the impact that truth is intended to make on my congregation.

If significance is neglected, the preacher will never "bridge the gap between exegesis and homiletics."[3] One may masterfully explain the meaning of a passage (the second component of expository preaching), yet still fail miserably to persuasively communicate the significance of the passage for life in the real world (the third component of expository preaching). In such a case the connection is missed, and genuine biblical preaching has not taken place.

I recently took the liberty of doing some lab work at a large suburban church. The pastor opened his sermon with a summons to consider "five observations" regarding the morning's text. Afterwards, I decided to ask some congregants how God would want them to respond to the passage they had just heard. There were blank stares, uncomfortable pauses, and even excuses as to why they didn't track well on that particular morning. Realizing the preacher had failed to construct any bridges between a great passage and their lives, the more thoughtful among those I questioned cobbled together a hasty applicational connection. In those cases, I fear it was my question more than anything in the sermon that had prompted them to give their pastor an assist.

Certainly those who attend that church would hail their pastor as an "expository preacher" because he moves week by week from one biblical passage to the next. I would respectfully disagree with their assessment. While there were several insights shared from the pastor's week of study, implications of that study never saw the light of Sunday morning—much less that of Monday or Tuesday morning! Real expository preaching should continue to echo in the minds and hearts of congregants not for a day or even a week, but for a lifetime.

Liberals long have targeted the irrelevance of evangelical preaching. A century ago, Harry Fosdick chided, "People do not come to church with a burning interest in what happened to the Jebusites, but with their own questions and problems."[4] Instead of bridging the two worlds, liberals have opted for a convenient and catastrophic solution to the problem by blaming the Scriptures themselves and, in the end, persuading many that the Bible has no inherent authority.[5] On the contrary, those of us with confidence in the authority and sufficiency of the Scriptures dare not sell them off for a supposed pot of "cultural relevance" in our sermons. Instead, we must do the hard work of keeping ourselves diligently engaged in *both* worlds. As Stephen Neill states:

> Preaching is like weaving. There are two factors of the warp and the woof. There is the fixed, unalterable element which for us is the Word of God and there is a variable element. . . . For us the

38

variable element is the constantly changing pattern of people and situations.[6]

To weave a true expository message, the text *and* our audience must be repeatedly crossed in the course of the sermon. The unalterable truth and the life patterns of our congregants must be intertwined and tightly woven before we send them on their way.

You cannot truly begin to craft your sermon until you discover God's intended impact of the passage on people's lives. Boil it down to these questions: "Why did the Holy Spirit put this text here?", and "What is the Holy Spirit's purpose?"[7] Don't fail to keep two audiences in view during this discovery process:

(1) the original recipients: *"What was this text intended to change in their lives?"* and

(2) my audience: *"What should this text change in my life, and in my congregants' lives?"*

Let's look at each target more closely.

WHAT WAS THIS TEXT INTENDED TO CHANGE IN THEIR LIVES?

Haddon Robinson contends that more heresy is spread in the preacher's attempt to apply Scripture than in his presentation of Scripture's meaning. He blames much of this on our lack of training in the area of making application:

> Preachers want to be faithful to the Scriptures, and going through seminary, they have learned exegesis. But they may not have learned how to make the journey from the biblical text to the modern world. . . . Sometimes we apply the text in ways that might make the biblical writer say, "Wait a minute, that's a wrong use of what I said." This is the heresy of a good truth applied in a wrong way.[8]

It is therefore critically important to consider the original audience and understand what the Scripture text intended to convey to them. Jumping from the text directly to your audience, even after investing hours in painstaking exegesis, enhances your chance of making basic, applicational mistakes.

Ironically, the kind of errors made from our pulpits parallel those of the cult groups across town.[9] The difference is that our application still falls within biblical orthodoxy while theirs most often does not, but the horrifying similarity lies in a loose interpretational approach to the texts we are preaching. Our shoddy handling of the text's application in fact can nullify our rigid handling of the text's meaning. For example, to use Philippians 4:13 ("I can do all things through Christ who strengthens me") to excite a congregation to give to a church building project would be a gross misapplication of scriptural intent. In truth, Paul intended to secure something quite the opposite in the Philippians. By this claim he modeled God's empowerment to live contentedly *without* the things so many others thought he needed—so to use the verse as a fund-raising tool would be both inaccurate and wrong.

If we are to "be diligent" as unashamed "workers" who "rightly divide the word of truth" (2 Tim. 2:15), the same vigilance we demonstrate in interpreting a passage's meaning *must* be shown in interpreting its significance. A shameful handling of a text's applicational elements usually comes down to how we spend our time studying the passage (more on this in chapter 7). It is not unusual for pastors to lament over hours spent wrestling with a text's meaning, then confess to having spent only minutes on its intended application. Or, what's more amazing, some confess to Spirit-inspired "lightning bolt" applications hitting them while *in the pulpit!* To avoid these dangerous scenarios, we must honestly balance our study schedules to provide fair and ample time for both exegesis *and* discovering application.

Principles for Study

The principles for discovering a passage's intended impact on the original audience are much the same as those for uncovering a passage's meaning. The following is a summary of principles that should be carefully applied *after* the meaning of a passage has been ascertained.

1. Put Yourself in Their Sandals

To put ourselves in the sandals of the original audience means that we carefully consider the historical, grammatical, and literary context of the passage we are studying. This is the primary guideline for deciphering the passage's meaning *and* its intended application. Carefully noting the author's intentions will prevent us from short-changing the power of the text and keep us faithful to the reason for the text's placement in Scripture. This discovery then will govern the direction and parameters of the application we eventually will tailor for our own audience.[10]

When Satan came to Jesus in the wilderness, he quoted Psalm 91 to tempt Jesus to throw Himself from the temple. Jesus quickly refuted his ploy as a misapplication of the passage. In the psalm, the psalmist hails the loving protection of Yahweh, telling how He serves as a refuge and protector of those who trust Him. Satan quotes the part of the psalm which promises that Yahweh "shall give His angels charge over you, to keep you in all your ways. They shall bear you up in their hands, lest you dash your foot against a stone" (Ps. 91:11–12). Satan's application suggests it would be the "biblical thing" to jump from the pinnacle of the temple, just as though it would have been the "biblical thing" for the psalmist to throw himself in the path of an oncoming spear. Think of it—the angelic rescue would validate Jesus' messianic claims in the eyes of the people! What was so bad about that?

Satan extracted the verses of Psalm 91 from their context to prompt an action that was unrelated to the initial purpose for that Scripture. The psalmist embedded examples in the context of Psalm 91:1–13 to help the original recipients (and subsequent ones) discover his intended application. His examples included protection from sickness and disease (vv. 3, 6), dangers encountered on an ancient battlefield (vv. 5, 7) and hazards of traversing the wilderness (v. 13). The example contained within the quoted section itself also helps to define the parameters of the promise when it refers to stubbing one's toe on a rock (v. 12). Safety from unforeseen dangers of illness, enemies in battle, attacks from animals, or even the unanticipated road hazard have nothing in common with throwing oneself in front of an oncoming arrow—or jumping from the pinnacle of the temple. To use this verse to justify entering harm's way would undoubtedly provoke an objection from the psalmist and those who understood his original message in its context.

You must ask yourself, from a historical point of view, "What did the psalmist or prophet or apostle have in mind?" or "What did the Holy Spirit intend to prompt in the people who initially heard this?" or "What action did He expect the people to perform as a result of this teaching?" Believe that every Scripture was given for a purpose and don't give up until you find it. Indications as to the author's intent will become more obvious with practice, so look and keep looking each time you study a passage. Put yourself in their sandals and highlight the verbal indicators like "for this reason," "because of," "like," "just as," and "therefore," which help mark parameters to the appropriate application of the truth in its original setting.

2. Camp on the Imperatives

Since verbs are the keys to understanding the meaning of any text, we should target them for study first in any passage of Scripture. When it comes to determining the passage's intended impact on life, we should revisit the imperative verbs.[11] Oftentimes the passage's imperative verbs will help to govern the length of the passage to be preached.

When you encounter an imperative verb, particularly in the didactic portions of Scripture, the application to the original audience is usually obvious. Here is something they were told to do, or in many cases, not do. "Love your

41

enemies and bless those who hate you" (Matt. 5:44), "Do not lie to each other" (Col. 3:9), "Be diligent to come to me quickly" (2 Tim. 4:9) all clearly prompt the original readers to action. These imperatives provide the handles for working our way toward an appropriate application of the text to our modern hearers.

3. Decide If a Narrative Passage Was Given to Serve as a Template for Them to Follow

Luke wrote in Acts 8:4 that "those who were scattered went everywhere preaching the word." It is important for us to determine whether this statement was simply made to explain the current situation, or presented to serve as an example to those who initially received his book. Earlier Luke recorded Jesus' words, "Sell all that you have and distribute to the poor" (Luke 18:22). The reason for any statement's inclusion and its applicability to the initial recipients of the book must be carefully considered before it is preached from your pulpit to avoid creating problems the passage never intended to incite.

4. Use and Compare Other Clear Imperatives to Keep Your Determinations on Track

Studying the detailed list of widows eliminated from the financial rolls of the church at Ephesus (1 Tim. 5:4–16), you may conclude these first-century Christians were to help as few people as possible! However, by consulting other parts of Scripture we conclude this could not have been an accurate or intended application for the early church. Jesus clearly instructed His followers to be openhanded toward the needy (Luke 6:34–35). The Bible always equates godliness with generosity (Prov. 11:25; 22:9). Paul even boasted about the Corinthians' generosity toward others in need (2 Cor. 9:1–5). In light of all these clear statements from Scripture we can be certain that whatever the application derived from 1 Timothy 5:4–16, one cannot possibly imply that Christians are to be tightfisted with their material possessions.

Visiting other clear imperatives confirms to me that the application for the initial recipients of a text is truly what the Holy Spirit and the human author had in mind. Cross-referencing may send me back to the drawing board, and it is certainly time consuming, but it will always keep me from preventable error. In the case of 1 Timothy 5, it helped me determine that the application for the church of Ephesus related to its church budget and *not* the individual practice of generosity.

Expending the effort to thoroughly consider the implications of a particular passage for its *original recipients* is a step that deserves our time and attention. It will prevent us from drifting too far afield in our quest to find an appropriate application for our contemporary audience.

WHAT SHOULD THIS TEXT CHANGE IN *OUR* LIVES?

As stated earlier, bringing an application over the centuries from "then" to "now" is not to be improvised in the pulpit, or even left to a few fleeting moments in the study. This is, in fact, the essential discipline that separates an aimless sermon from a truly life-changing sermon.

Having determined how the passage at hand was to be applied by the ancients, we are poised to think about the generation to which we are called to preach. Lest we bemoan this step as a modern dilemma, we need only to open the New Testament to see how the true pioneers handled it. They, too, had to discover how Old Testament passages were applied to New Testament teachings, and few did so as deftly as the apostle Paul. After recalling the disastrous events of Israel's wilderness wanderings to the Corinthians, he states, "these things happened to them as examples, and they were written for our admonition" (1 Cor. 10:11). He tells the Romans that "whatever things were written before were written for our learning, that we through the patience and comfort of the Scriptures might have hope" (Rom. 15:4).

The apostle shows us that it is not only legitimate but also necessary for us to utilize recorded events of Scripture to serve as applicational templates for subsequent generations. Though an example by itself does not always serve as a direct point of application (e.g., Paul wore sandals on missionary journeys, so modern missionaries should?), the ancient example ought to be carefully considered in every instance as a potential contemporary example of what should or should not be followed. Again, corresponding imperatives or prohibitions in other parts of the Bible will always help to clarify whether or not the biblical example is an appropriate application template for modern times.

The remainder of this chapter will summarize principles that will help us decide when and how to transfer an ancient application from "then" to "now." Along the way, we will need to note factors that may limit the transfer of the application as well as factors that call for the direct transfer of the application. Finally, we will add our knowledge of our own audience to the mix as we crystallize how best to target them with the application.

Note the Factors That Limit the Transfer of Application

Once we have determined how the initial audience was to respond to a particular passage, we need to examine several factors before rushing that application into a sermon as a directive for our hearers. While we believe the Book of Leviticus is part of sacred and inspired Scripture, we recognize that the command to "slaughter the young bull" before Yahweh and "sprinkle his blood" (Lev. 1:5) should not replace the Sunday afternoon nap for our congregants. Yet we know that "all Scripture," including

43

Leviticus 1:5, "is given by inspiration of God, and is profitable for doctrine, for reproof, for correction, for instruction in righteousness, that the man of God may be complete, thoroughly equipped for every good work" (2 Tim. 3:16–17). But what good works are to result from the preaching of Leviticus 1:5? Obviously not the "good work" of slaughtering an animal. Why? Because there are factors that limit the direct application of that passage to our target audience. (More on this later.)

1. Does the Immediate Context Limit the Target of the Application?[12]

Once you derive an application from a passage, ask yourself, "Is there anything in the context of the passage that might show why this application is limited to a particular target audience?" Some contexts give us clues to limitations, but they are not as obvious as the previous example. The original target audience of the application may partially overlap with your contemporary audience (e.g., the elderly, women, the poor, deacons), or it may not overlap at all with your target audience (unless it includes Levites, Edomites, or the apostles). We must always be mindful of this factor in order to make appropriate application.

The Pastoral Epistles provide a good example. Many of the commands to Timothy and Titus are seemingly timeless principles regarding the Christian life. Yet note that some of the intended application is directed specifically to pastors and their ministerial leadership in the church. This is a very important and limiting observation that may call for a more abstract or generalized character when the application is preached to your audience.[13] The call for Timothy to present himself as "a worker who does not need to be ashamed, rightly dividing the word of truth" (2 Tim. 2:15) is found in the context of Timothy's preaching commission. Therefore, direct transference of the application with all its contextual implications is an appropriate preaching goal if you are preaching at a pastor's conference. However, when preaching to a congregation of lay men and women, the application would need to take a step back from the context of church leadership to an appropriate level of applicability for the congregation being addressed. Of course, the pastoral epistles ought to be preached to those who are not in ministry, and the principles ought to make a difference in every hearer's life, but the *level of abstraction* for each text's application will be determined by the contextual clues that limit the application to a specific target audience.

2. Does Any Other Part of the Bible Limit the Target of the Application?

It may be that the immediate context does not limit the application of a passage, but a wider consideration of the whole of Scripture does. Our Leviticus 1:5 example applies here. The application of Leviticus to my audience is even further removed from the immediate context of the pastoral epistles because the rest of the Bible shows us that the sacrificial and ceremonial system of Leviticus has been fulfilled in Christ (Heb. 10:1–14; Matt. 5:17). Plenty of application may to be proclaimed to a contemporary audience regarding dietary laws and Israel's festivals or Sabbath regulations, but our application here must look different from the original one, or else we will not be faithful to the whole counsel of God.

3. Does a Cultural Condition Limit the Target of the Application?

While some may use this question as an excuse to avoid the application of a difficult passage, in *some* cases it is clearly a valid reason for limiting a text's application. At first glance, Paul's instruction to Timothy to "use a little wine" for his stomach and his frequent illnesses (1 Tim. 5:23) may lead us to conclude wine was used in the first century for medicinal purposes. Like Timothy, the people we preach to will be ill and have stomach problems. Since Scripture instructs Timothy to drink wine to remedy the problems, should we then directly transfer the application to teach our congregants to use the same remedy? In this case it is appropriate to modify the application in light of the first-century culture of medicine and that of today's. Here we can step away from a direct transference and instead present an application to our hearers that reflects that truth without the original cultural remedy attached. (Thankfully, today there are much more effective medicinal substances to apply to problematic stomachs.) Therefore, to direct Christians to seek medical attention when they are sick does not constitute a violation of Scripture or reflect a lack of faith. Here it is an appropriate and authoritative application of God's Word.

4. Does a Unique Historical Condition Limit the Target of the Application?

Much like our second question, the rest of Scripture will help us determine if the passage at hand offers a historical or theological reason why the specific application was presented to the original recipients.

When Jesus called the rich young ruler to follow Him with the words "sell all that you have and distribute to the poor" (Luke 18:22), the historical setting and its comparison with the rest of Scripture provide clues as to the reason for this kind of summons. Jesus did not require the others he called to sell everything they had, nor does the rest of New Testament teaching instruct would-be followers of Christ to sell all their possessions. In this case the specific nature of the request along with its specific historic occurrence should lead the preacher to avoid a direct transference to his audience and make a more abstract application here. Jesus demanded a break from the hold that money had on the rich man, hence this distinctive command. His reaction to the command, and Jesus' ensuing words regarding rich people and the kingdom of heaven, show us

45

there is much to apply to modern audiences regarding this passage, but the historical condition modifies and limits its presentation.

Note the Factors That Call for the Direct Transfer of Application

While some aspects of a passage may limit the transferability of a text's application, others call for its direct transfer. Several factors need to be considered to determine whether the direct transfer of an original application is appropriate, and if not, which aspects of the application should be transferred.

1. What Aspect of the Application Is Rooted in God's Character?

We must always take special note when a text's original application is grounded in the nature, character, or attributes of God.

When Jesus taught, "love your enemies, bless those who curse you," He rooted His lesson in the nature of God's character: "that you may be sons of your Father in heaven; for He makes His sun rise on the evil and on the good" (Matt. 5:44–45). The application of this passage will be directly transferable because Scripture bases its practice on the nature of God. This is an elaboration of the common theme that we are to be "holy because God is holy" (Lev. 11:45; 1 Pet. 1:16), and is specifically linked to timeless application of several biblical teachings (e.g., love, 1 John 4:7; forgiveness, Col. 3:13; acceptance, Rom. 15:1).

Similarly, Peter calls the women of the early church to exhibit "the incorruptible ornament of a gentle and quiet spirit" and then adds that such beauty is "very precious in the sight of God" (1 Pet. 3:4). The application of this passage is directly transferable because God Himself admires this character trait in women of any dispensation. Similarly, 2 Corinthians 9:7 connects our actions to God's heart when Paul writes that Christians should give "not grudgingly or of necessity, for God loves a cheerful giver." These clear indications rooted in the preferences of God should drive the preacher to keep the transfer of that application as direct as possible. The implication for the modern audience will undoubtedly need to be explored, but the descriptive adjectives must be preserved with the same impact intended for the original audience.

2. What Aspect of the Application Is Addressing Man's Depravity?

Preaching the Bible is designed to equip people for every good work (2 Tim. 3:16). That kind of preaching is used by God to accomplish a progressive pattern of sanctification—men and women becoming more and more like Christ (Rom. 8:29). Therefore, the effective preacher must continually consider how a given application addresses the universal need for all Christians to "put to death . . . whatever belongs to [their]

46

earthly nature" (Col. 3:5 NIV) and "lay aside all filthiness and overflow of wickedness" (James 1:21). Bryan Chapell refers to this concern as the "fallen condition focus"[14] and Haddon Robinson calls it the "depravity factor."[15] While many of today's preachers avoid this topic, both men highlight an essential interest in how the application of the passage addresses people's sin, their need for Christ, and the guidelines for Spirit-empowered obedience.

Asking how the ancient application addresses and remedies the universal problem of human sin will quickly uncover the most obvious and urgent aspects of the passage to be applied in any age.[16] The topic may be culturally distant, as oxen and fields, but the call to deny our sinful desires of greed and selfishness is an applicational truth we must address to our modern audiences. Is apathy, covetousness, independence, or laziness the concern behind the truth being presented in the passage? Once identified, the purposeful concern of the text will clearly call for a direct transference to the hearers of our day.

3. What Aspect of the Application Is Reflecting God's Created Order?

In Matthew 19:5 Jesus quotes Genesis 2:24 in His defense of monogamy, as does Paul in Ephesians 5:31.[17] This argument is based on the foundation of God's created order and therefore proves to be an applicable standard for every age.[18] Biblical applications regarding sexual ethics based on the created order need not be abstracted to some lesser degree, as some have done in defense of homosexuality. Rather, passages that find their application rooted in the created order, whether they pertain to the distinction of the sexes, the establishment of the family, or the structure and form of marriage, should alert us to find a universally relevant transfer of application. While not always politically correct, they are faithful reflections of God's intent and therefore require communication.

4. What Aspect of the Application Is Delivered as Counter-cultural?

In putting ourselves in the sandals of the original recipients, it is helpful to consider how the application fit the cultural context in which they lived—and more importantly, how it countered it. In His Sermon on the Mount, Jesus' words ran contrary to conventional, accepted practice. He repeatedly pointed out to the crowd "you have heard that it was said," but quickly raised the bar by adding "But I say to you . . ." (Matt. 5:21, 27, 33, 38, 43). The specific life-change He was calling for in these passages ran against the grain of the culturally accepted mores of the day. This is a helpful indication suggesting the application He was seeking was not bound to the specific context in which it was delivered. If the application was originally counter-cultural, then it often calls us to make a relevant transfer to our audience regardless of its cultural stance.

Not all counter-culture directives are as easily discernable as those in Matthew 5. Often it necessitates careful study of the historical and cultural background of the people to whom the passage was initially directed. Grasping the ancient Near East's social structure or understanding the Roman view of marriage can help us realize when a biblical writer is not attempting to address mere provincial concerns, but is driving home timeless points with universal application.

Add Your Knowledge of Your Audience to the Application

Thus far, the attention has been on the ancient application in its historical and cultural context. Our focus now shifts to the contemporary audience you are called to address.[19] The challenge now is to thoughtfully determine how you can best unite the relevant application of the text to your specific audience. At this point, the carefully analyzed application made to the original audience may be abstracted to a more general principle, or it may be directly transferred without any modification based on the criteria discussed above. Of course, this assumes a certain knowledge of your hearers. A wise preacher learns what is important to his congregants, and why it is important. The presumption that "all of us Americans think alike" is a dangerous one for any preacher to hold, particularly new ones moving out of their own neighborhoods to other parts of the country! The more insight you gain into the lives of your congregants, the better you will connect them to the life-changing implications and contemporary relevance you have discovered in the passage to be preached.

Here are four important questions to prepare you to formulate the specific goal of your sermon:

1. What Specifically Does Your Audience Have in Common with the Original Audience?

We now understand that the previously discussed points regarding the character of God and the depravity of man call for a more direct transfer of the ancient application to all people in all places. It is a given that we are all sinful people and must answer to the same immutable God. This was true then, it is true now, and it will be true for all future generations, so there is little question surrounding the direct transfer of the application to our audience.

Those two universalities are invariable, but many others can and should be noted that will allow me to strategically craft effective applications for our sermon.[20] A few minutes spent observing commonalities assist us in choosing the best road for the sermon to take. Make some simple comparisons regarding the initial recipients of Colossians 2:16–17 and the audience to which we are going to preach. The text reads:

48

> Therefore let no one judge you in food or in drink, or regarding a festival or a new moon or sabbaths, which are a shadow of the things to come, but the substance is of Christ.

Some observations might include the following: (1) the original recipients and my audience are both professing Christians; (2) they are both exposed to religious forms and prescriptions that are not biblically pertinent; (3) they are often expected and sometimes pressured to participate in those religious forms; (4) when they refuse to do so they are sometimes ridiculed for their attempts to live truly godly lives; (5) they both feel a personal and perhaps emotional cost exacted for not conforming to the religious expectations of others; and (6) those who pressure and ridicule them are in error regarding the necessity of following those religious forms.

Putting similarities into terms like these will help you to begin to identify scenarios in your own congregation which rightly reflect the scenarios of biblical times. This will assist you in drawing straight lines between the two.

2. In What Specific Areas Does Your Audience Lack Commonality with the Original Audience?

Equally important as identifying their commonalities is the need to identify the differences that exist between my audience and the original recipients. Look again at the Colossians 2:16–17 example and carefully note some of the differences: (1) unlike the original recipients, my audience is not pressured to engage in Jewish or Old Testament customs; (2) my audience is not likely to have participated in the same religious forms they are now pressured to participate in (as was the case for most in the original audience); (3) the proponents of the religious forms in our day are generally not as powerful as those in the time of the original recipients; (4) failure to conform to the proposed forms does not involve the same severity of alienation and ostracization today as it did back then; and, (5) while the pressure may be less severe, my audience is likely to be exposed to a greater variety of religious pressures than were the original audience.

Itemizing dissimilarities will help you take hold of the essence of how God will utilize this truth in your audience while keeping you from camping on an aspect of the text that has little bearing on how the passage is to be applied.

3. How Is My Audience Currently Practicing the Application?

Noting the established track record of your hearers is tremendously important if you are to avoid the "preaching to the choir" boredom that so quickly settles over modern-day audiences. Even when the application is rightly derived from a text, spending too much time exhorting them to do what they already do, or to believe what they already believe, will cause you to lose valuable time as well as the interest level necessary to effect change in their lives.

This need to analyze your audience cannot be stressed enough. Your pastoral finger must constantly feel the pulse of your audience. Don't just ask how much they know about the topic, ask yourself how well they are *practicing* this part of Scripture. If you are preaching on generosity and you have a church that has faithfully and generously sustained an expanding church budget, then you must naturally target your application toward a kind of generosity that has little to do with putting money in a plate on Sunday.

Yes, it is important to preach "the same things . . . again . . . as a safeguard" (Phil. 3:1). However, it is important to note that Paul did so in Philippians 3 because there was a continual flow of temptation in an area that he goes on to specifically identify. Even when he exhorts his readers in an area in which they excel, as he does in 1 Thessalonians 4:1, his call involves clear direction as to how they are to do so "more and more."

4. How Is My Audience Currently Neglecting or Abusing the Application?

Even Jesus pointed out the problem caused by the compartmentalization of application. As usual, the Pharisees provided an easy target. Their convictions led them to bind their word with complex oaths, but they obviously allowed themselves loopholes not afforded others (Matt. 23:16–18). Therefore, when Jesus preached to the Pharisees He was quick to drive His application to facets of their lives where truth was neglected. He specifically identified their neglect and called them to be bound by their word as they prescribed others to do so (Matt. 23:19–22). His knowledge of their neglect in this area drew the bull's-eye for His application regarding honesty.

Compartmentalization is not solely a problem of the Pharisees. In truth, all of us tend to apply Scripture in the most convenient and expedient ways. This reality must be ever before you as you seek to target your audience with the text you are preaching. If the transferable application deals with the Christian forgiving those who have wronged him, use your knowledge of the audience to pinpoint where forgiveness is most urgently needed within family units, workplace relationships, or church groups. If the congregation demonstrates a great deal of gracious forgiveness in the home but its tone and attitude toward employers is malicious and unforgiving, then that context for application should be considered as a potential target of your preaching goal.

The misunderstanding or misapplication of the application is another common problem you need to address. In the following example, the abuse of a biblical principle becomes a primary concern. When Paul had initially told the Corinthians to avoid associating with sexually immoral people in 1 Corinthians 5:9–11, some believers apparently misunderstood his intent and withdrew from *any and all* sexually immoral people. The intended application had limitations that, when missed, led to abuse of the principle. Therefore Paul explained they had missed the point and that their attempted application was in fact impossible.

As you prepare every sermon, make sure you explore areas where your audience may be attempting to live out application in inappropriate or misguided ways. With the prevalence of "bumper sticker theology" in contemporary Christendom, we must make a concerted effort to address these kinds of problems and misunderstandings in our sermons. This opens the door for your applications to have an eye-opening, freeing, and life-changing effect on those who hear them.

Crystallize How You Will Target Your Audience with the Application

Having laid your groundwork, you can now carefully articulate the specific goal of your sermon. Take the transferable application from your passage, as well as the gathered information regarding the original audience's relationship to that application, and seek to articulate the applicational goal for the audience to which you preach.

It is helpful to address the intellect, emotion, and will, but not necessarily with the broad brush used by many of today's preachers. It is not enough to ask myself what my audience should know regarding the meaning of the passage, but rather, it is important to ask more specifically what my audience should know regarding the *application of the passage*. This obviously includes a well-explained knowledge of the passage, but just as importantly, it must reveal the passage as it relates to the intended impact or life-change it calls for. The expected emotional response and the volitional response must be similarly handled, as we will see. Before we go there we must ask a preliminary question that will help pull together our overall applicational direction.

1. What Is the Greatest Need My Audience Has as It Relates to the Application?

After assessing both your audience's commonality with the original audience, and their practice, neglect or abuse of the transferable application, you must now determine the most pressing need to be addressed. This does not mean that the application is so specific that it only applies to one narrow context of life, but it must be more specific than a general conclusion from

51

Colossians 3:12–14 like, "my hearers need to reflect the love of Christ." In a sermon that is driving in that direction, it may be appropriate to conclude that "my hearers need to learn to love irritating people the way Christ loves us." With this goal, the message now widens its scope to include the wife with an insensitive husband, and the man with the unreasonable boss (both of which may be included in the specific applications I see my congregation currently neglecting). This focuses on the contemporary context while capturing the essence of the transferable application.

The greatest need of my audience may lead me to relate the transferable application to a shared life stage, a common temptation, or a common pressure they face. Or, it may hone in on the widespread misapplication or abuse of the truth being presented in an observed area of life. This will often drive the content and direction of the introduction as contemporary needs surface.

It may be helpful to articulate this need by completing the sentence, "My hearer's greatest need regarding this passage is. . . ." Forcing myself to identify this need for every sermon I preach keeps my sermons purposeful and on track. It provides the bead that aligns the parts of the sermon. It gives aim to my passion and draws my people to the uncovered relevance of the passage I seek to proclaim.

Further, we must consider what an appropriate response from our hearers will look like. Pondering an appropriate pattern of biblical obedience can be a helpful step in guiding the contemporary application. Ask yourself, "How will the hearer act, talk, think, or behave if he or she loves people who are irritating in the way Christ would love them?" If you cannot provide a solid answer, chances are your hearers cannot either.

2. What Should My Audience Know About the Application?

Though we seek to make application in a contemporary context, the "earthy" context itself often does not provide the elements critical to the framing of the application. I might conclude that if my hearers are going to love irritating people the way Christ loves them, then they must understand something of the quality of divine love as set against the backdrop of their sin. To crystallize this for my audience I teach how abhorrent sin is to a holy God. I teach the depth of Christ's love for us. Once they understand the nature of divine love, ignorance is no longer an excuse for their continued disobedience.

My goal at this stage is to state their intellectual need in light of the intended application. It may relate to the truth or the rationale behind the intended application, or it may simply seek a proper understanding of what is meant by the application. Either way, explicitly stating, "I want my audience to *know* that it cost Christ a lot to love us" helps me focus my attention on the challenge that lies before me as I preach to my congregation.

52

3. What Should My Audience Feel About the Application?

The hearer's emotional response is an oft-neglected aspect of preaching for life change. When we fail to address the emotional elements of the person, we neglect to preach to an integral part of the person. As Ian Pitt-Waltson writes:

> Unless there is some measure of emotional involvement on the part of the preacher and on the part of his hearers the *kerygma* cannot be heard in its fullness for the *kerygma* speaks to the whole man, emotions and all, and simply does not make sense to the intellect and the will alone.[21]   *EMOTION*

We must realize that seeking to connect the emotive wires of our hearers is not "emotional preaching." It is instead preaching to the entire person. All too often, our congregants confess, "I know I should do this or that, but I don't." Though they heard several sermons that convinced their minds regarding the application, it's obvious they have never been captivated by God's Spirit through a sermon leading to obedience in the matter. Simply, their heads and hearts are not in sync.

The emotional need should be articulated by finishing the statement, "I want my audience to *feel*. . . ." The statement should elicit an appropriate emotional response that rightly reflects the application in view. Statements such as "I want my audience to *feel* compassion toward irritating people" or "I want my audience to *feel* attracted to the love of Christ" or "I want my audience to *feel* agitated and uneasy about injustice" can provide focus as I preach the text at hand. It should not be a veiled intellectual or volitional goal, but it should clearly relate to the emotional aspect of their lives.

I WANT THEM TO FEEL . . .

4. What Should My Audience Do About the Application?

It may seem redundant to articulate what the audience should do in response to a proposed application, but it is an important step in the overall process. In explicitly stating their expected response, I trace a clear direction as to how my contemporary hearers are to incorporate this truth into their lives. I will seek to form the kind of statement that the biblical author might make were he to intimately know my audience and preach the passage to them. Imagining how the author of a passage would summarize its desired impact on your congregants will help you articulate a valid application.

You should articulate this goal with words that move beyond generalities to viable expressions of the application. You might state something like, "I want my audience to identify the irritating people in their lives and start extending tangible expressions of Christ-like love to them beginning this week." Make it something that can be acted upon in the upcoming week, but it should not be so specific that it limits application to one or two specific acts that can be checked off like items on a "to do" list. Though it will specifically target a particular sector or aspect of life, it should not exclude any segment of your congregation. Sometimes this is impossible, as when the primary thrust of your application focuses on singles, the married, or those with parents, but you should always seek to include as many in the congregation as possible.

Here the stated goal should focus on volition, even if the transferable application seemingly focuses on a truth to believe. We are usually too quick to elevate or relegate indicative truths to the intellectual realm, thereby failing to engage the volition. Biblical authors often addressed indicative statements in a volitional framework. Rather than putting a truth on display (e.g., "God cares for you"), or eliciting purely intellectual responses (e.g., "know and believe that God cares for you"), they often stimulate a *response* to the truth ("casting all your care upon Him, for He cares for you"—1 Pet. 5:7). This remains our task today.

Studying a passage in view of its intended impact on life—and bridging it with the needs and the understanding of a contemporary audience—lies at the heart of life-changing preaching. At first it may feel involved and laborious, especially on the heels of painstaking exegesis. Yet those who are disciplined to study a text's application as well as their audience, and are able to join the two together, will quickly learn to value the indispensable nature of this stage of message preparation.

CHAPTER FIVE

Frame an Outline that Will Change Your Audience

AN OUTLINE IS NOT A SERMON. THAT MAY SEEM LIKE AN ODD OBSERVATION, BUT it is an important one to make as we attempt to rethink the nature and purpose of outlining. While it is true that most sermons have a structure that has been (or could be) mapped out, the fact remains that the outline itself is not the sermon. The sermon is the totality of what is delivered; the outline is intended to govern and guide the preacher in his presentation, while maintaining a logical order and coherence to what is ultimately delivered.[1]

My dad has always been a stickler for using the right tool for the job. When as kids we raided his toolbox for a quick bike repair, woe unto us if we were ever caught using a pipe wrench when we should have been using a pair of pliers! If the bolt was metric, we dared not employ a standard socket. If the task called for a pair of channel locks, then we'd better not utilize needle-nose pliers.

Dad's concern wasn't so much for his tools as for our projects. He knew that the right tool always does the job better and more efficiently than the tool that is *almost* right. Searching for the right tool, shopping for the right tool, or even crafting the right tool is a smart and worthwhile investment.

When we preach we'd be wise to apply this axiom. Far too many times I have settled for an outline that I assumed would adequately accomplish my preaching goal, yet felt inside it really wasn't the right tool for the job. At times I found the toolbox I acquired through seminary didn't always have the kind of sermonic structures that best fit the passion and goals of the preaching I observed in the Bible, yet I felt awkward about crafting ones that did. I've concluded our preaching will be well served if we boldly rethink conventional outlining methods we have inherited and trade in good tools for better ones—even if we have to make them ourselves!

The primary points on the preacher's outline will be those chosen to highlight what is to be delivered. These might include phrases or sentences that reflect the explanations of the text, the logical points of an argument, or even the illustrations or the applications of the sermon. Don't underestimate the importance of those points to your audience. They are truths that you naturally emphasize. They are truths you have brought to the forefront in your speaking. And they are truths most likely to be remembered by those who hear your sermon.

If you are like most preachers, you likely choose the same kind of material as main points of your outline week after week. If you have been trained in common forms of expository preaching, your "points" probably reflect the structure and content of the text of Scripture. Pull out your last preaching outline and examine the essence of each main point. What did you try to capture as you formed those phrases or sentences? Did your statements explain the text, summarize the content, or advance an argument?

Those of us trained to preach "expositorially" probably follow, to some degree, the textbook examples of our forerunners. See if your outlines follow the pattern of this example of an Isaiah 6:1–8 "expository outline" from Broadus' classic book, *On the Preparation and Delivery of Sermons*:

  1. A Young Man's Vision of God

  2. A Young Man's Vision of Sin

  3. A Young Man's Vision of Cleansing

  4. A Young Man's Vision of Service[2]

Broadus' textbook, initially published in 1870, became the standard for several generations of preachers. Though there have been some variations on his theme, this basic format has been mimicked and replicated in millions of sermons ever since.[3]

A DIFFERENT APPROACH

If the exclusive goal of preaching is to transfer the content and structure of a passage to an audience, then this classic approach to outlining should continue to influence our methodology. But if preaching is meant to do more than merely teach content, if it is truly designed by God to persuasively rebuke, correct, and train in righteousness so that our people may be thoroughly equipped for every good work (2 Tim. 3:16–17), then we need to change our view and method of outlining our sermons.

Good ol' Scholasticism

As noted in chapter 2, scholasticism has had a lasting impact on the face of modern preaching. Ironically, most contemporary sermon outlines would be right at home on the lecterns of the medieval churches, since their shared goal was not transformation of lives but comprehension of truth. Listeners knew more, but did not necessarily do more. The sad and often unrecognized fact is, people do not leave scholastic sermons as doers of the word, but hearers with a deeper level of understanding.

I recently heard a sermon from a veteran pastor which, from the first word of the introduction to the final "amen," failed to present us with a single directive, guideline, or suggestion as to how God might want us to respond to the passage that had been carefully analyzed and discussed. This is scholastic preaching at its best, but biblical preaching at its worst. As Sidney Greidanus points out: "Without genuine relevance there is no sermon. Relevance for the church here and now is the final goal of sermon preparation."[4]

We can use our sermon outline to keep us from underscoring the high-points that simply reflect content or structure, and thus move us toward our final goal of relevance.

Pin the Tail on the Puritan Sermon

While many have abandoned strict scholastic preaching, they have perhaps unwittingly adopted a modified form of the same. The Puritans perfected this modified style of preaching that, in its form, rejects the sermon outline that had failed to address real life issues.

If you have read reprints of Puritan sermons from John Cotton, Thomas Hooker, Jonathan Edwards, or their contemporaries you have surely become acquainted with *the* Puritan sermon outline. Whereas the main points of a modern sermon usually reflect aspects of the passage, the four points of the Puritan outline were always the same regardless of the passage. They were laid over the top of whatever passage the preacher sought to exposit:

1. The Text

2. The Doctrine

3. The Usage

4. The Applications[5]

This format was called the "plain style" of sermon outlining. First, the *text* was explained word for word. Second, the theological axioms were highlighted or drawn from the passage. This generally constituted much of the sermon. Third, the "uses" of the doctrine were delineated in third person language. And finally, the sermon would conclude with the "uses" formed into second person applications that required the hearers to take the "doctrine to heart."[6]

These sermons were undoubtedly applicational and they did bring the text to bear on the "here" and "now" of the congregant's life. In practice, however, the pattern essentially consisted of a Bible lecture with an applicational addendum. While this addendum was tremendously important to the Puritans, and was no doubt a marked improvement over scholastic preaching, it failed to weave the relevance of the text throughout the fabric of the sermon.

Let the Entire Sermon Reveal the Bible's Relevance

If the purpose of preaching is to change lives, and if outlining is underscoring the highpoints of our sermon, then we should make the passage's applicational thrust the underscored points of our outline, accentuated throughout the entire sermon.

Jay Adams, an advocate of this kind of revolutionary outline, writes:

> It is in the message format that a preacher's true theory and practice of preaching can most clearly be discerned. When discussing how he preaches, he may say much about many things, but what he actually believes about preaching most plainly appears in the way he finally organizes his material. Those preachers who understand that preaching is application organize their points for application.[7]

Elsewhere he writes:

> The preacher . . . using a genuine preaching outline applies all along the way; indeed, in one sense the whole sermon is application. The preaching format is an applicatory format by nature.[8]

This simple shift from outlining a text's *content* to outlining its *application* can radically transform a sermon *and* the people who hear it.

In training untried future preachers, I have taught them to outline their sermons according to the passage's transferable application. As their instructor, I review their outlines before they step into the pulpit to preach and satisfy myself as to with the direction of their sermonic roadmap. Sometimes the novice preachers struggle—occasionally with every facet of delivery imaginable! I have watched introductions crash, illustrations cast a fog on the audience, and conclusions burst into flames before my eyes. However, if the would-be preacher managed to spit out his carefully worded main tenets, each poignantly addressing the audience's biblical responsibility, then the sermon was salvaged. At least its main points were engaging, convicting, and life changing. How much better was this than a

58

smoothly delivered sermon which endlessly dices up a text and carefully categorizes informational points yet never engages the listener with the "so what" of the passage?

To those who fear that this kind of applicational outlining jeopardizes true expository preaching, Jay Adams brusquely responds:

> Often, preachers, especially those who try to "stay close to the text" and so-called "expository" preachers will tell you that they use the structure of the passage to determine the structure of their sermon. Typically you will hear them say things like, "Now this text naturally falls into three divisions." So, it falls into three divisions; so what? Does that mean that sermons from Revelation will have seven points? Will a message from Proverbs always have two because proverbs "naturally" fall into two divisions? Will all preaching from John, with his many contrasts (light/darkness, truth/error, etc.), also be two-pointed? To say that a passage falls into so many divisions may be good literary and rhetorical analysis, but what has that got to do with preaching forms? What is the purpose of following the "natural textual divisions"? To be more biblical? To do so doesn't make you more biblical but *less* biblical.[9]

Some preachers have a missile lock on communicating Scripture's structure that prevents them from converting to applicational outlining. Others believe that the prominence of true explanation, and thus the hearer's understanding of Scripture, will somehow be jeopardized, and that keeps them from changing. To this Bryan Chapell responds:

> Recognize that the chief purpose of application is not simply to give people something to do. *Application gives ultimate meaning to the exposition.* Even if the explanation of a sermon were to define every Greek and Hebrew word for prayer, were to quote at length from Calvin, Luther, and E. M. Bounds on prayer's meaning, were to cite fifty passages that refer to prayer, and were to describe the prayer practices of David, Jeremiah, Daniel, Paul, and Jesus, would the listeners truly understand what prayer is? No. Until we engage in prayer we do not really understand it. Until we apply a truth, understanding of it remains incomplete. This means that until a preacher provides application, exposition remains incomplete.[10]

I see no better way to bring biblical relevance to bear on the congregation than to be faithful to the text's intended impact on lives. This causes me to state the main points of a sermon in terms of what the text and its Author expect from people who hear it.

Start with the Primary Preaching Point

Start with "the proposition,"[11] "the big idea,"[12] or "the *telic* purpose"[13] of the sermon. This is the overarching and governing concept of the entire message. I prefer to call this "the preaching point."

The preaching point of most sermons slides over from the preacher's exegesis, often with little or no modification at all. Once the passage has been synthesized and encapsulated into a phrase or sentence (utilizing questions such as "what is this passage talking about?" and "what is this passage saying about what it is talking about?"[14]), it often becomes the preaching point by default. In attempting to "preach the passage" (i.e., its content) preachers innately conclude that there is no better way to do it than to enlist the raw textual idea and enthrone it as the preaching point. Thoughtful preachers proceed from there with main points that further parse the text's summary statement.

It should be clear by now that a preaching point that governs an applicational outline must be more, and accomplish more, than a statement that serves as a synopsis of the textual content. A synopsis of the textual content (what I call "the textual point"), no matter how well done, cannot adequately govern the sermon if the sermon is to accomplish the goal of true biblical preaching.

Bringing a textual point to the place where it is ready to be stated as a preaching point was the basis of chapter 4. That chapter began with the assumption that a text's meaning has been accurately discovered and the textual point succinctly stated. That textual point was then to be considered in light of the passage's applicational impact on the lives of the original recipients. Next, the transferability of that application was to be carefully analyzed and considered in light of a specific contemporary audience. Then, and only then, the preaching idea is ready to be formulated. More than simply restating the meaning of the text, the preaching point encapsulates both the meaning and its contemporary significance in a single sentence.

Here are some sample preaching points:

> From Hebrews 10:24–25; "It is more urgent now than ever that we Christians get together and help each other be more godly!"

> From Colossians 3:5–11; "The Christian life is a battle against sin—one that requires a daily revitalization of the new heart that God has given you!"

> From 2 Samuel 17:1–29; "Confidently believe and rejoice that, because of Christ, God loves you even when you feel the most unlovable!"

60

An applicational statement of the preaching point is critical to understanding the relevance of the passage you are preparing to preach. It brings the truth of the passage face-to-face with your audience. Joseph Stowell comments:

> No doubt the most important aspect of clarity is the formation of a concise, memorable, applicational statement of the central idea. While the exegetical statement of the central idea may be "Christ elevates servanthood as an imperative," an applicational version might be "The authentic Christian descends into greatness." . . . Ask the question, "How can this point focus on the listener?" Craft the statement in a precise and penetrating way. . . . Work hard at this.[15]

GUIDELINES FOR OUTLINING THE MAIN POINTS

Once the preaching point can be articulated in a clear and applicational way, the main points should be worded applicationally. Remember the importance of these points. They are statements that, by their placement and presentation, form the elements of your message that will be highlighted and most likely remembered. Spending significant amounts of time on their construction will always be worth the effort.

The following guidelines will help you frame these important statements.

Connect the Main Points to the Preaching Point

The preaching point should provide unity and cohesion for the message. If you have established a preaching point that accurately reflects the meaning and contemporary significance of your passage, then it may rightly serve as a *hub* of the main points of your sermon. It is a common practice of some preachers to *link* one main point of their sermon to the next as a chain. Doing so can easily result in a sermon that drifts away from the intended preaching point. An outline that only gives thought to the preceding material may show the relation of each point to the next, but in the end, the sermon may conclude with a point that has little or no perceivable relation to the first.

While narrative and inductive forms of preaching which seek to arrive at the preaching point at the conclusion of the sermon are obvious exceptions, the cohesion and sequence of the kind of outlining I am describing can be visualized by the following diagram. (See fig. 5.1.)

Figure 5.1
The Preaching Point as the "Hub"

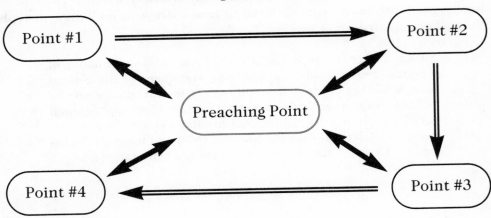

There is generally a greater applicational impact on God's people when the preacher is careful to show the connection between all major parts of the sermon to the central preaching point. When the main points are worded with logical proximity to the preaching point, the transitions naturally fall into place and the cohesion of the message is preserved.

Use Second Person Pronouns in the Main Points

It has been rightly noted, "the preacher is not to speak before the people but to them."[16] This simple and obvious discourse feature rarely is heeded when wording main points of sermon outlines. It is an effortless adjustment, yet dramatic changes take place in a sermon outline when one shifts from the scholastic third person ("he," "his," "they," "them," "theirs") to the more direct and intimate second person pronouns (e.g., "you," "your," yours").

Framing your main points in the third person allows the hearer to side-step the issue and apply it to someone else. At best, third person propositions are presented for the hearer to analyze and consider, not to heed and obey. At worst, use of third person pronouns distances the truth from the very people we hope to provoke to become doers of the Word. Consider Broadus' textbook example again from Isaiah 6:

1. A Young Man's Vision of God
2. A Young Man's Vision of Sin
3. A Young Man's Vision of Cleansing
4. A Young Man's Vision of Service[17]

This kind of third person outline deals with an enthralling passage of the Bible in subdued terms relating to someone else's life—and that of a "spiritual giant" no less! The actual message may inspire some to action, but it does so at a cultural and historical distance. The simple shift into the second person changes the feel of the entire outline:

1. A Young Man's Vision of God

     \ 1. Your Vision of God

2. A Young Man's Vision of Sin

     \ 2. Your Vision of Sin

3. A Young Man's Vision of Cleansing

     \ 3. Your Vision of Cleansing

4. A Young Man's Vision of Service

     \ 4. Your Vision of Service

A personal challenge emerges as you use the outline points to talk directly to the listener. All with the help of one small grammatical shift! But even more can be done to bring our hearers face to face with the truth of Isaiah 6.

Make the Main Points Imperatives

It takes more than just stating main points in the second person to make an outline truly applicational. True application calls our listeners to respond to the Word, and it is your job to make that response clear to your audience.

Again, simple English grammar is the key. Simply move the wording of your points out of the indicative mood (the way things are) and into the imperative (a call to the way they should be). While some preachers worry about sounding heavy-handed or oppressive, we must never ignore our calling as heralds. If obedience to God's Word is the intended goal of bringing the message, then we ought to frame our outlines in a way to be clear about the listener's responsibility.

Assuming that Dr. Blackwell's example in Broadus should include application in each point, watch what happens to the outline when that application is made explicit:

1. A Young Man's Vision of God

     \ 1. Elevate Your View of God

63

2. A Young Man's Vision of Sin

\ 2. See the Ugliness of Your Sin

3. A Young Man's Vision of Cleansing

\ 3. Embrace the Cleansing of Forgiveness

4. A Young Man's Vision of Service

\ 4. Dive into the Challenge of Service

These simple grammatical shifts are easy to make, but the roadblock to implementing them just may be within you. You may not want to be perceived as a confrontational authoritarian, so you may want to hide behind the softer, generic third person. After all, don't "preachy" preachers turn people off?

Unfortunately, our culture has made a baneful caricature out of preaching. While in seminary, I briefly backed off from even using the word "preach." I succumbed to society's pressure to avoid that unpleasant and disliked company of "preachers." I wanted to avoid using the tabooed word, as well as avoid the act itself. But sooner or later, all preachers must come to the conclusion that preaching is their job. People may knock it. They may preface their statements over coffee with words like, "I don't mean to preach . . .". They may even equate what you do with soapboxes and big black Bibles. The simple truth is, if you are called to be a preacher, then you must preach! If you don't, you will degenerate into something truly worse. You might find yourself sliding into the ambiguous "Neverland" of Bible-talker or spiritual adviser. But if you know the lofty New Testament calling resides on your life, then fulfill your calling and unapologetically call people to obedience of God's Word. Call sinners to repentance and Christians to conformity to the image of Christ. Don't suggest it. Don't advise it. Preach it!

Luther in typical fashion writes:

> The Gospel ministry should spare no one, no matter how high the position may be which he occupies, but should rebuke wrong in everybody. This is why ministers and preachers exist. A very heavy burden is placed on them. They should so conduct their office that they stand ready to answer for it and give an account of it on Judgment Day. If they do not speak to you and rebuke in you what their office requires them to speak and to rebuke, God will require your blood from their hand. Tell me, why should we preachers burden ourselves still more by preaching to you as you desire? It is not our word. Nor do we live for your sake, as though you had ordered us, and we had to preach what you like.

> Preachers can, will, and should not do this. Therefore he who will not listen is free in God's name to walk out through the church door and let our Lord God keep His ministry unhindered.[18]

Though preaching is to be direct, it is not a task to be discharged with dictatorial glee or angst. It is a humble task, born in a heart of the preacher who has a burden for God's people. When second person imperative preaching is set against the backdrop of a loving pastoral ministry, the two sides of ministry are biblically complemented. Notice the description of Paul's ministry among the Thessalonians:

> We were gentle among you, just as a nursing mother cherishes her own children. So, affectionately longing for you, we were well pleased to impart to you not only the gospel of God, but also our own lives, because you had become dear to us. . . . You know how we exhorted, and comforted, and charged every one of you, as a father does his own children, that you would have a walk worthy of God who calls you into His own kingdom and glory (1 Thess. 2:7–8, 11–12).

Loving ministry complements the power of second person imperative preaching; it should not exclude it. Our calling and burden for people both demand it. As Paul wrote, "Knowing, therefore, the terror of the Lord, we persuade men" (2 Cor. 5:11). We are called to a persuasive ministry, empowered by God's Spirit and aided by the use of direct language.

Keep the Wording of the Main Points Simple

When attempting to craft the main points of the sermon into applicable, second person imperatives that are clearly connected to the preaching point, we have a tendency to make them too long and complicated. At times we unwittingly obscure our main points in an effort to word them as completely as possible. Carefully qualifying each of the applicational points can lead to statements often fifteen and even twenty words in length. Though it is important to express a thought completely, keeping it simple makes it more potent and effective.

Jesus' teaching reminds us that constantly qualifying our statements can detract from their power. He always spoke truthfully, and His teaching, especially His use of second person imperatives, was usually terse, pithy, and to the point. The imperatives were sometimes misunderstood and taken out of context, but Jesus' preaching preference was that of the clear and concise over the complex and circuitous. When He said "not to resist an evil person" (Matt. 5:39), He could have easily provided the crowds with a number of biblical exceptions and qualifications. But He didn't. When He taught, "Ask, and it will be given to you" (Matt. 7:7), He could have packed much more into that statement to avoid confusion. But He didn't. When He exhorted, "Do not lay up for yourselves treasures on earth" (Matt. 6:19) He could have expanded the thought to exclude appropriate provisions for one's evening meal. But He didn't. Instead Jesus allowed the power of His simple second person imperatives to resonate in the hearts of His hearers. Did He face "questions in the lobby" that began with "what about . . . ?" I'm sure He did. It was the unmitigated impact of concise preaching points, however, that characterized the teaching of Christ.

English Puritan Richard Baxter reminds us:

> All our teaching must be as plain and simple as possible. This doth best suit a teacher's end. . . . Truth loves the light, and is most beautiful when most naked. It is the sign of an envious enemy to hide the truth; and it is the work of a hypocrite to do this under pretence of revealing it; and therefore painted obscure sermons (like painted glass in windows which keeps out the light) are too oft the marks of painted hypocrites.[19]

The Puritans brought back a simplicity and clarity to the pulpit, part of a movement that had already begun among many preachers during the Reformation.[20] Because the Puritan preaching was intended (according to Robert Cushman) "to point out the Gospel in plain and flat English, amongst a company of plain Englishmen," the Puritan preachers opposed elaborate and flowery literary devices.[21]

Make the Main Points Clear

It is possible for us to be simple and concise and yet still ambiguous. If our pithy statement evokes shrugged shoulders and wrinkled brows, our time in preparation and our point are both lost.

I may sometimes rewrite my main points fifty or sixty times before I settle on wording that accurately and *clearly* communicates God's intended effect. Though all my attempts are short, they are not all clear. Arriving at main points that resound with clarity can be a daunting task, but the fruit of the challenge is always worth it.

John MacArthur talks of the effort clarity requires:

> It's very easy to be hard to understand, very easy. All you have to do is not know what you're talking about and nobody else will either. Sometimes you hear somebody speak and you think "It's too deep for me." Probably not. Probably you didn't understand it because they didn't understand it. It's very hard to be crystal clear because you have to have mastered your understanding. And when you respond to a preacher and you get the message, it's

66

because they have done the hard work of understanding it in their own mind so that they can convey it clearly to you because they understand it clearly. That is what has impact on people's lives. Just mumbling about the Bible with a lack of clarity doesn't have a positive effect. Speaking the word of God [so that it can be] clearly understood is what brings its impact to the heart. And that takes effort.[22]

Don't Create Too Many Main Points

It should be obvious that too many main points will dilute the effect of any one of them. Rarely does a powerful, memorable, or life-changing sermon contain seven or eight main points.

Most novice preachers tend to attempt to communicate too much material in too many points.[23] Experience bears this out. The more years of preaching experience one has, the more likely he will tighten the focus of material in order to create a stronger impact.

Fight the temptation to communicate everything you know about a passage. Hold back from exploring "just one more" angle on the text or its application. Settle on two, three, or four applicational statements to drive home to your audience. You likely will have the opportunity to revisit that particular text again in another sermon, so file away that nugget for another day.

Careful planning and hard work invested in the framing of statements that will provide the structure, unity, and focus of your message will yield tremendous rewards. God will use the reiteration of His applicational intent for your audience as a tool to bring His Word to bear on their lives. It is our awesome responsibility to pen the points the Holy Spirit will use in His transforming work.

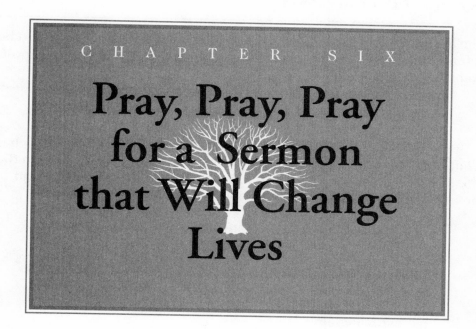

CHAPTER SIX

Pray, Pray, Pray for a Sermon that Will Change Lives

WHEN I WAS FIFTEEN AND A HALF MY FATHER BOUGHT ME THE DREAM OF EVERY soon-to-be-licensed teenager. To my adolescent eyes, that "pre-owned" 1967 VW Bug might as well have been a Ferrari. It looked great!

Just as I was about to ask if I could drive the car around the neighborhood and show it off to my friends, my adolescent dream crashed into reality. Dad informed me that, while the Bug had a lot of neat features, unfortunately, it had no engine!

My dad had figured that my after-school job would allow me not only to buy gas and pay for car insurance, but also to help pay for an old VW engine that he and I could rebuild in the evenings. That summer I learned a lot about carburetors and cam shafts. I also learned that often the stuff about a car that matters most is not apparent at first glance.

When it comes to preaching, most seasoned pastors have made a similar observation. Plenty of naïve anticipation has been dashed before noon on Sunday when a young preacher discovers that shiny accessories are no substitute for the power required to drive any sermon into the hearts and lives of our hearers. Without prayer, our sermons may look good on paper—they may even sound good in the pulpit—but you can bet that they will never leave the church parking lot.

God powerfully used the preaching of Martin Luther as a tool for dramatic change. It is no surprise then to discover that Luther's life motto was "To pray well is half the study."[1] Though many factors contributed to the revolutionary impact of his preaching, prayer was unquestionably the cornerstone. Luther knew that prayer "is not a matter that is to be left to our choice," but if we are to do anything that will be eternally profitable we should and must pray.[2]

THE INDISPENSABLE INGREDIENT

It should be no secret that prayer is the tool with which the preacher crafts and effectually delivers his sermons. Its ubiquitous presence in the life of every effective preacher reminds us that we dare not attempt to preach without it. As E. M. Bounds observes:

> A ministry may be a very thoughtful ministry without prayer; the preacher may secure fame and popularity without prayer; the whole machinery of the preacher's life and work may be run without the oil of prayer or with scarcely enough to grease one cog; but no ministry can be a spiritual one, securing holiness in the preacher and in his people, without prayer being made an evident and controlling force.[3]

Prayer must be the "evident and controlling force" in preaching because the goal of preaching is supernatural. No human can attain the goal of spiritually transforming lives through preaching without divine involvement. Ardent study, intelligent outlines, or persuasive presentations will not ensure that true biblical fruit will result from our preaching. The message, the messenger, and his audience must all be impacted by the Spirit of God.

Jesus makes this crystal clear in His parable of the seed and the sower. Christ describes a potent seed which is properly cast. The sower does all the right things to secure a crop. But as the story unfolds it becomes obvious that preaching requires more than mere human proclamation. Jesus lays out for us the spiritual battle that wages when the biblical sermon encounters the soils: "Some people are like seed along the path, where the word is sown. As soon as they hear it, Satan comes and takes away the word that was sown in them" (Mark 4:15 NIV). Christ's tersely stated reason for the sermon's failure to change these lives is chilling. While you battle in your study to craft a biblical sermon, remember that another battle will be waged in the pew, and still another in the hours and days that follow. Unless God fights all of the spiritual battles that rage whenever we purpose to preach His word, our efforts will surely fail. God *must* be thoroughly involved.

The enemy would gladly accept a variety of "positive responses" when you preach. He'd happily allow people to be impressed with your outlines, as long as people aren't changed. He'd gladly foster their interest in what you have to say, as long as they aren't changed. He'd cheerfully pass out warm feelings about your message, as long as people aren't changed. Surely he would settle for anything short of your biblical sermon affecting permanent transformation in peoples' lives. That is the goal of your preaching, and it is a goal beyond your reach. God must do it—and prayer is the way He says it will get done. Luther understood this when he wrote:

> Therefore, putting aside the foolish confidence as though we had some ability to help the Word along in the hearer, let us rather engage in the prayer that without us He alone may perfect in the hearer what He speaks in the teacher. For it is He who speaks, and it is He who hears and works all in all people. We are His vessels and instruments, powerless either to receive or to give unless He Himself gives and receives.[4]

The work is God's. Therefore, our petitioning of Him must take precedence.

MAKE PRAYER THE PRIORITY

The first-century leadership of the Jerusalem church demonstrated the importance of the preacher's priorities when they delegated a variety of leadership responsibilities to others so that they could give themselves "continually to prayer and to the ministry of the word" (Acts 6:4). They clearly understood that the ministry of the word and a devotion to prayer were inseparable disciplines. They knew that effective preaching would require significant blocks of time in which the preacher would give himself "continually to prayer."

Participation in the "ministry of the word" comes with a built-in accountability. Sunday and Wednesday arrive and we are on the docket, so if we fail to step up to the plate and preach, the vacuum is glaringly obvious. If we stand up to preach without adequate effort in preparation, our ad-libbed attempt is just as obvious. We are therefore compelled, by the public nature of the act, and the calendar, to apply ourselves to the tasks of message preparation and delivery. Unfortunately, our calling to pray does not have the same level of built-in accountability. In fact if the average preacher were to neglect his calling to pray for the entire week, few people would even notice. A well-reasoned, creatively illustrated message can carry the day with few complaints or concerns from the congregation. It is possible to preach carefully crafted sermons for weeks and even months without giving any time at all for prayer, and few in your church would ever suspect you are failing to fulfill your calling.

But don't fool yourself. Your sermons are unlikely to accomplish their God-ordained task. You may not fail to inform your people, but you will fail to change them. You may not fail to keep their attention, but you will fail to achieve the true purpose of preaching. John Piper diagnoses the problem of prayerless preaching when he writes: "The aroma of God will not linger on a person who does not linger in the presence of God. . . . Without prayer the God of our studies will be the unfrightening and uninspiring God of insipid academic gamesmanship."[5] Our times cannot afford pulpit gamesmanship.

If powerful, life-changing preaching is your aim, then like Luther you must resolve that open books and open eyes can only constitute half of the study. David Larsen is right when he asserts that "we have not prepared until we have prayed."[6] Yet surveys consistently reveal that while pastors spend hours in any given day studying a passage of Scripture to be preached, on average, they spend less than 30 minutes praying. Presumably, much of that meager half hour is spent on issues unrelated to the sermons they are preparing.[7] If this is true, it is little wonder that such a small amount of preaching today makes any lasting impact on the lives of those who hear it.

SCHEDULE IT

Praying specifically for the sermons we prepare is a spiritual exercise that must be scheduled. We cannot expect to find time to do it; we must make the time to do it! And then we must vigilantly guard that time. We must get serious about blocking out parts of the days within our allotted message preparation time and must learn to say "no" to every competing distraction.

Consciously or subconsciously, you have probably structured various sub-schedules within your current preparation schedule. You have most likely allotted times to ponder the text at hand, read commentaries, craft an outline, and create appropriate illustrations. These sub-schedules prompt you to flow from one task to another. Since we all have learned that 90 percent of our preparation time cannot be dedicated to any one aspect of message construction, you have established a certain rhythm (and discipline to maintain that rhythm) to move you from text to sermon each week. The point here is that prayer must be included—or better yet, interlaced—in this rhythm.

You may choose to schedule a time of focused prayer at the top of every hour during your preparation. If you do, you may also need a regular prompt to keep you to it. Try an hourly alarm on your wristwatch or clock radio. If you have scheduled prayer between your reading of each commentary, use a sticky-note on the cover of every book to prompt you. If you've assigned certain hours for uninterrupted prayer time, ask your secretary or another staff member to call and remind you to pray at the specified times. Be creative. Use any means available until focused and fervent prayer moves from a mere scheduled item to an irreplaceable aspect of your message preparation.

If ever you are tempted to feel as though your prayer time is an intrusion on your study time—if you kneel to pray and think, "I need this time to 'make progress' on this message"—then remember that prayer can actually be the most instructive part of your study. Martin Luther's assertion that prayer constituted half of his study was bolstered when he testified, "I have often learned much more in one prayer than I have been able to glean from much reading and reflection."[8] Any thought that would oppose your prayer time should be suspect. The urgency of sermon deadlines should not lure us *away from* our time of prayer, but rather *to it*.

BE SPECIFIC IN YOUR PRAYING

During message preparation it is important that our prayer time be focused and strategic. Wandering minds and widely varied topics that intrude upon our sermon prayer time may reflect a deficiency in our devotional lives. Stay up to date with your personal prayer list so that you don't find your message preparation prayer time inundated with items unrelated to the task at hand.

Though our ultimate concern is for God's people to rightly respond to God's Word, the focus of our prayers, like our preaching, is threefold. We must specifically pray in regards to the crafting of the sermon, the delivery of the sermon, and the intended response to the sermon. (See Appendix 1 for a reproducible list of the prayer items that follow.)

Pray for the Crafting of the Sermon

There are at least five basic requests that can and should be made in relation to the preparation of the sermon.

1. Pray that the message you are preparing will be an evident part of your own life. Pray to step up to preach the message you are preparing without any trace of hypocrisy. Ask the Holy Spirit to convict you of sin regarding the practice of the truth you are seeking to understand and proclaim. Request that he thoroughly evaluate your own life to ferret out any pockets of compromise that exist as they relate to the passage you are preparing to exposit.

2. Pray for the protection of your sermon preparation time. The timing and variety of distractions that assault our study time should remind us that "our struggle is not against flesh and blood, but against . . . the spiritual forces of evil in the heavenly realm" (Eph. 6:12). Ask God to fight the battle against unnecessary interruptions and phone calls that would steal time from your sermon preparation.

73

3. Pray that you will be given grace and illumination to rightly divide His Word. Pray God's Spirit will guide your insight into the passage and grant you understanding and an accurate interpretation of the passage.

4. Pray that the words you choose to frame your outline will be effective tools for the Holy Spirit to employ. Pray that the vocabulary you use to build the structure of your sermon will assist in producing a biblical response to the message. Pray that the words used to present the sermon will not be misleading, distracting, or in any way prove to be stumbling blocks to the people who hear them.

5. Pray that you will have insight into the needs of your audience as they relate to the sermon you are preparing. Pray that the ways you seek to apply God's Word will perfectly address the current needs of the people who hear your sermon.

Pray for the Delivery of the Sermon

Several aspects that relate to the actual delivery of the sermon require God's specific intervention. Remember these six aspects of the preaching event during your preparatory prayer times:

1. Pray that people will attend the preaching event. Your audience's spiritual battle commences the moment they wake up on Sunday morning. It is easy to assume that people will simply show up to hear the Word preached. Don't assume it; ask for it. Pray that God will bring to your church this Sunday all those who need to hear and respond to the sermon you are preparing.

2. Pray that your audience will arrive in the right frame of mind. Pray for protection for those God is calling to hear the sermon. Remember, their battle is being waged in their homes, on the roads to church, and maybe even in the church parking lot! Pray that their time prior to the preaching event will help to enhance their receptivity and not detract from it. Pray that they will reach their seats with well-prepared hearts.

3. Pray that God will guard against preaching distractions. It is important to keep in mind that the enemy fights against the clear preaching of God's Word with the most common of weapons. A crying baby, a ringing cell phone, an allergy attack, or a dead microphone can effectively steal attention and deflate a powerful moment in a sermon. Implore God to protect the sermon from all potential distractions.[9]

4. Pray for clarity in your vocabulary. Since effective preaching rarely springs from manuscripts or memorized scripts, there is always a certain amount of spontaneity in one's vocabulary, and that vocabulary can be affected by a wide range of factors. Pray that God's Spirit will govern your words and keep your mouth and mind on track. Since your mind can formulate thoughts much faster than you can express them, pray that those

74

"extra thoughts" will be focused in productive areas and not found roaming on useless sidetracks.

5. Pray that God will give your audience understanding. Pray that your audience will be alert, attentive, and eager to understand what you present. Pray that God will prevent the enemy from stealing away the word you sow. Ask him to illuminate His Word and allow those present to mentally track with the truths you preach.

6. Ask God for the most effective and fruitful sermon you have ever preached. This is admittedly a bold prayer, but it is a reasonable prayer for those hoping to make continual progress. Most preachers readily admit that their preaching gifts have not yet been fully developed. If that's true of you, then humbly ask God to make your progress a discernible reality each and every time you preach.

Pray for the Response to the Sermon

It is supremely important that we pray for victory in the spiritual battle that ensues *after* the sermon has been delivered. Here are four specific items worth praying about as we prepare to preach:

1. Pray that people will put the sermon into practice. This is by far the most obvious petition to bring before God each week, yet it is frequently neglected in our prayers. It's not an overstatement to say this single request might well occupy the bulk of our praying. Like Christ, we should long to see our hearers build their lives on the truth. This was not only His stated concern, but also His passion, so it needs to comprise a great deal of our time and energy in prayer. Herein lies the central spiritual conflict each time we preach—when the hearers walk away, will the sermon make any lasting difference? We ought to labor in prayer that those who hear our sermon would prove to be doers of the word and not merely hearers of it.

2. Pray that the sermon will not be compartmentalized. Ask God to prevent your hearers from relegating the application of the sermon to only one aspect of their lives. People frequently apply truth to areas of life that are convenient. Or, they limit application only to the few areas suggested in the sermon. To combat these tendencies, pray that God will drive the application of the message into any and every area of your hearers' lives.

3. Pray that the application of the sermon will be contagious. The far-reaching impact of effective preaching is naturally transmitted through the lives of faithful congregants, so pray that your hearers will be enthusiastic about passing it on. Consider the reverberation of the apostle Paul's preaching. He expected its effects to go far beyond the immediate audience: "And the things you have heard from me among many witnesses, commit these to faithful men who will be able to teach others also" (2 Tim. 2:2). Ask God to impact your congregation so profoundly that they will become ambassadors of the truth you preach.

4. Pray that the sermon itself will be delivered repeatedly. For centuries, effective biblical sermons have been preserved in some form for the purpose of being reused and relived. In the early days of the church, sermons were transcribed to be reread. Today most of us make audiotapes available. Though rereading or rehearing cannot possibly capture important dimensions of the live preaching event, both mediums have been used greatly of God to bear fruit in the lives of those unable to hear the sermon firsthand. Ask God to multiply your efforts by directing recorded copies of your sermon to those who need it. A heightened sense of responsibility and anticipation emerges when we prepare a message that may have an effect on people we may never meet this side of eternity.

Praying through this list each time you prepare a sermon will no doubt require a good chunk of your study time. However, you will truly experience what it means in Acts 6:4 to *pray* and preach. It will also put your efforts in perspective. Serious prayer preparation will convince you that God is the victor in the entire preaching process. If a biblical outline is well constructed, if people show up and comprehend your sermon, if they actually leave and practice it, if it bears far-reaching fruit, then you are never tempted to take the credit. Instead, you realize you have prayed well, and that God has done something marvelous and mysterious. You will quietly and humbly comprehend that, for this moment in time, you have been used as a tool in the hand of God to bring His message of grace to the lives of His people—and you will bow in the light of His glory.

DEVELOP A "MESSAGE PREP" PRAYER TEAM

Few things have emboldened my preaching and preparation more than knowing I have a team of committed people praying for the fruitfulness of my next sermon. Trust God for an ever-widening circle of friends who will bring these weekly requests before God. Again, Martin Luther provides encouragement and insight as he exhorts us to pray *together*:

> No man should be alone when he opposes Satan. The church and the ministry of the Word were instituted for this purpose, that hands may be joined together and one may help another. If the prayer of one doesn't help, the prayer of another will.[10]

As part of my preparation I have made it a practice to partner with one or two men who will pray with me in my office. Scheduling prayer partners to come in the thick of the study and preparation battle can provide refreshment and perspective as they pray for God's involvement and intervention in every aspect of the sermon.

Broaden the Circle

After years of personally praying with a fellow pastor or layman for my weekly sermons, I ventured to broaden the circle even wider. This resulted in a prayer team of over twenty-five people who cover every hour of my weekly preparation. My single most heartening comfort amid the labor of study is knowing that there is a godly person grappling in prayer for me, the sermon, and its impact.

Remarkably, this inestimable benefit is simple to arrange. Begin by mapping out the hours in your week committed to study and message preparation. If you study for three hours on Tuesday mornings, five hours on Thursday afternoons and all day Friday, then create a table that breaks down that schedule hour by hour. The resultant chart provides sixteen or seventeen "hour blocks" which correspond to the hours you spend preparing the sermon each week.

Next, note something of the process you go through in preparing your message during those time slots. Of course, every hour cannot be surgically distinguished from the next, but attempt to reflect the time period in which you generally work with the text, the time period you usually consult reference works and commentaries, and the time period in which you draft the outline. (See Appendix 2 for a sample chart.)

Enlisting a Team

Finding those whose schedules allow them to pray at the same time each week will prove to be an important part of this prayer plan. With this breakdown of your weekly study schedule and a general description of the progress you make from text to sermon, identify faithful, godly people who you believe will consistently pray for you and the impact of the sermon. Considering each person's insight, experience, and most importantly his/her weekly schedule, match people with appropriate time slots. These prayer team members usually will not be asked to pray *with* you, but they will pray *for* you and for the sermon where they are during their assigned hour. I have found that homemakers, retirees, and shut-ins often are best-suited for this kind of prayer ministry.

In the recruiting of prayer team members I do not ask the men and women to pray the entire hour without interruption, but I do hope to instill a sense of stewardship whereby their assigned hour is, at the very least, punctuated by thoughtful and fervent prayer.

Some may initially question the importance of having people pray during specified hours of the week, but I believe that after a few weeks of faithful prayer coverage you will be reluctant to leave a single hour of your preparation uncovered.

Communicating with the Team

Giving specific and regular guidance to your Message Prep Prayer Team provides the fuel for keeping their prayers fresh and consistent. You may choose to start by giving them the list of the fifteen prayer items suggested in this chapter (and itemized in Appendix 1). Spending just two minutes in prayer for each of these items would require half of the hour they have been assigned. Reproduce the prayer list for them, or challenge them to construct their own list to use during their scheduled prayer time.

I also communicate weekly with my Message Prep Prayer Team through email. It's a quick and easy way to update the entire team. In it I give them a sense of where I am headed in the sermon. It lets them know what special challenges are contained in the passage at hand, and what my hopes and desires are for the intended impact of the sermon. This email, sent near the beginning of the week, helps to provide each person on the team with specific items and information for his or her scheduled prayer time.

I have found that most consider it a privilege to join with me in prayer during a specific hour of the week for something of such eternal value. Their concern for its fruitfulness is increased while their anticipation for God's work in their own lives each week is heightened. Their privilege is a benefit to the entire congregation.

DEVELOP A "PRE-DELIVERY" PRAYER TEAM

The sense of need and urgency regarding the sermon naturally shifts into high gear just prior to the preaching event, making this a critical time for prayer. Many preachers already have a prayer team that meets during this time. If you do not, consider drafting one as soon as possible. To segue from a prayer meeting into a scheduled time of preaching makes for a perfect transition. Rearrange your preliminary routine if necessary in order to gain the strength, perspective, and grace which come through prayers that call for God's power in your preaching.

In my own ministry, I have limited this group to a small number of handpicked men who arrive 30 minutes before the service begins. Some are church leaders, some are staff, and others are laymen. We don't shoot the breeze before we begin, or provide donuts and coffee. We briefly greet one another and get immediately to the work of prayer.

The expectations and enthusiasm generated in that concentrated half hour of prayer are contagious. We experience a heightened sense of dependence on God to work in our midst. We feel a deepening burden to see God's Word communicated accurately. We ignite within our hearts a passion to see God's truth transform people's lives. It also greatly encourages the preacher to know godly men are standing with him as he goes forth to proclaim God's Word.

Of course, these are all collateral benefits of this prayer time. The real joy is watching God respond. When we see God graciously do what we have humbly asked Him, we rejoice in His work. And if we are faithful to pray before every sermon, it becomes increasingly impossible to mistake whose work this really is. When lives are changed, clearly God alone has done it.

DEVELOP AN "AS YOU PREACH" PRAYER TEAM

If the entire preaching process is a spiritual battle, we should naturally assume that much of it is waged while the preaching actually is taking place. Jay Adams describes an ancient scene from the fourth century in which the renowned preacher, John Chrysostom, interrupts his sermon with the following rebuke:

> Please listen to me—you are not paying attention. I am talking to you about the Holy Scriptures, and you are looking at the lamps and the people lighting them. It is very frivolous to be more interested in what the lamplighters are doing. . . . After all, I am lighting a lamp too—the lamp of God's word.[11]

Frustration over the spiritual warfare during preaching can tempt every preacher at times to interrupt the flow of his sermon with a pastoral reprimand. Yet we usually resist, concluding that a mid-sermon censure would be counterproductive. On top of that, we understand our real struggle extends far beyond the symptomatic intrusions of cell phones or lamplighters. It is our enemy who is at work, and God must intervene to thwart him.

Seeing the battle from the pulpit is not difficult, but personally praying for God's intervention while absorbed in the task of preaching is most difficult. To simultaneously pray and preach is nearly impossible, so this one aspect of life-changing preaching must be delegated entirely to others.

If your church has multiple services and a small, unused room, then this ministry is very easy to establish. Invite groups of godly people to pray specifically for the preaching *while* it is actually taking place. If you hold two services, a small group which attends the early service can pray during the later service, and vice versa. If you have only one service, find people who will forfeit their opportunity to sit under your preaching once every two or three months in order to pray for its effectiveness. In so doing they will quickly grow in their understanding of the critical impact prayer has upon effective biblical preaching.

To preach with every facet of your preparation and delivery girded by the faithful prayers of godly men and women is a powerful experience. Once you engage in a pulpit ministry that has been bathed in prayer, you won't dare preach without it.

PRAY EXPECTANTLY

We must approach our preaching task with an attitude that anticipates God's active involvement. Consider how Jesus beckons us to pray with a set of incredible promises:

> Ask, and it will be given to you; seek, and you will find; knock, and it will be opened to you. For everyone who asks receives, and he who seeks finds, and to him who knocks it will be opened. Or what man is there among you who, if his son asks for bread, will give him a stone? Or if he asks for a fish, will he give him a serpent? If you then, being evil, know how to give good gifts to your children, how much more will your Father who is in heaven give good things to those who ask Him! (Matt 7:7–11).

Here Jesus clearly demonstrates that He wants those who come to Him to come with expectant hearts. James summons us to pray with the same appeal—God is generous and willing to give! Notice his enticing call to prayer: "If any of you lacks wisdom, let him ask of God, who gives to all liberally and without reproach, and it will be given to him" (James 1:5).

To know God stands poised to participate in our quest to preach life-changing sermons provides incredible hope. To know he is a generous God toward those who ask motivates us to labor in prayer as diligently as we do with the text. But James was quick to add that we must "ask in faith, with no doubting" (James 1:6). Doubt offends God and thwarts the fruitfulness of our prayers.

Not long ago I preached one of those sermons that left me thinking, "What in the world happened?" It looked so good in the study but came out a disaster. Of course, I, and many others, had faithfully prayed for the effectiveness of the sermon, but after hearing myself preach I never gave those prayers a second thought. I unconsciously assumed that this time God did not answer. Certainly He could never use a sermon like that one.

I moved on, as we all must do after a "bad" sermon, and set my sights on the next. Just as I was forgetting my debacle, God sent a Christian couple to chide me for my lack of faith. They didn't realize they were God's reprimand for my heart, but that didn't matter. We "happened to meet" at a restaurant days after the dreaded sermon. Enough time had elapsed to free them from the obligatory "nice sermon" comments, so you can imagine my shock when they began to say how incredibly God had used the sermon in their lives. They went on and on about how life-changing it had been. They asked about getting tapes so they could share the blessing with their friends and relatives. They were so adamant, so sincere, that I honestly wondered if we were talking about the same sermon!

Suddenly it dawned on me. This was exactly the type of response we all had prayed for the previous week! We brought this specific request before God day after day and hour after hour, yet I had failed to expect it. Once again God impressed on me that life-changing preaching is not about flawless deliveries, or illustrations that "work," or perfect verbiage. He reminded me that effective preaching is all about His powerful and undeniable involvement. Oh that we would learn to ask for that involvement with sincere anticipation—the kind that is not surprised when He moves mightily in the hearts of people.

The psalmist showed us the way we ought to pray when he wrote, "in the morning I lay my requests before you and wait in expectation" (Ps. 5:3 NIV). May God teach us to confidently and expectantly pray for His transforming power to invade our preaching and our lives. May we experience what E. M. Bounds described when he wrote:

> A prayerful minister has passed beyond the regions of the popular, beyond the man of mere affairs, of secularities, of pulpit attractiveness; passed beyond the ecclesiastical organizer or general into a sublimer and mightier region, the region of the spiritual. Holiness is the product of his work; transfigured hearts and lives emblazon the reality of his work, its trueness and substantial nature. God is with him. . . . His long, deep communings with God about his people and the agony of his wrestling spirit have crowned him as a prince in the things of God. The iciness of the mere professional has long since melted under the intensity of his praying.[12]

Choose today to renew your passion for prayer. Make it your priority. Enlist those around you to join in asking God for His transforming work in the lives of those who will hear His Word proclaimed this week.

CHAPTER SEVEN

Come to Grips with the Time It Takes to Prepare a Life-changing Sermon

PREACHING TO CHANGE LIVES IS TIME-INTENSIVE. WITHIN THE CONTEXT OF AN effective overall pastoral ministry, the task appears daunting, if not impossible. But take heart. You can do it once you straighten out a few things in your mind and schedule.

PRIORITIES

A change in my medical insurance forced me to find a new doctor. A deep cut on my leg prompted me to contact the new doctor's office sooner than I had expected. Within the hour I was introduced to a no-nonsense former Army captain who said he'd fix me "as good as new." As I left the office with four fresh stitches, I was satisfied that I had found a forthright and down-to-earth physician.

From then on, when I had a medical need, I called their office and asked for him by name. He treated me for this and that over the next couple of years, until one day when I was sitting in the waiting room I overheard the receptionist refer to my doctor as "Mister Johnson." I thought to myself, "How rude and unprofessional!"—but then the other receptionist referred to him in exactly the same way.

My mind started to spin. After a minute or two of mental gymnastics, I walked over to the receptionists and said, "I couldn't help but overhear you refer to "Doctor Johnson" as "Mister Johnson." "Oh," one responded, "he's not a doctor, he's just an assistant. Would you like to see a doctor today?" I quickly answered, "Yes, I think I would,"

On the way back to my seat, part of me felt bad for so quickly abandoning "Mr. Johnson." But another part of me—the more rational part—couldn't stop thinking about the importance of medical students burning the midnight oil, giving themselves fully to the arduous task of passing their medical exams! My resolve grew with each thought, becoming fully convinced that I always preferred doctors, surgeons, pilots, and architects who had done their homework, endured and prevailed in their course of study.

If we expect such from those who correct and protect our physical bodies, why would we ever think our congregants should lower the bar for us? If we are to be involved in the weekly correction and protection of spiritual lives, does it not follow that we too must do our homework, enduring and prevailing in our weekly course of study?

A study of the Pastoral Epistles or the Book of Acts quickly reveals that few endeavors are more "honorable" than devoting much of our time and effort toward this primary task. Consider Paul's reminder to Timothy: "The elders who direct the affairs of the church well are worthy of double honor, especially those whose work is preaching and teaching" (1 Tim. 5:17 NIV). This must be seen as our ultimate weekly priority. We must ruthlessly eliminate the distractions that would hinder us from keeping this as Job One. As G. Campbell Morgan warned his generation of pastors:

> The supreme work of the Christian minister is the work of preaching. This is a day in which one of our great perils is that of doing a thousand little things to the neglect of the one thing, which is preaching.[1]

Even if you preach multiple times throughout the week, the actual delivery of the sermon constitutes only a small fraction of your schedule. To say that preaching is time-intensive is not quite accurate. Message preparation is time-intensive. Therefore, to become proficient at the honorable work of preaching and teaching, you must commit long hours to the labors of study and prayer.

Resign Yourself to Many Hours of Study Each Week

There is no way around it—to preach well, you must necessarily sacrifice a "normal life." Face it. Your schedule is out of sync with your congregation's—as their week winds down, yours kicks into high gear. Your weekdays, imagined by the naïve to consist of pastoral chitchat, hours of pleasure reading, and afternoon rounds of golf, are in fact days of intensive study that culminate in a spiritual battle called a sermon. As Bruce

84

Thieleman writes, "The pulpit calls those anointed to it as the sea calls its sailors; and like the sea, it batters and bruises, and does not rest. . . . To preach, to really preach, is to die naked a little at a time and to know each time you do it that you must do it again."[2] The life of preaching requires dedication to the ongoing rigors of weekly preparation and delivery.

The preparation itself may in the end prove to be the most challenging aspect, considering the self-governed schedule most pastors keep. The appointed preaching hour comes, whether we are ready or not. That hour is unavoidable; yet the available preparation hours often pass us by before we know it. It doesn't take much discipline to show up when the crowd expects you, but keeping those divine appointments and choosing the quiet work of preparation both require a tremendous amount of self-discipline and perseverance.

It helps to continually keep in mind your lot in life and your calling from God. Envision yourself as one who is to be constantly found in prayer and study. This image should govern your perception of your role and help you remain in your chair with your mind on your task. John MacArthur comments on this mindset when he says:

> Somewhere along the line you have to do the hard work. The difference between mediocre preaching and good preaching is effort. . . . The struggle to understand the Bible is a struggle that basically you're willing to make or you're not. I think if you're serious about the word of God—you believe it is the word of God—you just pay the price. You just make the effort because you know that that is the priority of your life.[3]

The Priority Reflected in Your Schedule

John Calvin was right when he wrote, "the teachers of the Church ought to be prepared by long study."[4] While some have attempted to quantify the hours required,[5] I have discovered that it will take as much time as you give to it and then some. Maintaining a high view of the Scripture and feeling the awesome responsibility of the task, I never sense that a sermon is completely prepared—rather the time for preparation simply runs out. Sermon preparation time must be given top priority in the preacher's weekly schedule, for all would agree that the "sermon prepared on Saturday evening reveals an attitude that is unworthy of the work."[6]

The supremacy of preparation in your weekly schedule must be evident to everyone—your family, your staff, even your congregation. Indeed it must be clear that you are called to preparation—not exclusively, but to a very significant extent.

The Priority Reflected in the Place You Study

If message preparation is truly your priority, then your place of study ought to reflect that priority. Constantly referring to it as a "study" is helpful. The label of "office" conjures up a business or administrative atmosphere, while the word "study" serves as a perpetual reminder to everyone, from your secretary to visitors, that your *primary* weekly task is sermon preparation. If space or funding allow only one room, call it a study. If you are able to acquire two rooms, intentionally create a contrast between the two.

I do have an office that adjoins my study. The office is very small, with only a desk and a couple of receiving chairs; its sparseness reflects the fact this is not my primary work place. There I meet with people, answer mail, and engage in administrative tasks, but it is not my primary domain. Just behind my small office desk is a door that leads to my study—and when I open that door I enter an entirely different world. There is nothing passive about this environment. My books, files, and computer are all arranged for action. This space has been well thought out and everything in it assists in my reading, prayer, study, and meditation.

Do all you can to gather what you need to do the job. Investment in this room and the tools within it is of paramount importance. Fred Craddock colorfully relates the problem when he writes, "the one room in the house of God which, judging by its size, furnishings, and location, is an afterthought, is not the parlor but the pastor's study."[7] If the arrangement and equipping of your study is an afterthought, think again. It ought to become a place your heart longs to be—a place that provides every reasonable advantage to tackle the challenge of message preparation. Budgets for books, software, equipment, and furnishings should be generously established and the money wisely spent. If the leadership of your church has not seen the value of this type of work environment as a priority then it must become a matter for honest discussion and prayer.

The Priority Reflected in the Messages You Preach

To lobby for support that allows preparation and preaching to become your top priorities demands you do all you can to make the investment pay off. If a congregation supplies the time, tools, and resources that allow the pastor to give himself to study and prayer, then the result ought to reflect their trust. As MacArthur warns, you don't want your church or its leadership to say regarding your sermon, "It took you three days to come up with that?"[8]

Writing to Timothy regarding the labor of preaching, Paul said, "Be diligent in these matters; give yourself wholly to them, so that everyone may see your progress" (1 Tim. 4:15 NIV). It was important for Timothy to make measurable and evident progress in his pulpit ministry; it is important that your congregants, those who allow you to commit more time and resources to

86

preparation, likewise see you making advancements in your preaching. In short, there ought to be noticeable progress in the life-changing effectiveness of your sermons.

One way to track this progress is through regular evaluations. Every six months I assign a team of six people to evaluate one of my sermons. The team includes four church leaders, one layperson and my wife. I provide them with a preaching evaluation form and a list of known weaknesses I am seeking to strengthen. I encourage them to be brutally honest and provide me with feedback that I can use to make progress that can be evident to everyone. (See the Appendix for a sample evaluation form.)

PRINCIPLES FOR SCHEDULING

Few practical skills are more important to the pastor than time management. It is critical that he be able to keep the main things *the* main things. Yet much of what is written on the topic of time management is presented from a secular perspective and, in many points, does not reflect biblical values.[9] There is a great need for more to be written on this topic, especially for those in the ministry—those who may need it most. It is my prayer that the following principles will be utilized to keep your focus and your energy centered on the high calling of preaching sermons that change lives.

Schedule!

If you don't make your own schedule and keep it, others will dictate and dominate it. Of course God always maintains veto power (and often exercises it with an impromptu evangelistic encounter, a counseling crisis, or a funeral), but for the most part you'll either protect your schedule or you'll allow others to maintain it by default.

It is important to remember that God, the Master Planner, is pro planning. He says, "The plans of the diligent lead to profit as surely as haste leads to poverty" (Prov. 21:5 NIV). Again God says, "Make plans by seeking advice" (Prov. 20:18 NIV). We must shun any temptation to "go with the flow" and let circumstances drive our schedules. We must take charge of how our week is to unfold, deferring only to God's intervention. If there is a sudden left turn in our week we must be certain it is God diverting us from the path we have laid out.

Of course there will be plenty of necessary, God-ordained diversions from our schedules and we must honor them. However, a pastor must discern their source and must never sacrifice the best for the sake of the good. Temptations must be creatively and diplomatically rerouted. If God has called you to preach then He has implicitly, yet very clearly, called you to prepare yourself to preach. *His* interruptions will be few.

Tenaciously guarding your study schedule is especially important in light of what your congregation likely believes regarding the disciplines of study, preaching, and pastoral ministry. Fred Craddock insightfully highlights the challenge:

> One of the ironies in the history of the church is the fact that the person who is expected to speak every week on issues of ultimate importance—God's will and human freedom, evil and suffering, grace and judgment, peace and covenant—has been in many quarters begrudged the study time necessary to prepare. Not everywhere, of course, but in many parishes there is strong resistance to granting a pastor any study leave. . . . "What do you mean, study? I thought you had already graduated."[10]

People commonly believe the pastor should perform a myriad of obligations that would preclude long hours of study. *After* fulfilling those tasks they feel you can simply rely on your innate ability and your preexisting knowledge of life and Scripture to produce next Sunday's sermon. This situation should never be—but unfortunately, it often is. Therefore we must fight these misconceptions by diligently focusing our weekly schedule on the high priority of personal, private study.

Some will dismiss this advice as unrealistic, applicable only to those few who preach in large churches, those insulated by an army of support staff. Don't be one of them. If the grass looks greener, I can assure you it is not. Having had the weekly responsibility of preaching in a small church as the sole staff member, as well as preaching each week surrounded by a crew of capable ministers and staffers, I can testify that there is not a stage, size, or staff configuration that can free you from the attacks on your study and prayer time. Regardless of the size of your church or the size of your staff, it is a constant battle. Get used to the challenge and learn to lovingly say "no." Be convinced you can rightly protect the schedule that will allow you adequate time to study. As Spurgeon once advised, "Learn to say 'no;' it will be of more use to you than to be able to read Latin."[11]

We must realize that saying "no" is neither ungodly nor unbiblical. Situations arose in which Christ wanted His disciples so focused upon their task at hand that He ordered them to say "no" to anything that might pull them away from their goal. When Jesus commissioned the seventy-two to go before Him into the towns as His representatives, He told them, "*Greet no one* along the road" (Luke 10:4), and "Do not *go from house to house*" (v. 7). Their task was so urgent, so much a priority, that they were to fulfill it even at the risk of perceived rudeness.

Though our ministry of preaching the Word is likewise urgent, we never want to disgrace Christ by intentionally shunning His sheep. Make sure to schedule a manageable amount of counseling time and faithfully keep your appointments. However, we must recognize that we cannot consistently sacrifice the needs of our entire congregation for the needs of the few who insist on rearranging our schedule, and thus diminish our time in study. D. A. Carson rightly observes:

> Many of our people expect us to be counselors first, administrators second and thirdly to be preachers. And we're supposed to do that without much study—we learned all of that in seminary, didn't we? Sometimes we fit into this expectation by the sheer dictatorial power of the urgent. I do not know of a single minister in a substantial sized church anywhere who maintains a healthy preaching habit who does not limit his hours in the counseling room. . . . Somehow or other as part of our commitment to preaching, however much counseling we do, once we've agreed to the number of hours, apart from crisis [we must] draw a line. Or else our preaching becomes flatter and flatter, staler and staler, and the pressure of the immediate gradually squeezes out the importance of the transcendental.[12]

Don't Be Lazy!

Creating time is one dilemma—stewarding it well confronts us with yet another. It may be that in protecting our schedules we are, in effect, creating new opportunities to waste our time. The study hours can be accumulated, only to be squandered by laziness. Often laziness is cloaked in busyness and procrastination. A favorite poem illustrates the problem:

> I've gone for a drink and sharpened my pencils,
> Searched through my desk for forgotten utensils,
> Reset my watch and adjusted my chair,
> Loosened my tie and straightened my hair,
> Filled my pen and tested the blotter,
> Gone for another drink of water,
> Adjusted the calendar, raised the blinds,
> Sorted erasers of different kinds.
> Now, down to work I can finally sit
> Oops! Too late, it's time to quit![13]

Scripture chides the lazy with a simple comparison:

> Go to the ant, you sluggard;
> Consider her ways and be wise,
> Which, having no captain,
> Overseer or ruler,
> Provides her supplies in the summer,
> And gathers her food in the harvest (Prov. 6:6–8).

We cannot afford to be distracted from the time we have scheduled for study and prayer. Like the ant of Proverbs 6, we must go about our task without a supervisor looking over our shoulder. The crack of the whip must be internal. Laziness and procrastination must become our mortal enemies.

Beware of wolves in sheep's clothing! Some aspects of study can easily become counterproductive. Access to the Internet is one example. The Net can be a useful research tool, yet it can easily become a time-waster, beckoning us to check last night's scores, read trivial news articles, or explore interesting but useless websites. When your tool becomes a toy, take heed!

Before I was able to hire staff to help utilize this vast resource, I formed a team of laypersons who were Internet-savvy and willing to do research for me. I would e-mail them a single communiqué requesting a specific piece of research (e.g., "How much time does the average American watch television?") and ask them for a response within twenty-four hours. Often by that afternoon I would have two or three responses from different web sources, automatically confirmed and crosschecked. It was a win-win situation. I would benefit from current statistics and fresh information from the web *without* being sidetracked by superfluous information. My research team would perform an enjoyable, practical ministry—plus see it bear fruit each weekend!

Keep in mind that newspapers, periodicals, the radio, or television all can end up stealing more time than they are worth. Guard your environment with vigilance. Jettison anything you suspect might be keeping you from the work at hand. If you are in doubt, pull the plug or cancel the subscription!

Martin Luther was right when he challenged his generation with the stinging reminder that "God certainly has not instituted the office of the ministry in order to produce secure and lazy preachers for Himself."[14] Let us be sure that we don't fall into that category.

Know Where Your Time Goes

Before I make some suggestions for pacing your study time, plan a fact-finding tour of your preparation schedule. Purpose to discover how your time is currently being spent. This is always an eye-opening experience, yet knowing where you are is an important first step in determining what changes will be required to get you where you should be!

Try this. Make a list of elements involved in your weekly study (e.g., reading and rereading the text, consulting commentaries, praying for the sermon, wording an outline, finding illustrations). Keep a list that logs the time spent on each activity. Remember to enter a column for "interruptions." Each week analyze your time chart, then after a month compare your charts. Any imbalances will quickly surface—as will areas unforeseen when you started out. Correct any obvious negative tendencies, and if you need to add new profitable categories, do so. Just remember to follow a balanced diet. For instance, many preachers spend far more time hunting for illustrations than they can afford, and far less time praying than they can afford. Or you may discover you spend too much time in commentaries and not enough time preparing application. These and other problems can be detected when we accurately track and analyze how we are spending our prep time.

Pace Your Weekly Study

The preparation of life-changing sermons involves three general stages. If these are balanced and paced, we can remedy much of what is deficient in today's preaching. In the broadest sense, these stages consist of the following: (1) time spent grappling with the text's meaning; (2) time spent grappling with the text's significance; and (3) time spent actually crafting the message itself.

Of course, in one sense, your next sermon begins immediately after the last one is preached. It is only natural to cogitate on this week's sermon(s) and contemplate the next week's passage from Sunday evening onward.

In my own study, however, I prefer to relegate each of the general stages to a different day of the week. I have found it invaluable to give Thursday, Friday, and Saturday to each respective stage. Though each day has a primary task, every day should be interlaced with prayer as discussed in chapter 6.

1. Time to Study Meaning

Thursday is the day I have chosen to grapple in depth with the text's meaning. On this day I lay out my commentaries, word study tools, and Bible dictionaries and I attempt to become an expert on the passage I am going to preach. I study the text in its original language, its original literary context, and its historical setting. I apply the principles of sound hermeneutics to understand the text's meaning as completely as possible. By the end of the day, I hope to be so well versed in every facet of the passage that I could write my own commentary on it.

This is a very important day, and is often my longest. It is the foundation upon which all subsequent preparation is built; therefore it cannot be compromised. If I am not finished or some significant interpretive questions still remain at the end of the work day, I do not wait until Friday to deal with them. Instead I retreat to the kitchen table after my family is asleep and study until I am satisfied that I have grasped what the author was saying to that generation. Before I sleep I should be able to articulate the "textual point" which fully, yet concisely, encapsulates the proper interpretation of the passage. If I can accomplish that much, I know I can begin Friday with a mastery of the passage that is indispensable to the next two stages of study.

Personally, I cling to the deadlines for each of these stages with a great deal of tenacity. If I become lax and the task lines become blurred, the entire process of preparation suffers. The importance of keeping to deadlines can hardly be overstated.

2. Time to Study Significance

My Friday is given to the oft-neglected task of carefully deciphering the text's significance and framing the application-worded main points. This process was explained in some detail in chapters 4 and 5. If Thursday's work of determining meaning was done well, then determining the text's significance to the original audience does not consume much of my day. That leaves the bulk of the day to the meaningful transferal of the application to my own congregation. I want to concentrate my attention on how God intends to impact my particular listeners with this Scripture passage. The afternoon concludes with the exercise of strategically wording the main points of the outline and creating the materials to assist in the follow-through of the message. (More on that in chapter 15.)

I supplement Friday's study with something of a "working dinner." Each Friday evening my wife and I sit across the table from people new to the church, or a couple with whom I am not well acquainted. This provides me an opportunity to come face to face with the real people and real lives that I am seeking to impact with God's Word. The conversation doesn't always turn to the weekend's sermon, but I find that almost subconsciously I latch on to appropriate strategies and implications for the message as I bring a mind brimming with exegetical and applicational thoughts to the restaurant.

3. Time to Craft the Message

Saturday is the day I craft the message. I already have determined the text's meaning, carefully thought through the text's intended impact, and built the basic framework of the sermon in the form of an outline. My next task is to determine the wisest and most appropriate way to communicate the sermon to my audience. I do this through the development or discovery of illustrations, examples, and transitions. Finally, I write the introduction and a conclusion to the message.

With the entire day spent on this work I am able to give thought to every part of the sermon. If all goes well, by evening I have the flow, the logic, and much of the material already committed to memory—and I'm ready to face the congregation.

To reiterate, setting and honoring deadlines provides my weekly study with the balanced preparation needed to preach a message that doesn't cheat the text or its application. Of course, the principles presented here are the ideal. Real life, with its funerals, staff crises, family needs, and added speaking engagements, may dictate modification of this schedule.

Nevertheless, as stated earlier, I attempt to make sure those breaks remain the exception and not the rule.

Make Time to Study Your Audience

My Friday dinners are purposeful opportunities to truly understand my audience, yet for many preachers this element often gets squeezed out of the schedule. The fact remains, keeping a finger on the pulse of the church is critical to effective preaching. Becoming an office-bound hermit may result in a great tract ministry, but preaching will always be a face-to-face venture. If the preacher loses touch with his congregation, the gulf between them will become far greater than the distance between pulpit and pew. Grant Osborn poignantly makes the case for congregational analysis by chiding those who feel too busy to stay in touch with their congregations:

> So-called super-pastors at times believe that their major calling is to feed their flock and so spend all their time in the study preparing their message(s), leaving the day-to-day ministry to their staff. The problem is they never get to know their flock, its needs and interests. At best they receive it secondhand from the staff or board . . . [and] the specific needs of the congregation remain untouched—at least in the pastor's pulpit ministry. Pastors and missionaries must know their flock and take time to discover their specific situation in life. This will lead to a sermon style that eschews technical jargon as well as generalizations. . . . Application will not be dry or cliché-laden but will zero in on the people's specific needs, suggesting ways to make the text meaningful in the concrete situations encountered in the days following.[15]

As tempting as it often is to allow the study of the text to squeeze out our interaction with our congregants, we must stubbornly fight that temptation and do the time-consuming work of audience analysis.

My wife and I have found these dinner-dates to be of great help to this end, especially when we meet with folks we don't know well. Keeping the age demographic varied on those Friday evenings has also proven valuable for me. When I listen to the challenges of a young couple with a brand new baby, or hear the discouragement of a recently retired worker, I am freshly challenged by the needs to which I preach each week.

Making the time to occasionally visit people at their place of employment will also cast a new light on the life situation of the congregants you face every Sunday. When I step into the executive's office or mechanic's garage I enter his world—where he must live out the Christian life day after day. There I gain a fresh appreciation for the challenges people face, and I sense specific needs unnoticed from the safety of my study. Charles

Kemp is right when he observes that time invested with our people drives us back to the study with a "new earnestness and a deeper sense of need." He reasons, "[If] a man merely reads books, he may become a scholar, but, if he separates himself from people, he will not become a preacher."[16]

Haddon Robinson testifies to this problem among pastors when he tells of his encounter with a businessman who confessed, "As much as I appreciate my pastor and enjoy his sermons, it's not often that he speaks about my world."[17] If so indicted by a jury of our listeners, then we must realize the magnitude of the disadvantage from which we preach. If people sense a "holy detachment," then we enter the pulpit with little hope of our preaching becoming relevant to their lives. Yet the Bible *is* relevant and *every* passage has vast implications for every Monday-through-Friday environment represented in your congregation. It is part of your job to become acquainted with those environments so you can persuasively build a bridge between truth and application.

Beware of the Self-preservation Trap

Giving adequate time to the work of message preparation and to his other required responsibilities will keep the faithful pastor more than busy. I realize it is trendy to be "busy" (everyone says that they are), but statistics indicate people today have more leisure time than any previous generation in our history.[18] The average American spends over ten years of his or her life watching television[19] and six hours each week surfing the Internet.[20] More people than ever before are finding the time and energy to engage in expensive hobbies.[21] Over 60 percent of Americans spend "significant time" engaged in some form of physical fitness.[22] In stark contrast, our grandparents and great-grandparents labored in the fields from sun up to sun down. Their evenings were spent repairing equipment, sewing clothing, or preparing the next day's food. We must realize that although our generation professes busyness, it is an altogether different kind of busyness.

Putting in more hours than our neighbors at the good work of preaching does not make us candidates for "burnout." In most cases, we barely scratch the surface of our potential capacity. To his disciple Timothy, Paul said, "Be diligent in these matters; give yourself wholly to them (*en toutois isthi*), so that everyone may see your progress" (1 Tim. 4:15 NIV). *Isthi* is the second person imperative of *eimi*, the verb "to be." Paul is presenting Timothy with a command, literally, "to be in these things." Some translate this unique phrase "to be absorbed in them,"[23] "to be immersed in them,"[24] or "to throw yourself into them."[25] Paul is challenging Timothy to be fully engrossed in the work of Christ—to a level of commitment attainable but rarely seen in any worker or in any career of our day.

Paul tells the Corinthians, "Always abound in the work of the Lord, knowing that your labor is not in vain in the Lord" (1 Cor. 15:58). Again, here is a strong admonition to give our all to the work of Christ—because it is a good and profitable quest.

Our soft society is overly concerned with "burnout" and "fatigue." Often these words are used as a cover for sin and laziness. Sometimes these words become self-fulfilling prophecies, more imagined than real. Either scenario results in an ardent devotion to self-preservation—"I must protect *my* time, preserve *my* peace of mind, promote *my* leisure and recreation—offering nothing more than a litany to self. Unfortunately, this mentality has filtered into ministry training. Instead of being told to "be absorbed in these things," or to "always give yourself fully to the work of the Lord," we are told in seminaries and pastors' conferences to do *the opposite*. My flesh rarely needs encouragement to take coffee breaks or mornings off—yet my unredeemed flesh requires constant reminders to give myself fully to the work I have been called to do.

When the term "burnout" was becoming a popular buzzword, J. Vernon McGee, who kept a packed schedule of faithful service to Christ, did his best to nip it in the bud. He told his Christian radio audience, "I'd much rather 'burnout' than 'rust out.'"[26] I fear that many of us can become convinced, albeit deceptively, that we are too busy to give message preparation the hours it needs. What a perfect strategy of the enemy to get pastors to neglect the hard work of study and prayer!

May Satan's intentions be thwarted as we shun lesser things to wholeheartedly and diligently engage in the awesome priorities of biblical study and sermon preparation.

PART
THREE

PREACH TO
CHANGE
LIVES

CHAPTER EIGHT

Realize They Won't Change What They Don't Hear and Understand

MANY PASTORS TAKE ON THE DIFFICULT TASK OF ENSURING THE PROPRIETY AND excellence of the musical aspects of the worship service. This can be an awkward assignment when well-meaning and enthusiastic volunteers want to share their "talents" or "gifts" with the congregation. What pastor hasn't had to graciously redirect the crooning accordion player or the banjo quartet from a Sunday morning disaster?

Pastors who seek to promote an effective worship experience will not buy into the "make a joyful noise" argument because they recognize that good lyrics, poorly executed, can be worse than no music at all! Worship is rarely achieved when a good hymn is offered with the dissonance of the corner karaoke.

And the same may be said for those of us who preach. A good truth poorly delivered rarely hits the homiletical target. We must recognize that the greatness of the truths we proclaim demands nothing less than excellence in the manner and mode of our presentation.

A biblical sermon must be heard—I mean truly heard—if it is going to bring about any change in a person's life. It does not matter how masterfully the sermon has been prepared or how strategically the outline or illustrations crafted. If the sermon is not delivered in a compelling manner the ultimate goal of preaching will likely be thwarted.

Paul unapologetically told the Corinthians that his goal was to "persuade" them (2 Cor. 5:11) and yet his methods were not simply made up of "persuasive words" (1 Cor. 2:4) or manipulative tactics (2 Thess. 2:5). From such passages we understand we cannot allow biblical preaching or the study of homiletics to be reduced to a set of rhetorical devices or oratorical tips.

Yet appropriate delivery of the message has always been a rightful concern.

For example, Paul asked the Colossians to pray he might "proclaim it clearly as [he] should" (Col. 4:4 NIV). He asked the Ephesians to pray he would "fearlessly" proclaim the gospel (Eph. 6:19). In the exercise of spiritual gifts of teaching, Peter instructed, "If anyone speaks, he should do it as one speaking the very words of God" (1 Pet. 4:11 NIV). It was understood there was a manner of delivery that was appropriate to the task of proclaiming Scriptural truth and its intended application.

It has been correctly observed that "a speaker who holds the attention of his listener does not necessarily succeed—but no speaker can succeed unless he does hold their attention."[1] Without falling into the abuses of delivery tactics and devices, let us briefly consider a handful of general elements that are essential if our sermons are to be truly heard by those God calls us to address.

PREACH WITH URGENCY

The importance of preaching with urgency can hardly be overstated. This is clearly not a tactic but rather an orientation of the preacher to his sermon. Urgency cannot be added by the simple inclusion of certain phrases or gestures at well-timed junctures. It is a component of preaching that exists when the preacher himself is captivated by the sermon he is standing up to deliver, and it permeates his delivery with an unfeigned, unrehearsed sincerity.

It makes sense that one can hardly expect a sermon to impact people who don't sense the critical nature of the sermon. If you are not moved by the message, they likely will not be moved. Unfortunately, it does not take the audience long to process whether your message is marked "urgent," or if it's just another piece of mail to file away.

You must be so personally occupied by the content and application of the passage that your heart has naturally been burdened with the concern that *everybody* appropriate these biblical truths as earnestly as you have. There comes a point in preparation when you know you have crossed into this rarified air. Your enthusiasm for the passage increases, your interest in communicating its implications heightens, and your desire to see your listeners "get it" makes it difficult to wait for Sunday! You would be frustrated if for any reason your message would be preempted. Your concern for the delivery and comprehension of the message is akin to the bottled up feelings of Elihu when he said:

100

> For I am full of words,
>   and the spirit within me compels me;
> inside I am like bottled-up wine,
>   like new wineskins ready to burst.
> I must speak and find relief;
>   I must open my lips and reply.
> I will show partiality to no one,
>   nor will I flatter any man (Job 32:18–21 NIV).

When a sermon reaches this point you don't think about being careful or diplomatic or flattering. You just have to get the word out because it has so captivated your own heart! That is one reason I cannot take a day off between preparing the sermon and delivering it. My Thursdays, Fridays, and Saturdays crescendo into the preaching event with an urgency that creates a passion to get that message into the lives of those who come to hear it.

The sense of urgency in the sermon is difficult to describe but easy to identify. Bill Hybels adds his description of this dynamic:

> What are some of the common denominators of great preaching and teaching? . . . When I was listening to great communication, repeatedly I would be struck with how this person was preaching as though the subject matter [he was] talking about was the most urgent subject matter on the planet. Everything else kind of went away.[2]

If our listeners are to have that experience, then we must have it in the days before the sermon. Prior to the sermon that message ought to be on your mind and in your prayers. It should be sprinkled throughout your conversation and bouncing around in your imagination. Once you own it at this level you will naturally unleash the passion of a message your heart is eager to share.

If you sense a lack of urgency in the days prior to the sermon, then linger in earnest prayer until God grants it. Ask Him to give you His perspective of the text you will present. Plead with Him to show you what's at stake for your congregation if they choose to ignore it. This is a prayer He won't ignore.

Urgency in Introductions

The sermon's sense of urgency must be evident right out of the gate. Urgency compels you to discard long, drawn-out introductions that delay presentation of the preaching point. Those critical opening moments of the sermon provide us the opportunity to give our listeners a whiff of why this message is so important. In these moments we should give them a compelling reason to lean forward and listen. Mark Galli is right when he testifies that a "good introduction arrests me. It handcuffs me and drags me before the sermon, where I stand and hear a Word that makes me both tremble and rejoice."[3]

An introduction will not arrest your congregation if it doesn't address the question, "What difference does all this make?" It must immediately show the relevance of the text to be preached. Therefore, the introduction is the place where your applicational thrust begins. It cannot wait for the conclusion. Many of the preaching events recorded in the Bible flow out of settings in which a particular question or concern has already been raised by the audience (e.g., "Teacher, tell my brother to divide the inheritance with me"; "Why do you stare at us as though by our own power or godliness we made this man walk?"; "Is it lawful for a man to divorce his wife for any and every reason?").[4] However, our people may not have entered the parking lot with a particular concern or question in mind; it is our job to raise one in our introductions.

Because the introduction addresses questions and concerns explored in the body of the sermon, introductions should never be crafted first. They should always come late in our preparation, only after we have nailed down the flow and direction of the sermon.

Urgency in Conclusions

The closing words of your sermon will likely linger the longest in your hearers' minds. Those final statements can drive the preaching point home in a way that few other parts of the sermon can. While most preachers innately recognize the importance of conclusions, we often cheat them out of the time and attention necessary to infuse the needed urgency. When this happens, the sermon's impact is minimized. Jay Adams says, "Without a good conclusion, the (otherwise) best sermon is a dud."[5] A ho-hum or matter-of-fact conclusion, or worse, no conclusion at all, can take the applicational punch right out of the message. It will give your audience license to think, "I guess it really wasn't that important after all."

A conclusion that nails the appropriate urgency of the message does more than summarize what preceded. It does more than simply restate the preaching point from another angle. Like Paul's last letter to Timothy, it should be filled with passion and concern. It ought to reflect the challenge a coach gives his team moments before they break out of the locker room onto the playing field. If the hearer has not yet responded to the truth that has been preached in the body of your sermon, and the conclusion doesn't prompt a response, it is unlikely that he will respond once he leaves the church building.

With that in mind, some preachers tend to drag the conclusion out with restatement after restatement. Reiterating the call to action does not

102

strengthen the conclusion, however, but can actually weaken it. We must, as the saying goes, land the plane without endlessly circling the airport.[6]

Though there are many ways to develop a conclusion (i.e., direct appeals, questions, stories, and quotations), the chosen avenue must convey an urgency that this sermon must be understood and responded to without excuse or delay.

PREACH ENTHUSIASTICALLY

Few things derail a sermon faster and more effectively than a boring preacher. All preachers should adopt the oft quoted resolve that "it is a sin to bore people with the Bible."[7] The urgent truth of each message we preach should enflame our personalities and spread with a fervor that befits God's powerful Word.

To say that we should preach enthusiastically is not to say that we act like circus clowns who dance and cajole to garner the attention of our audience. I am saying that God's Word should absorb our entire being when we preach. We should not be so focused on mechanics or so self-conscious that our hearts cannot become intertwined with the truth we attempt to proclaim.

The dictionary defines "enthusiasm" as the "absorbing or controlling possession of the mind by any interest or pursuit."[8] Webster notes that the English word had its origin from the Greek idea of having "God within" or "being possessed by a god"—an apropos revelation as it relates to the lofty nature of our task.[9] The Bible requires preachers to be soberly consumed by a keenness and fervor that are equal to the assignment. Recall Peter's exhortation: "If anyone speaks, he should do it as one speaking the very words of God" (1 Pet. 4:11 NIV). Paul said that when he preached it was "as though God were pleading through [him]" (2 Cor. 5:20). Whether their message was accepted or rejected, the record shows their enthusiasm bred enthusiastic responses.

Martin Lloyd-Jones describes the substandard preaching that lacks this kind of enthusiasm:

> A dull preacher is a contradiction of terms; if he is dull he is not a preacher. He may stand in a pulpit and talk, but he is certainly not a preacher. With the grand theme and message of the Bible dullness is impossible. This is the most interesting, the most thrilling, the most absorbing subject in the universe; and the idea that this can be presented in a dull manner makes me seriously doubt whether the men who are guilty of this dullness have ever really understood the doctrine they claim to believe, and which they advocate. We often betray ourselves by our manner.[10]

Like urgency, enthusiasm cannot be manufactured, faked, or contrived. We find it, as Lloyd-Jones suggests, when we become absorbed and enamored with the truth that we preach and with the God who gives it. We must learn to despise anything less.[11]

PREACH EXPECTANTLY

Given the repetitive nature of pastoral preaching it is easy to lose our sense of expectancy. After delivering hundreds of sermons each year it is a challenge to expect that the next one I deliver will truly change lives . . . again. Yet we should never lose hope in the power of God's Word, which is "living and powerful" and "sharper than any two-edged sword, piercing even to the division of soul and spirit, and of joints and marrow, and is a discerner of the thoughts and intents of the heart" (Heb. 4:12).

When we realize transformational power lies wholly in the truth of the message, and not the messenger, then we can always preach with anticipation that God *will* work in the lives of our people. William Carey's exhortation certainly holds true in the pulpit; we must learn to "expect great things from God!"[12] When we do not, our lack of expectancy is contagious and our preaching efforts are crippled. J. I. Packer observes:

> Low expectations become self-fulfilling. Where little is expected from sermons, little is received. Many moderns have never been taught to expect sermons to matter much, and so their habit at sermon time is to relax, settle back and wait to see if anything the preacher says will catch their interest. Most of today's congregations and preachers seem to be at one in neither asking nor anticipating that God will come to meet his people in the preaching; so it is no wonder if this fails to happen. According to your unbelief, we might say, be it unto you![13]

May God infuse us with a fresh sense of expectancy. May we truly believe that God wants to meet our people in our preaching. May God bolster our confidence in the power and effectual nature of His Word. Review the psalmist's observations regarding the Book we exposit to people each week:

> The law of the LORD is perfect, converting the soul;
> The testimony of the LORD is sure, making wise the simple;
> The statutes of the LORD are right, rejoicing the heart;
> The commandment of the LORD is pure, enlightening the eyes;
> The fear of the LORD is clean, enduring forever;
> The judgments of the LORD are true and righteous altogether;
> More to be desired are they than gold,

Yea, than much fine gold;
Sweeter also than honey and the honeycomb.
Moreover by them Your servant is warned,
And in keeping them there is great reward (Ps. 19:7–11).

Being mindful of the nature of God's Word can alter the attitude with which we present our sermons. Bonhoeffer paints a picture of expectant preaching when he writes, "A truly evangelical sermon must be like offering a child a beautiful red apple or holding out a glass of water to a thirsty man and asking: Wouldn't you like it?"[14] There should be no room for a "take it or leave it" attitude when we hold out the word of life.

Take time to imagine how lives can and will be changed through your proclamation of the message. Envision the intimacy with Christ that will be established. Try to foresee the acts of righteousness that will be produced or the marriages that will be transformed by the appropriation of the truth. Get excited about how God will use His word to change the hearts of His people.

Perhaps Richard Baxter summed up the posture of expectation best when he wrote:

> If you would prosper in your work, be sure to keep up earnest desires and expectations of success. If your hearts be not set on the end of your labours, and you long not to see the conversion and edification of your hearers, and do not study and preach in hope, you are not likely to see much success. . . . Let it be the property of a Judas to have more regard to the bag than to his work, and not to care much for what they pretend to care; and to think, if they have their salaries, and the love and commendations of their people, they have enough to satisfy them: but, let all who preach for Christ and men's salvation be unsatisfied till they have the thing they preach for. He never had the right ends of a preacher, who is indifferent whether he obtain them, and is not grieved when he misseth them, and rejoiced when he can see the desired issue.[15]

PREACH LOGICALLY

While much of my appeal has been targeted at the heart of a preacher, let me now focus on his mind, and in essence propose a marriage of the two.

There is great power in the sermon delivered with urgency, enthusiasm, and expectancy, especially when it is wrapped in tight and reliable logic. A study of New Testament preaching reveals this tightly woven fabric of reason and good sense in the way God's truth is presented. Recall how

Paul hangs the preaching of the resurrection in Corinth on the rationale of Christ's Resurrection:

> But if there is no resurrection of the dead, then Christ is not risen. And if Christ is not risen, then our preaching is vain and your faith is also vain. Yes, and we are found false witnesses of God, because we have testified of God that He raised up Christ, whom He did not raise up—if in fact the dead do not rise. For if the dead do not rise, then Christ is not risen. And if Christ is not risen, your faith is futile; you are still in your sins! Then also those who have fallen asleep in Christ have perished. If in this life only we have hope in Christ we are of all men the most pitiable. But now Christ is risen from the dead and has become the first fruits of those who have fallen asleep (1 Cor. 15:13–20).

It is not just the work of New Testament apologetics that calls, as Peter did, for the logical expression of the "reasons for the hope that is in you" (1 Pet. 3:15). It is also the work of preaching, whether to Christians or non-Christians. Jesus made regular use of logic and reason to teach the divine guidelines regarding marriage (Matt. 19:4–8), and to dispel anxiety (Matt. 6:28–30), and to bolster faith in the afterlife (Matt. 22:31–32). Though it may be argued that life-changing preaching appeals to the conscience and not the intellect, Christ's ministry shows that the intellect is often the avenue through which the conscience is confronted.

While it is true that logic and reason have their limitations, one cannot deny they hold a very important place in the work of biblical preaching. Without them our sermons may be perceived as the passionate pleas of an illogical and irrational person. But God is neither illogical nor irrational, and His Word should never be presented as such. Those who quickly default to a form of modern mysticism in the pulpit often do so because they simply fail to do their homework. When we fail to adequately think through the logical nature of our presentation we can hardly hope to create it on the spot. Sound reason in preaching must be carefully formulated first in the study, then diligently articulated on the platform.

Preaching in our modern culture requires rational support for every main point. Somewhere between explaining and applying each assertion we must adequately prove it. We must satisfactorily answer the question, "Is this really true?"[16] Haddon Robinson warned that it is "an initial impulse of those who take the Bible seriously . . . to ignore this question and assume the idea should be accepted as true because it comes from the Bible."[17] This is a catastrophic mistake.

Today more than ever people have a faltering view of the Bible.[18] We must recognize the deplorable state of our post-modern culture and its effect on our churches and respond by preaching with appropriate reasoning and proofs. If we continue to preach without them, our preaching will become part of the problem instead of the solution. People will fail to even hear our preaching because we fail to present it cogently.

If you sense your logical skills are weak, then read authors who present concise, logical arguments. Reading good systematic theologies, apologetics, or even some forms of Puritan preaching with their arguments and propositions can help enhance our preaching logic. Even a community college course in logic or a local seminary course on apologetics can help you make sound assertions from the pulpit.

Don't forget that when we preach we are calling people to abandon existing beliefs, values, and behaviors, and adopt new ones. Even the most faithful follower of Christ responds with some level of skepticism when the security of the familiar is torn from him. We must expect that level of skepticism and be willing to preach with the skeptic in mind. While this should not lead us to a kind of preaching that attempts to substantiate every sentence, we must always remember that life-changing preaching speaks to people's reason as well as their conscience.

PREACH CONCRETELY

To preach concretely is to preach with the real world in mind. If we are preaching to change lives, then the nature of our preaching must be truly relevant. Our sermons cannot remain in the arena of principles and propositions but must descend into the streets, offices, and homes of those sitting before us. It is easier for us and more comfortable for them if our sermons remain ethereal and abstract. But real preaching that guides people to actually be "doers of the word" (James 1:22a) must form those principles into models that show people how it's done.

Concrete Illustrations

The use of meaningful illustrations and stories is immensely helpful along these lines. Jesus, of course, was known for a unique and effective form of persuasion that found its expression in story form. His parables were instrumental in bringing conviction to His hearers and driving them to action. He masterfully used stories to paint real life images of the truths He wanted appropriated in His listeners' lives.

It is important to underscore that Jesus' stories were never utilized as an end in themselves. His stories were strategic. They were a means to an end. It is increasingly popular these days to equate biblical preaching with mere storytelling. While stories are important, we must know how they function. The Bible and its preachers utilized stories for life-changing purposes and we should do the same. Paul explains that even the extended stories of the Old Testament have a practical purpose:

Now these things occurred as examples to keep us from setting our hearts on evil things as they did. Do not be idolaters, as some of them were; as it is written: "The people sat down to eat and drink and got up to indulge in pagan revelry." We should not commit sexual immorality, as some of them did—and in one day twenty-three thousand of them died. We should not test the Lord, as some of them did—and were killed by snakes. And do not grumble, as some of them did—and were killed by the destroying angel. These things happened to them as examples and were written down as warnings for us, on whom the fulfillment of the ages has come (1 Cor. 10:6–11 NIV).

If we are to enlist stories and illustrations in our preaching, they must be employed to give life to the principles we are expounding.

Many of Christ's stories so obviously depicted how truth was to be lived out that He would conclude them with the words, "Go and do likewise" (Luke 10:37b). When the principle of loving one's neighbor was being presented, the story said, "and this is what it looks like."

In some cases He conveyed a story to illustrate what His followers *would not* look like. When Jesus told the stories about the lost sheep, the lost coin, and the lost son (Luke 15), He was presenting concrete examples of the arrogant and whining attitude of the Pharisees. He was trying to show through the elder son who refused to rejoice when the lost had been found, that "this is how not to do it!"

As you may know, many illustration books and websites provide countless cute and clever stories. Before you enlist one in your next sermon, be sure it serves an important purpose. Though they can be used for other valid purposes, like explaining or proving a point, make sure to enlist them for their most powerful purpose—to provide a template that will show your listeners what the truth should (or should not) look like. Your stories, by nature, will be one of the most memorable components of your sermon, so make it your pattern to use illustrations that give applicational direction to the message you are preaching.

Concrete Examples

Illustrations can add clarity to the kind of application a passage is calling for, but specific examples show how it ought to be done, here and now. In other words, illustrations may be presented with analogous elements or placed in an unrelated setting and still powerfully highlight the general application of a truth being preached. Examples, on the other hand, seek to retain a one-to-one correspondence to the lives of your hearers. Whereas sheep, goats, and jealous brothers may constitute an effective illustration, a concrete example drives your point out of the first century and into Monday morning!

108

Note the kinds of specific examples offered by John the Baptist in his preaching regarding genuine repentance:

> The man with two tunics should share with him who has none, and the one who has food should do the same... Don't collect any more [taxes] than you are required to... Don't extort money and don't accuse people falsely—be content with your pay (Luke 3:11, 13, 14b NIV).

John was showing his first-century hearers what repentant living should actually look like, not with a story but with concrete examples from the daily occupations of shepherds, tax collectors, and soldiers.

When we offer examples of application in our sermons we must also seek to invade the daily activities and responsibilities of our hearers. Because the lives of our listeners are varied it is usually difficult to find an example that crosses into each person's life setting. Therefore, a good example is rarely presented by itself. As in John's preaching we need to give a variety of applicational examples—in your congregation you might explore the specific application for the business executive, the self-employed entrepreneur, the stay-at-home mom, and the student.

Examples can be taken a step further by relating an exemplary incident that has actually happened. Often a "perfect example" of what this can look like in a contemporary setting will be uncovered in your reading or research. Sometimes a great example of a truth in action will surface from the experience of someone in your congregation. They're likely all around you—you only need to look for them!

Examples "from the parsonage" should be handled with care. Use them with caution and discernment. If an example from your own life distracts or deflects the focus of your point or application, then don't use it.[19] You also should be sensitive to how personal examples can put a dishonest spin on you or your family.[20]

Concrete, real-life examples, when wisely used, can be one of the most effective ways to animate a biblical truth for your listeners. They should be frequently used, always carefully thought out, and wisely presented.

The comment was made after hearing the powerful preaching of Harry Ironside, "He preached for an hour and it seemed like twenty-minutes; others preach for twenty-minutes and it seems like an hour."[21] Good preaching will impress people in this way. It engages the listener, pulling him through the door, so to speak, and he becomes an eager participant. The urgency and passion of the sacred event do not allow him to drift into boredom or preoccupation. Reason and relevance refuse to yield the mind to daydreaming. It is the kind of preaching that is heard—really heard! It is the kind of preaching that transforms lives.

CHAPTER NINE

Keep the Life-changer at the Center of Your Sermon

WHAT ASPECT OF YOUR LIFE NEEDS IMPROVEMENT? WHATEVER IT IS, CHANCES are there's a seminar or class starting in your neighborhood this week that will help you become "a better you." Men and women all over your community will step up to microphones and share principles that will help you quit smoking, drinking, and overeating. They will teach you how to manage your anger and your money. You'll learn how to enrich your marriage and your inner self. By week's end hundreds of thousands of people nationwide will testify how their lives have been changed for the better because of these meetings and seminars.

Though these messages clearly target areas of ethical behavior related to Scripture, they certainly are not Christian sermons. Motivational self-help or "higher power" lectures may share some common results (i.e., people living more civil or charitable lives), but they cannot produce the types of changes brought by the preaching of God's Word.

Behavioral reform has a place in the biblical equation, but God's objectives for men and women are much broader and more profound than simply exchanging sinful activities for righteous ones. God's transforming and sanctifying works are predicated upon the helplessness of our sinful state and our reconciliation to our holy Creator. All regenerative work is ultimately done to the praise and honor of the Sovereign God of the universe.

A biblical sermon might well result in the management of one's anger or the enrichment of one's marriage, but it must begin with a proper understanding of and connection to the Author of all true reformation.

Therefore, Christ is the focal point of all Christian preaching. God is the Source, Reason, and Enabler for all that is prescribed. In Christian preaching there is something categorically distinct from all other forms of life-enhancing lecturing.

BEWARE OF PEOPLE-CENTERED SERMONS

In theory most would agree that Christian preaching is to be categorically distinct from self-help seminars, but in practice the distinctions may not be so obvious to our congregants. This is especially true when the preacher is passionate about seeing change in his hearers, yet inadvertently reverts to the role of self-help guru. God does want and expect changed hearers, but He never secures change apart from His rightful place in their lives—and His rightful place in your sermons.

Stated simply, preaching *can* miss the point of biblical life-change by pushing God to the fringes of the sermon and moving people to the center of it. This happens when God is no longer the source or reason for what is being taught but rather becomes ancillary to it. He is consciously or unconsciously relegated to a supporting role as the congregants slide to the center of the sermon. This is a role God does not tolerate.

People-centered Ministry

People-centered sermons are often symptomatic of people-centered ministries. People-centered ministries are those that have adopted the belief and/or practice of making people and their benefit the ultimate goal of their ministries. The pursuit of God's glory and honor has been displaced by the ambition to meet people's needs. When programs, projects, and sermons are constructed, little thought is given to God's desires or interests. Instead the carefully researched interests of the congregation become the controlling factor. Although the Bible demonstrates that human interests often are targeted by divinely governed ministry (Phil. 2:20–21), the ultimate controlling factor in biblical ministry should always be the glory and pleasure of God.

People-centered ministries are often accompanied by a lack of church discipline, an avoidance of difficult or demanding texts, and a general evasion of anything that does not grant immediate gratification or benefit to those targeted by the ministry. Hence, commitment levels are generally low and requirements for ministry participation or leadership are either nonexistent or not enforced.

People-centered ministries often can be traced to years of faulty evangelism. Consider ministries that proclaim a gospel that urges people to come to Christ for their own personal benefit. Their message of salvation comes with promises to enhance people's daily lives, dispel their aches and pains, and give meaning and purpose to replace their loneliness and despair. While there are countless destructive implications of this kind of evangelism,[1] perhaps the most prevalent is the kind of preaching emanating from pulpits each Sunday.

Now imagine churchgoers who have cut their teeth on this kind of gospel suddenly being presented with a kind of preaching aimed at their sanctification! In essence, God is no longer making *their* life more bearable. He's making them able to live like Christ! This type of message would be a shock to their spiritual systems. If they are presented with a man-centered gospel it is likely they will expect to be fed a weekly diet of man-centered sermons. And it becomes incumbent upon those who preached that gospel to satisfy them—and so many, week after week, try to do just that.

As Malachi did in his generation, it's time for preachers in ours to boldly stand up and declare that God does not exist for us, but rather, we exist for Him; He is not our servant—we are called to be His; we do not obey Him for our sake—we obey Him for His sake. Only when we truly understand that we exist for the glory of God can we end the slide toward people-centered ministry and restore a God-centered ministry characterized by God-centered preaching.

Simplistic Moral Instructions

When sermons are not grounded in a proper view of God and wider context of Scripture they are often reduced to lectures on ethical behavior or moralistic principles. These may be true biblical ethics and good morals, yet if they are detached from Christian theology they will ultimately miss the true intention of the text.[2] Biblical instructions on sobriety or marital fidelity must be seen in the larger context of God's purpose in order for Christian preaching to remain distinctly Christian.

When our ethics-based instructions fail to "save the marriage," "yield happiness," or bring some other desired result, the error of simplistic moral preaching begins to surface. Honest men and women rightly object, saying they have been sold a bill of goods. "If this was supposed to make me happy," they complain, "it didn't work!" People-centered preaching that does not grasp the broader understanding of biblical obedience puts an unbiblical spin on Christianity. It fails to incorporate the whole picture. Part of that picture includes promises that cannot be reconciled with a people-centered theology: "All who desire to live godly in Christ Jesus will suffer persecutions" (2 Tim. 3:12); "In the world you will have tribulation" (John 16:33); and:

> If the world hates you, you know that it hated Me before it hated you. If you were of the world, the world would love its own. Yet because you are not of the world, but I chose you out of the world,

therefore the world hates you. Remember the word that I said to you, 'A servant is not greater than his master.' If they persecuted Me, they will also persecute you" (John 15:18–20).

People-centered preaching may alter people's behavior but it will eventually fail at the most significant point. When Scripture is not accurately presented, God will not be properly honored, and needy people will end up disillusioned.

AIM FOR GOD-CENTERED SERMONS

There is a better way to preach. It secures change in people's lives because it gives them the right perspective, adequate resources, and a biblical motivation to change. It is preaching that keeps God and His agenda at the center of our sermons. A steady diet of this kind of faithful preaching will transform men and women into a congregation of servants equipped by grace to follow the Master's lead.

Each year when I was a boy my elementary school held a carnival that brought out colorful clowns, a dunking booth, and twenty-five cent pony rides. Of course I made the rounds, but most of my quarters ended up at the crazy bikes course. The challenge was to successfully navigate one of their "crazy bikes" through a maze of cones and chalk lines sketched out on the playground asphalt.

My determination and repeated attempts were fueled by how easy the course looked while standing in line. As simple as it seemed from the sidelines, the problems became evident when you mounted the bike. The many flags, plastic windmills, and the extended forks on the bike were mere distractions compared to the mischief caused by the intentionally displaced hubs in both wheels. The spokes on the top side of each wheel were three to four inches shorter than the spokes on the bottom, causing the bike to bob and wobble. Needless to say, steering the bike with any amount of control was next to impossible.

Sometimes our sermons do the same in that they fail to guide our hearers down the path that looks so attainable from the sidelines. Though the course may be carefully marked out, our sermonic vehicle, like the crazy bike, is hopelessly out of balance! If we hope to see our preaching reach its biblical goal we must take pains to keep central things central and first things first.

God-centered Preaching Is Always Christ-centered Preaching

The indispensable ingredient in God-centered preaching is Jesus Christ. God is in the business of glorifying His Son and calling people to abide in Him. This in turn glorifies the Father Himself. At the end of His ministry Jesus prayed:

> Father, the hour has come. Glorify Your Son, that Your Son also may glorify You, as You have given Him authority over all flesh, that He should give eternal life to as many as You have given Him. And this is eternal life, that they may know You, the only true God, and Jesus Christ whom You have sent. I have glorified You on the earth. I have finished the work which You have given Me to do. And now, O Father, glorify Me together with Yourself, with the glory which I had with You before the world was (John 17:1–5).[3]

The inspired hymn of the early church contained in Philippians 2:9–11 expresses God's intent to exalt the Son, and the resultant glory that comes to the Father:

> Therefore God also has highly exalted Him
> and given Him the name which is above every name,
> that at the name of Jesus every knee should bow, of those
> in heaven, and of those on earth, and of those under the earth,
> and that every tongue should confess that Jesus Christ is Lord,
> to the glory of God the Father (Phil. 2:9–11).

The Holy Spirit, too, purposes to exalt Christ:

> However, when He, the Spirit of truth, has come, He will guide you into all truth; for He will not speak on His own authority, but whatever He hears He will speak; and He will tell you things to come. He will glorify Me, for He will take of what is Mine and declare it to you. All things that the Father has are Mine. Therefore I said that He will take of Mine and declare it to you (John 16:13–15).[4]

Understanding this, Paul set out to glorify the Triune God by exalting Christ in his preaching. He wrote the Corinthians, "For I determined not to know anything among you except Jesus Christ and Him crucified" (1 Cor. 2:2).

Some applicational preaching attempts to be "relevant" to modern life without ever connecting the mind of the listener to the Christ who changes lives. Karl Dijk exposes the problem when he writes:

> [Preaching which] again and again equates Abraham and us, Moses' struggle and ours, Peter's denial and our unfaithfulness; which proceeds only illustratively, does not bring the Word of God and does not permit the church to see the glory of the work

115

of God; it only preaches man, the sinful, the sought, the redeemed, the pious man, but not Jesus Christ.[5]

This kind of preaching is the kind of ethical lecturing that would be at home in a variety of non-Christian meetings. Jay Adams explains:

> If you preach a sermon that would be acceptable to the members of a Jewish synagogue or to a Unitarian congregation, there is something radically wrong with it. Preaching, when it is truly Christian, is *distinctive*. And what makes it distinctive is the all-pervading presence of a saving and sanctifying Christ. Jesus Christ must be at the heart of every sermon you preach.[6]

Put Christ on Display in Every Sermon

Upon completing the review of my life and doctrine, the team of pastors who conferred the ordination of my pastoral ministry concluded with the words, "We have one final exhortation for you. *Preach Christ!* Make Him the theme of your preaching ministry."[7]

Regardless of how it is said, true Christian preaching establishes Christ as the hub of every sermon. Spurgeon worded his exhortation to young preachers in this way: "Of all I would wish to say this is the sum; my brethren, preach Christ, always and evermore. He is the whole gospel. His persons, offices and work must be our one great, all-comprehending theme."[8] We must remember our preaching is ultimately about Him!

Commenting on Paul's resolve to "preach Christ" (1 Cor. 1:23), Sidney Greidanus clarifies that doing so is not some kind of homiletical redundancy:

> Paul's preaching of Christ is not simply a constant retelling of Jesus' life, death and resurrection. . . . Rather, Paul takes his *starting point* in Jesus Christ and preaches Christ as his person and work illumine all other vital issues and questions. "Jesus Christ and him crucified" is the heart of God's plan of redemption; from this heart, renewing power pulses into every area of life.[9]

Don Carson explains what preaching Christ looks like in an expository sermon.

> At its best, expository preaching is preaching which, however dependent it may be for its content on the text or texts at hand, draws attention to inner-canonical connections that inexorably move to Jesus Christ.[10]

If our preaching doesn't set one's thoughts and focus on Christ we have failed at New Testament preaching. This, of course, means more than simply

116

mentioning His name throughout our moral instruction. Christ must remain the theological axis of all that we teach. As Edmond Clowney writes:

> The Scriptures are full of moral instruction and ethical exhortation, but the ground and motivation of all is found in the mercy of Jesus Christ. We are to preach all the riches of Scripture, but unless the center holds, all the bits and pieces of our pulpit counseling, of our thundering at social sins, of our positive or negative thinking—all fly off into the Sunday morning air. . . . Let others develop the pulpit fads of the passing seasons. Specialize in preaching Jesus.[11]

It's not always easy to proclaim Christ (and inexorably move to Him in our preaching) so that the truth about Christ holds the bits and pieces of our sermons into a cohesive whole. In some cases the text we are preaching provides clear connections; at other times it does not.

Easy in the Epistles

The didactic sections of the Epistles provide us with many preaching texts that are, even on the surface, rooted and grounded in Christ's work. For example, note the opening statements of Colossians chapter three:

> If then you were raised with Christ, seek those things which are above, where Christ is, sitting at the right hand of God. Set your mind on things above, not on things on the earth. For you died, and your life is hidden with Christ in God. When Christ who is our life appears, then you also will appear with Him in glory (Col. 3:1–4).

Exploring the connection between a truth or an application and Christ and His work is no great challenge when the association is so plainly worded.

Hard in Some New Testament Narratives

Some narratives in Acts, and surprisingly even some in the Gospels, present the preacher with the challenge of pointing the sermon to the appropriate Christological connection. The Sermon on the Mount will require a purposeful handling, even though the words are spoken by Christ and are sometimes related to Christ. For example, Christ says:

> Blessed are you when people insult you, persecute you and falsely say all kinds of evil against you because of me. Rejoice and be glad, because great is your reward in heaven, for in the same way they persecuted the prophets who were before you (Matt. 5:11–12 NIV).

To understand the blessing Jesus is talking about, to be able to rejoice in the midst of persecution, to understand the basis for heavenly reward, and to know how one shares a fraternity with the Old Testament prophets, one must understand the work of Christ not explicitly stated in this passage. Therefore, we must constantly look for these connections and purpose to preach them if we are to remain true to our calling as heralds of Christ.

Challenging in the Old Testament

The call to soundly preach Christ from the Old Testament brings us face to face with our greatest challenge. The nature of the challenge has drawn a fair bit of hermeneutical attention.[12] Graeme Goldsworthy observes:

> [P]reaching from the Old Testament presents many problems for the Christian preacher. . . . It is plainly easier as a Christian to preach from the New Testament than from the Old. Some may feel that preaching from the Old Testament is the same in principle as preaching from the New. Of course, if we are diligent in the choice of our texts, that may well appear to be the case. But even at the level of ethical teaching in the prophets, or the praise of God in the Psalms, we instinctively recognize that the material still emanates from the period before Jesus came into the world. How much more, then, is the gap obvious when we deal with some ceremonial prescriptions in the law of Moses.[13]

This being the case, the practice is fraught with hermeneutical dangers. Greidanus is right when he observes that "Christological interpretation [of the Old Testament] can easily slide into eisegesis."[14] Therefore, we must be faithful to the text without forcing upon it a Christological idea that is contrary or foreign to the text.

Though the task carries inherent hazards and difficulties, it should not discourage us from preaching Christ from the Old Testament. We know that it is entirely possible and most certainly appropriate. We must not forget the practice of the apostle Paul:

> Then Paul, as his custom was, went in to them, and for three Sabbaths reasoned with them from the Scriptures, explaining and demonstrating that the Christ had to suffer and rise again from the dead, and saying, "This Jesus whom I preach to you is the Christ" (Acts 17:2).

I stand, witnessing both to small and great, saying no other things than those which the prophets and Moses said would come—that the Christ would suffer, that He would be the first to rise from the dead, and would proclaim light to the *Jewish* people and to the Gentiles (Acts 26:22b–23).

118

And Apollos:

> Now a certain Jew named Apollos, born at Alexandria, an elo-
> quent man and mighty in the Scriptures, came to Ephesus. This
> man had been instructed in the way of the Lord; and being fer-
> vent in spirit, he spoke and taught accurately the things of the
> Lord . . . for he vigorously refuted the Jews publicly, showing from
> the Scriptures that Jesus is the Christ (Acts 18:24–25, 28).

And Philip:

> So Philip ran to him, and heard him reading the prophet Isaiah,
> and said, "Do you understand what you are reading?" Then Philip
> opened his mouth, and beginning at this Scripture, preached
> Jesus to him (Acts 8:30, 35).

And, of course, Jesus himself:

> Then He said to them, "O foolish ones, and slow of heart to believe
> in all that the prophets have spoken! Ought not the Christ to have
> suffered these things and to enter into His glory?" And beginning at
> Moses and all the Prophets, He expounded to them in all the
> Scriptures the things concerning Himself (Luke 24:25–27).

It is interesting to note that Jesus did not sympathize with their inabil-
ity to discern the Christological truths from the Old Testament passages.
Rather, He chided them and called them fools for not recognizing the
truths He was apt to point out to them.[15]

The Wrong Way to Do It

In our eagerness to follow the biblical pattern we must be careful to be
true to the texts we exposit, whether from the Pentateuch or the Epistles.
When we attempt to inject Christ by spiritualizing or allegorizing the
Bible, we undermine the authority of our sermons and, of greater concern,
the authority of Scripture. Even the greatest of preachers have tripped
over this one from time to time.

In their zeal to preach Christ, some popular preachers make poor exegesis their habit.[16] We can twist and contort the meaning of a passage, or
at times fail to exposit its context in our efforts to show a "redemptive connection." Take care not to use Scripture as a quick springboard to unrelated or more comfortable passages. We may move "inner-canonically"
and "inexorably" to Christ, but we must always do so with a sworn fidelity
to the passage at hand.

The length of the preacher's passage can be a clue to error in this regard. The shorter it is, the more suspect you should be.[17] If you tend to isolate a phrase or a single verse from the Old Testament and from that phrase form an outline that speaks exclusively of Christ, it is likely that the context has been forgotten and the text's intended meaning has been violated.

When the Proverbs instruct us, "Do not forsake your own friend or your father's friend" (27:10), there is an obvious concern regarding relational loyalty. The intention of the text cannot be rightly applied without a sermonic connection to Christological truths, but a sermon should not disregard the text's intention in favor of preaching exclusively on Christ as our friend.[18]

GUIDELINES FOR "CHRISTIAN" PREACHING

Keeping applicational sermons centered on God's glory and rooted in the work of Christ requires a set of governing principles; otherwise, our preaching text will become a mere springboard to preach topically about Christ. The following guidelines can help to ensure that our sermons remain distinctively Christian.

Clarify the Effect of Sin

One of the principles used to discern the transferability of a biblical application from "then" to "now" is to draw from the ancient application those aspects which address man's depravity (discussed in chapter 4). Identifying this unchanging human condition serves to preach Christ as it clarifies the desperate need we cannot meet ourselves.

Without Christ Our Best Is Not Good Enough

When human sin and depravity are uncovered in a preaching text, it should remind our listeners of their helpless state before God. As our sin is addressed it should be clear there is no remedy but Christ. Our best is never good enough:

As it is written:

> There is none righteous, no, not one;
> There is none who understands;
> There is none who seeks after God.
> They have all turned aside;
> They have together become unprofitable;
> There is none who does good, no, not one. . . .

Now we know that whatever the law says, it says to those who are under the law, that every mouth may be stopped, and all the world may become guilty before God. Therefore by the deeds of the law no flesh will be justified in His sight, for by the law is the knowledge of sin (Rom. 3:10–12, 19–20).

Highlighting our sinful condition drives us back to the Cross in our preaching. Bryan Chapell writes:

> No passage tells us what we can do or should do to make ourselves holy (as though we could lift ourselves by our own bootstraps to divine approval). The Bible is not a self-help book. The Scriptures present one, consistent, organic message. They tell us how we must seek Christ who alone is our Savior.[19]

We dare not leave the impression that compliance to the practical teaching contained in the sermon is in any way a means to secure God's divine approval. When facing any divine directive, proper emphasis and regular explanation of our utter helplessness before a holy God will keep our need for Christ front and center in our preaching.

Without Christ Our Best Will Never Be True Obedience

There are no truer words about sanctification than those written by Paul to the doctrinally imperiled Galatians. He wrote, "Are you so foolish? Having begun in the Spirit, are you now being made perfect by the flesh?" (Gal. 3:3). He explained further, "For you are all sons of God through faith in Christ Jesus. For as many of you as were baptized into Christ have put on Christ" (Gal. 3:26–27). To the Corinthians he wrote, "Now it is God who makes both us and you stand firm in Christ" (2 Cor. 1:21 NIV). The phrase "in Christ"[20] was frequently used by Paul to denote our union with Christ in relation to our justification *as well as* our sanctification.

While it is true that obedience can be an acceptable sacrifice that honors and pleases God (Heb. 13:15–16; Phil. 4:18; 1 Pet. 2:20; Rom. 12:1–2; 15:16; 1 Tim. 4:3; Eph. 5:10), it cannot be so without Christ as its source and hope. He makes us, and our offerings, acceptable. We are received, as are our gifts of service and obedience, solely upon our union with Christ, our position *in Him.* When Christ is removed from the equation (or the sermon), we are left with nothing of lasting value. As Jay Adams writes, "Preach Him plainly and gratefully, and you will not be tempted to preach about man and his pretended power and dignity."[21]

Display the Work of Christ

If the helplessness of our human condition before a holy God is the consistent backdrop of our preaching then the natural response is to, as Carson put it, "move inner-canonically" to display Christ's redeeming work.

To the charge that regular exposure to the effects of sin is too negative,[22] Chapell fittingly responds, "The Bible's ultimate aim is beautifully positive. Scripture addresses our incompleteness only because such a focus concurrently signals the work of God that makes us whole."[23] Great opportunities to deliver God's gracious solutions will surface when we are faithful to highlight the "depravity factor"[24] in our text.

Christ Paid Our Debt

The ultimate solution to this depravity factor is, of course, the substitutionary Atonement of Christ on the Cross. Scripture abounds with support of this truth. God has "made Him who knew no sin to be sin for us, that we might become the righteousness of God in Him" (2 Cor. 5:21). He turned aside the wrath that was due us and "forgave us all our sins, having canceled the written code, with its regulations, that was against us and that stood opposed to us; he took it away, nailing it to the cross" (Col. 2:14 NIV).

This truth can be demonstrated directly in the text itself in several epistles, or by a careful presentation of a legitimate "type" in the Old Testament, or by exploring the larger context of the preaching portion.[25] Chapell explains that in "its context, every passage possesses one or more of four redemptive foci. Every text is predictive of the work of Christ, preparatory for the work of Christ, reflective of the work of Christ, and/or resultant of the work of Christ."[26]

Goldworthy concurs:

> [A]ll texts in the whole Bible bear a discernable relationship to Christ and are primarily intended as a testimony to Christ. Lest a skeptic should ask how texts about sin and the devil testify to Christ, I would respond by saying that such texts are an important testimony to the victory and the salvation Christ has won for us, and to the fact that he was made to become sin for us.[27]

We must always answer the disclosure of our helplessness with a clear indication, in one way or another, of God's propitiatory solution.

Christ Provided Our Righteousness

The redemptive work of Christ involves not only the death of Christ but also His life. This may seem theologically pedantic but it is often missed in our preaching. When ignored, those truly justified by faith may needlessly seek a portion of "maintenance grace" through their own merit. Yet Paul's hope was to "be found in Him, not having my own righteousness, which is from the law, but that which is through faith in Christ, the righteousness which is from God by faith" (Phil. 3:9). Paul found no need to seek any further than the Lord Jesus Himself.

Our hearers should never be ignorant of the imputation of Christ's righteousness on their behalf as the sole grounds for their acceptance before God. Christ lived the life our listeners should have lived. He "fulfilled all righteousness" (Matt. 3:15 NIV), and imputed that righteousness to sinners. He has made us as acceptable to God as we will ever be.

When this aspect of our preaching wanes and our congregants do not embrace these truths, our call to be conformed to the image of Christ may be received with heretical results. It would be tragic to replicate a Galatian-style crisis whereby our listeners secretly rely on their own righteous deeds to pave their own way to God (Gal. 3:10). Be vigilant not to "set aside the grace of God" and by your preaching communicate that "Christ died in vain" (Gal. 2:21).

Call for People to Appropriate Christ's Work

It is not enough to expose ultimate needs and discuss ultimate solutions. As we preach we must appeal to people to embrace those solutions.

The Call to Non-Christians

Though I am convinced that evangelism is not the primary function of the assembled church, "gospel preaching" necessarily results when we preach Christ appropriately. That doesn't mean that sermons always end in "altar calls" or "sinner's prayers." It does mean there should be enough theological clarity for an unrepentant sinner to know that he needs to place his faith in Christ and throw himself on the mercy and grace of God. Surely there are appropriate times to be cognizant of the "unbelievers" among you, and to call them to initial repentance and faith in Christ. But as 1 Corinthians 14 describes, that call often takes place *within* the process of edificational "prophesying" *to believers* (v. 24). Perhaps prompted by a directed statement in our sermon, the non-Christian will be convicted that "he is a sinner," the "secrets of his heart will be laid bare," and he will come to faith recognizing that "God is really among you" (1 Cor. 14:24–25).

While this scenario may regularly take place in the course of our preaching, it should not become the applicational goal of every sermon. It is unwise to drive every sermon to the same Christological implication each week. Though many preachers have historically done this and others still do, whenever the church is assembled it is our explicit call to feed the flock (Acts 20:28–32). Jay Adams writes "While edificational preaching always must be evangelical, it must not become simply evangelistic. . . . Edificational preaching is no longer edificational in purpose if the purpose of the sermon becomes evangelistic instead."[28]

Nevertheless, the transformational elements of the gospel message will usually be present in good biblical exposition. Therefore the effective preacher will find many who will come to an initial faith in Christ through his faithful preaching to God's people.

The Call to Christians

As we edify and equip the body of Christ we need to be sure that our directives include a clear call for continued reliance on the work of Christ. As I have already said, our malfeasance in this area will have a devastating doctrinal impact on the lives of our listeners. Rather than leaving it unsaid, or even infrequently said, we must continually proclaim Christ as our all in all. As Chapell asks, "Why should we assume our listeners will understand what we rarely say?"[29]

Good preaching should regularly address godly motives for obedience. There should be a consistent call for them to trust in Christ's merited favor on their behalf. We must call God's children to trust in the secured love of the Father through the work of His Son. As we direct Christians to be Christ-like we must also direct them to fully trust in the finished work of Christ on their behalf.

Our listeners must understand both sides of the coin. God tells them to obey Him, but He also makes it clear that He is the agent of that obedience. Paul wrote to the Philippians:

> Therefore, my beloved, as you have always obeyed, not as in my presence only, but now much more in my absence, work out your own salvation with fear and trembling; for it is God who works in you both to will and to do for His good pleasure (Phil. 2:12–13).

God speaks through Ezekiel to underscore the source of the obedience of those whose hearts He would regenerate.

> I will give you a new heart and put a new spirit in you; I will take the heart of stone out of your flesh and give you a heart of flesh. I will put My Spirit within you and cause you to walk in My statutes, and you will keep my judgments and do them (Ezek. 36:26–27).

The writer of Hebrews concludes his lengthy exhortation with a reminder of God's role in our pursuit of His will:

> Now may the God of peace who brought up our Lord Jesus from the dead, that great Shepherd of the sheep, through the blood of the everlasting covenant, make you complete in every good work to do His will, working in you what is well pleasing in His sight, through Jesus Christ, to whom be glory forever and ever. Amen (Heb. 13:20–21).

Simply put, Jesus said, "No branch can bear fruit by itself" and "without me you can do nothing" (John 15:4, 5 NIV).

All of this is not to deny nor detract from preaching that passionately calls people to obey Christ. But the reason, the rationale, the motive, the power, and the goal of all obedience must always be crystal clear. It *is* difficult to expend the effort and time needed to regularly include these elements in our sermons, but true Christian preaching cannot afford to neglect them.

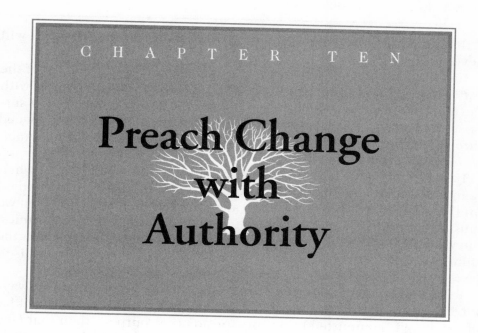

CHAPTER TEN

Preach Change with Authority

No doubt about it, today's preachers preach in difficult times. One might object to this assertion, pointing to signs of unprecedented peace and prosperity that surround us. True, few of us have been run out of town or had rocks thrown at us for proclaiming the Resurrection of Christ. This apathy is one reason I give to prove we preach in the *most challenging* environment the church has ever experienced. It is not that the truth of the message is violently rejected. Instead, truth itself has become passé.

The current state of our modern (or "postmodern") culture[1] allows our hearers to yawn their way through assertions that would have either encouraged and enlightened or enflamed and enraged former generations. So unique is this generation that a poignant truth cogently delivered fails to raise eyebrows, let alone the willing hands of those to whom it is directed. Therefore, we would be wise to "understand our times" (1 Chron. 12:32) so as to preach in a way that most appropriately and effectively reflects the eternal truth which was "once for all delivered to the saints" (Jude 3).

AUTHORITY IN THE PULPIT

Many years ago, after a particularly difficult sermon, a congregant met me at the lobby doors with a stern rebuke, leaving no doubt as to the degree of his disappointment in me as his preacher. As he began his critical remarks I thought to myself, "I knew this was coming," yet as he articulated his concerns, his exhortation surprised me in a way I will never forget.

His criticism had nothing to do with the demands or difficulties of the truth I had attempted to exposit. He even seemed willing to grapple with the blunt implications I had spelled out for our congregation. To my surprise, he said he was frustrated over the subtle apologies that I laced throughout the sermon. He wisely discerned that there was *far too much of the messenger* in the message.

I've always tried to remember the wisdom of that doorway lesson when tempted to show any hint of regret over the words of truth God prescribed for His children. It is important to be appropriately compassionate, but we must never be apologetic. Preaching to change lives may be hard at times, but we don't do our church or God any favors by being sheepish about the things He desires to communicate. God's Word is authoritative. If it is to be relayed with His power, we dare not diminish that authority.

Regardless of the cultural climate, good biblical preaching is always intrinsically authoritative. As John Calvin rightly pointed out, "The office of teaching is committed to pastors for no other purpose than that God alone may be heard there."[2] If God's thoughts, standards, and expectations are clearly expressed in a sermon, it inherently possesses His authority. When the Creator's voice is heard among the created, it commands respect. When the Judge of the living and the dead has His mind articulated He should not vie with any earthly information for our attention.

The Nature of True Preaching

Too often the preacher fails to recognize biblical preaching's intrinsic authority, or worse, he chooses to acquiesce to the current climate, thereby failing to deliver a message that clearly expresses the nature of biblical authority. The latter is a temptation that must be avoided, as D. A. Carson points out:

> We must not only declare the whole counsel of God, but do so in an environment where the subject is perceived to be vaguely or even explicitly irrelevant. In fact, if you seem too passionate about it, *you too* may appear to be vaguely irrelevant. To bridge this gap, many preachers succumb to the temptation to become entertainers (for entertainment is one of the categories people *do* understand), or to the temptation to transmute the gospel into something that helps us in our perceived inadequacies (for endless self-focus certainly dominates the national discourse). Other preachers, more robust, dig in and condemn, and gather a group of like-minded conservatives around them, but make little impact on the land.[3]

Your job as a preacher is not to entertain, augment lives with God-talk, or establish a bunker mentality in your church. Your calling is to articulate the truth of God and its implications to this generation. It is not your voice, your opinions, or your ideas that are to be heard from the pulpit. Only God's are. Carson explains:

> Authority is integral to the notion of what preaching is; namely, it is clear, human utterance of God's message. Its authority is bound up with the fact that this is God's message. Preaching that does not display divine authority both in its content and in its manner is thus profoundly inadequate.[4]

Application is a critical aspect of the proper authority of biblical preaching. When application is neglected it "precludes the possibility of authority."[5] It is not disengaged propositions that call people to attention, but the required implementation of God's Word.

I recently sat through a sermon filled with biblical concepts wrapped in ethereal, irrelevant statements. Aware of the severe abstraction of biblical truth, I decided to watch the reaction of the audience. They didn't appear to be the least bit interested! The preacher had failed to connect eternal truths to their earthly lives. By his preparation and preaching manner he convinced hundreds of people that there was nothing of importance being discussed that morning. The sagging eyelids, the men picking lint from their slacks, and the women playing with their daughters' hair made it clear to me that the preaching event carried little weight—and no authority—in their lives.

What a dreadful weekly experience for these people *and* their preacher. Spurgeon lamented this kind of powerless preaching when he said, "To stand and drone out a sermon in a kind of articulate snoring to people who are somewhere between awake and asleep must be wretched work.[6]

Authoritative preaching is an entirely different experience. Unfortunately, too many churches have never experienced it. J. I. Packer observes:

> Far too many pulpit discourses have been put together on wrong principles. Some have failed to open up Scripture; some have expounded biblical doctrine without applying it, thus qualifying as lecture rather than preachments (for lecturing aims only to clear the head, while preaching seeks to change the life); some have been no more than addresses focusing the present self-awareness of the listeners, but not at any stage confronting them with the Word of God; some have been mere statements of the preacher's opinion, based solely on his own expertise, rather than messages from God carrying divine authority. Such discourses are less than preaching, . . . but because they were announced as

sermons they are treated as preaching and people's idea of preaching gets formed in terms of them, so that the true conception of preaching is forgotten.[7]

When God's Word is rightly preached, clearly presenting God's mind and not our own, a dramatic shift takes place. Some may not fully understand it, and others may rebel against it. Nonetheless, that new form of preaching will carry with it *divine* authority. There will be no need to yell or pound the pulpit to make a point. As we shall see, God's authority comes clearly through other means.

What Authority Is Not

It is important to note that to preach with authority is not authoritarianism.[8] We do not desire to set up a dictatorship in which our personal views and opinions rule the lives of our listeners. Real pulpit authority comes from accurately presenting *God's mind* on a matter, not our own.

It is the tendency of some preachers to pervert the honor of being a messenger. They selfishly twist the role of the herald and assume an authoritative posture in areas that lie outside the Word they are authorized to proclaim. They often work in churches with little or no personal accountability and feel that, as "God's messenger," they answer to no one. This problem arises in smaller churches with solo-pastors, or in larger churches that have not adopted the biblical form of leadership comprised of a plurality of elders. Without these safeguards a preacher can lose perspective of his role. No longer does he see himself merely delivering the message—he begins to feel he has an integral part in *creating* it.

Pulpit authority is not simply the authority of "human religious expertise" or of a "knowledgeable person speaking with emphasis."[9] Nor does true preaching consist of offering sound advice or suggestions. We dare not assume the role of an amiable grandfather rocking away while kindly sharing bits of wisdom. Waxing profound and winding insights into your personal journey may grab the attention of some, but they should never be the focus of your message. Presenting God's revelation as a detached or sympathetic "fellow traveler" will only cloud the authority of the message.

THE CURRENT CLIMATE AGAINST AUTHORITY

Today's increasingly hostile environment against any and all forms of authority, human and divine, provides the greatest challenge to the authoritative preaching of God's Word. Lawmakers and the Creator of law are routinely scorned. Political leaders and the King of kings are dismissed as irrelevant. Police officers and Heaven's Enforcer are looked

130

upon with disdain. Parental authority and our Heavenly Father are viewed as confining and unnecessary.

People scorn submission and can't tolerate the thought of judgment. Rules in general are held in contempt while personal autonomy is exalted, as exhibited by the pro-abortion bumper sticker that reads, "Get your laws off my body!" The final lines of William Ernest Henley's *Invictus* have never been so universally claimed as they are today:

> It matters not how straight the gate,
>> how charged with punishment the scroll.
> I am the master of my fate.
>> I am the captain of my soul.[10]

John Stott observes:

> Seldom if ever in its long history has the world witnessed such a self-conscious revolt against authority. Not that the phenomenon of protest and rebellion is new... What seems new today... is both the world-wide scale of the revolt and the philosophical arguments with which it is sometimes buttressed.[11]

The Revolt Against Absolutes

The damning philosophical premise which has moved from the ivory towers to the man on the street states there is no absolute truth. In other words, you and I can assert two opposing beliefs about God, the world, or mathematics and both of us can be right. So prevalent is the acceptance of this premise that it has shaped an entire culture. Currently, 66 percent of Americans polled agreed with the statements "there is no such thing as absolute truth," and that "different people can define truth in conflicting ways and still be correct."[12] Nonetheless, 95 percent of Americans still believe in God,[13] and 86 percent believe that He "rules the world today."[14] The juxtaposition of these contrasting views underscores the complexity of our task.

Enter the preacher who comes talking about God. So far as he reflects the comfort, solace, and warmth of the Almighty, he treads on safe ground. Pro-God is widely popular, especially in these days when nationalism and God's grace are inextricably bound together. Now when God Himself speaks through this same man regarding what God requires and what He rejects, well, the party's over! Once you step into the biblical role of a "preacher" and present truisms, principles, and standards about that same God, your widespread popularity will quickly dissolve.

Rejecting the messenger is one thing. Rejecting the truth bears much greater consequences, and that is the real problem. Preaching that clearly presents absolute truth will not interface with current cultural expectations.

The altar of tolerance is filled with options for the sincere seeker, or so he is led to believe. Yet the Author of all Christian preaching was unbending: "I am the way, the truth, and the life. No one comes to the Father except through Me" (John 14:6). The earliest preachers also were unflinching about the exclusivity of their proclamation: "Nor is there salvation in any other, for there is no other name under heaven given among men by which we must be saved" (Acts 4:12). The very foundation of Christianity requires this view of absolutism,[15] and so does edificational proclamation. As Paul wrote to the Thessalonians in regard to their sexual conduct:

> For you know what instructions we gave you by the authority of the Lord Jesus. It is God's will that you should be holy; that you should avoid sexual immorality. . . . Therefore, he who rejects this instruction does not reject man but God, who gives you his Holy Spirit (1 Thess. 4:2–3, 8 NIV).

The Irrationality of Relativism

It is hard, if not impossible, to argue with an irrational person—whether he is drunk, on drugs, or just caught up in rage. Not far behind in degree of difficulty is reasoning with someone thoroughly entrenched in relativism. Paul said that he was engaged in demolishing "arguments and every pretension that sets itself up against the knowledge of God, and taking captive every thought to make it obedient to Christ" (2 Cor. 10:5 NIV). This is evident as we follow his ministry through the Book of Acts.

However, the "rules of engagement" for arguments in his day differ greatly from those employed today. Honed on centuries of Greek thought, there was a fixed and established framework for educated people to determine whether or not claims were true. While Greek rules of logic were admittedly imperfect, most of them have been discarded in recent times. Today's mores fluctuate and shift, and are protected by the mists of tolerance whenever threatened by logic.

It is important to see this and understand it for what it is. At the heart of the problem lies the self-contradicting "revolt against absolutes." Pondering such a statement should help us to see something of the irrationality of what we are up against when we preach. Consider carefully the assertion of those who revolt against the assertions of God. As Carson puts it:

> For the first time in the history of the church . . . the only heresy that's left is the view that there is such a thing as heresy—that is the one heretical view. And within this kind of framework to preach an unflinching truth, and to claim that apart from this truth men and women are eternally lost makes you not only sound "nineteenth century" and bigoted, but irrelevant and

132

hopelessly lost in an epistemology now dead just crying out for a decent burial.[16]

Before we acquiesce to the demands that we mute all biblical imperatives, let us consider the inconsistencies of these modern revolutionaries.

While the majority of people tenaciously hold to a belief in moral relativism, they exhibit a glaring inconsistency each time they are inflamed by the "wrongs" in their world. As Frank Beckwith and Greg Koukl point out, such people will still complain when someone cuts in front of them in line. They will continue to "object to the unfair treatment they receive at work and denounce injustice in the legal system. They'll criticize crooked politicians who betray the public trust; they will condemn intolerant fundamentalists who force their view on others. Yet these objections are all meaningless in the confused world of moral relativism."[17]

To preach absolutes in our day is not as unique as it may at first appear to be. Admittedly, we are not preaching the same message as the world, but we are presenting the same kind of absolute claim. Relativists are attempting to "force their *absolute* morality on us" so that we will not "force God's *absolute* morality on them." If we give in to this logic or scale back due to the pressure from relativism, we are not leveling the playing field by being more "open-minded" or "accepting"; we are, in fact, conceding the battle, allowing God's thoughts and arguments to be taken captive by those who want to silence His voice in our society.

God commissions you to "exhort and rebuke with all authority" and to "let no one despise you" (Titus 2:15). Yet, despite having the authority of Christ and the truth of God's Word, some preachers are intimidated by those who "rebuke us" to keep us from rebuking them! When someone asks, "Who are you to say this or that?" we might well reply, "Who are you to say 'Who are you to say'?"[18] Our authority and commission come from God, and these supercede the flimsy authority of one who attempts to "correct" God's correction.

PRACTICAL STEPS TO REGAINING PULPIT AUTHORITY

If our generation is to hear the Word of God with its intended force and clarity, we must pay special attention to the manner and practice of our preaching.

Don't Misplace Humility

The Bible repeatedly announces the necessity of humility. God warns that He is opposed to the proud, but will give grace to the humble (James 4:6; 1 Pet. 5:5; Prov. 3:4). We know this well, but as G. K. Chesterton once wrote, it is easy to misplace our humility:

> What we suffer from today is humility in the wrong place. Modesty has moved from the organ of ambition. Modesty has settled upon the organ of conviction, where it was never meant to be. A man was meant to be doubtful about himself, but undoubting about the truth; this has been exactly reversed. We are on the road to producing a race of men too mentally modest to believe in the multiplication table.[19]

Every effective preacher realizes that he is nothing more than a clay jar, but that should not detract from the power and confidence in his message. Paul clarifies a distinction that must be embraced by all Christian heralds: "For we do not preach ourselves, but Jesus Christ as Lord" (2 Cor. 4:5a). Earlier in that same letter Paul discussed the source of our ministerial confidence:

> Such confidence as this is ours through Christ before God. Not that we are competent in ourselves to claim anything for ourselves, but our competence comes from God. He has made us competent as ministers of a new covenant (2 Cor. 3:4–6a NIV).

Personal humility is essential, especially considering the awesome privilege of our position. However, we ought not be modest regarding our message. It must be proclaimed fearlessly with a confidence that befits its importance (Eph. 6:20). James Stewart writes:

> It is always thus in every age the ministers of the living Christ are made—the crushing, paralyzing sense of abject worthlessness, the self-esteem broken and rolled in the dust, and then a man rising to his full stature as God's commissioned messenger. "Chief of sinners," "least of all saints"—such was Paul's self-estimate; yet with what royal, unqualified authority he proclaimed the word and the will of the Lord![20]

Clearly Preach the Bible

Preaching authority comes from the authoritative word that is preached. Sidney Greidanus writes:

> By whose authority do preachers preach? Whose word do they bring? If preachers preach their own word, the congregation may listen politely but has every right to disregard the sermon as just another person's opinion. If contemporary preachers preach with authority, however, the congregation can no longer dismiss their sermons as merely personal opinions but must respond to them as authoritative messages. The only proper authority for

134

preaching is divine authority—the authority of God's heralds, his ambassadors, his agents.[21]

If God's voice is to be heard, God's Word must be the focal point. If you prominently display God's message in your sermons, His authority will permeate every point.

Authority in preaching is not attained by merely quoting strings of Bible verses. Even if Scripture quotations constitute 80 percent of a sermon's material, the message of God's Word may still be lost without skillful exposition.

I recently heard a sermon filled with Scripture references, yet it carried little authority because the intent and direction of any one passage was never revealed. Those in attendance may have considered the sermon thoroughly biblical, but the force and authority of Scripture was never unleashed because the Scripture was never accurately expounded. True expository preaching will set and explain a passage in its context, and connect proper application to it. Such a sermon has inherent power and never leaves the hearer groping for a response to it.

Preach the Whole Counsel of God

Proper biblical authority is fostered in a pulpit ministry that does not shy away from preaching the difficult portions or themes of Scripture. Leaders of the contemporary church growth movement have persuaded this generation of preachers to "never be controversial in the pulpit" and "always be positive".[22] Truly powerful and life-changing preaching, however, has never been governed by such nonsense. Preaching the whole counsel of God without apology will never hinder effective ministry or biblical church growth. On the contrary, the authority that such preaching inherently carries with it is essential for the advancement of God's kingdom.

In the infancy of the church, Peter preached a difficult and timely message and God added three thousand to the church through that one sermon. All authoritative pulpits from Jesus and Peter to Edwards and Spurgeon were committed to preaching the messages that needed to be preached. Their bold sermons did not hinder the work of God, but rather were greatly used by Him to change countless hearts and lives. Paul understood his stewardship was fulfilled when he could say to the Ephesian elders that he had proclaimed the whole counsel of God (Acts 20:26).

Consider the damage to God's authority when we avoid the "bad news" of His Word. Imagine finding your well-meaning mail carrier sorting through your mail to separate the bad mail from the good. He may explain to you that he had just returned from a mail carriers' convention where they suggested respect for mail carriers would be elevated if they weeded out all past-due

135

notices and "Dear John" letters. Their new resolve, he explains, is to deliver only the best mail so you will come to honor the postal service. Of course, this strategy would do the reverse, causing a loss of respect for the selective, though well-meaning messenger. Yet we are convinced that delivering consistently positive sermons or preaching only on "good" themes will restore the waning respect for our pulpits. It is not so.

In attempting to answer the question of why Christianity is not transforming people today, one church advisor warns:

> Adults will also find the call to sacrifice, obedience and selflessness to be out of line with their own directions in life. The commands of Jesus will seem like an appeal to asceticism to most Americans, an unappealing prospect at best. . . . They may not vociferously challenge or oppose the Christian lifestyle and belief structure, but they will dismiss our faith as impractical and unreasonable for today's world.[23]

Has this not always been the case? When have sinful men and women ever found the call to sacrifice, obedience, and selflessness to be "in line" with their own directions in life? Of course the call to follow Christ and His exclusive claims are unappealing to fallen people, but it is through that message that the power of God is manifest. It is through the preaching of the entire Christian message that our culture will find the unfiltered message from God. With J. C. Ryle, we may need to risk the fact that some people may "think me uncharitable, illiberal, narrow-minded, bigoted, and so forth. Be it so. But they will not tell me my doctrine is not that of the Word of God."[24]

Don't Distort Your Illustrative "Facts"

The authority of preaching is risked when we inaccurately present statistics, quotations, and a variety of collateral information into our sermons. The incorporation of peripheral material can lead to the twisting of information or the presentation of inaccuracies as "facts." In the course of our study, biblical information, including historical descriptions and background information, is usually checked and double-checked in multiple sources. We are generally less arduous, however, when we venture outside our area of expertise. When we seek illustrative or supportive material in the fields of astronomy or American history, for example, we often find one source, grab what we need, and go with it. In the end, the history major or the high school astronomy teacher hears our erroneous depiction of his or her field and assumes we don't do our homework. Now our entire week of work is held in suspicion—all because of our lackadaisical preparation in ancillary areas.

136

Recently I read an article in a theological journal that presented a view different from my own on a biblical topic. I needed convincing, and the author was in the process of doing the job. Later in the article the author quoted a source I happened to be familiar with. As I read and reread the quotation, I could not believe that the quoted source had said such a thing.

The next day, I tracked down the source and read the quotation in context. Not only was the cited author *not* saying what had been ascribed to him, when read in proper context he was suggesting *just the opposite!* Immediately my view of the author and his argument was tarnished. It was a natural reaction. Likewise, the distortion or misrepresentation of facts kills our credibility as well as our preaching authority.

Precision in definitions and descriptions is essential.[25] We can disqualify forty-five minutes of good preaching with a quick comment that contradicts the facts. Though everyone may not catch it, still it may cause irreparable damage to those who do. So don't trust one source; double and triple-check your "facts." Don't rely on the *Encyclopedia of Illustrations* or uncorroborated websites for Civil War statistics or rules of physics. Check out the veracity of every statistic before using it in the pulpit.[26] Research the facts before you incorporate them into your message.

I have also found it helpful to footnote my preaching notes to provide the source of any collateral information. It has often come in handy when someone has inquired after the service about something I said. I can quickly and easily refer them to my source of information, and at the same time demonstrate that I am conscientious about the accuracy of every part of my message.

Distinguish Implication from Application

Often the authority of preaching is undermined when the preacher does not distinguish types of application. When mere implications of a preaching text are consistently and authoritatively presented as necessary applications, the preacher soon gains the reputation for crying wolf. Pulpit authority is placed in jeopardy when the preacher insists on a response to a text that contains only a *possible* implication and not a necessary directive. Discerning listeners will naturally begin to relegate all the preacher's applications to suggestion level and pick and choose those that are most convenient to reach and follow. Worse, they may dismiss them altogether as one man's opinion.

Therefore, it is important to make clear distinctions between the types of application derived from the passage being presented. One cannot frame the various types of application in the same way and with the same force. The following are distinguishable categories of application that should be noted as we prepare and preach.[27]

1. Application That Is Certain

Some applications of a given passage should be preached with all the force and authority that come from God Himself. The certainty of the application stems from careful exegetical and hermeneutical principles applied as described in Chapter 4. Take for instance a sermon to pastors from Paul's instruction to Timothy regarding the study and handling of God's Word (2 Tim. 2:15). The forceful application to modern pastors is to give the study of Scripture high priority, and to work hard at it as faithful men of God. In this case a *certain* application has been made, so full authority and force should accompany it. If one disregards this application he does not disregard a man and his opinion, but God and His Word.

2. Application That Is Probable

In the same sermon to pastors a further application may be made that pastors ought to give a large percentage of their weekly schedule to the study of God's Word. While this application is made in a more specific way, it certainly is diminished somewhat because 2 Timothy 2:15 does not necessarily infer this. Other passages may be enlisted to strengthen this application, and a logical case may be made as well, but one should be cautious as to how he states such an application. He might be wise to frame the application in the following terms: *"It makes sense then* that we would give a large percentage of our weekly schedules to the study of God's Word."

3. Application That Is Possible

In an attempt to be more specific, an "application" from 2 Timothy 2:15 may state that pastors should spend more time in study of Scripture than in any other duty of the pastorate. Such a statement *might possibly* be inferred from the context of Timothy and the rest of Scripture, but it is clearly not an emphatic application of what this passage is communicating. Disregarding this "application" would not constitute disobedience to God, and therefore should be carefully distinguished from other applications in its tone and force when it is offered. It might best be presented as: *"It may be that most of us would be wise* to schedule more time for the study of God's Word than for any other duty of the pastorate."

4. Application That Is Improbable but Possibly Helpful

Hoping to be helpful, a preacher may offer an application from the passage that suggests that pastors schedule twenty hours of study in the course of their weekly ministry. While this may be a useful guideline for some who are hearing the sermon, it cannot be presented with the same force or authority as application that is certain. This kind of "application" must be the most carefully framed—if it is offered at all. Those who miss your disclaimers will leave thinking you said the Bible teaches pastors *must* spend twenty hours a week in study. If you determine that such specificity is needed to prime the pump and get people thinking in concrete terms, then it is better to present more than one option. For instance, such implications might be offered as: *"I have found it very helpful to schedule twenty hours per week for the study of God's Word. Other pastors have suggested that fifteen hours of study is adequate. Whatever the number of hours, we must be sure to make the study of Scripture a high priority in our pastoral duties and work diligently at it."*

There are, of course, improbable applications that will not help anyone but will afford you an opportunity to slip in that story or illustration that you've wanted to share. Or worse, you may be tempted to provide an impossible application, one which the text could in no way imply, simply to serve the purpose of some church program or project. Resist these temptations! When these gimmicks creep into your sermons your credibility and your pulpit authority will begin to erode.

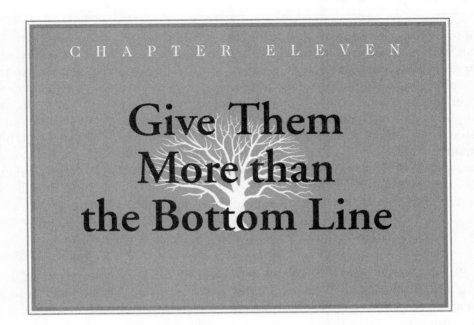

CHAPTER ELEVEN

Give Them More than the Bottom Line

LOOKS CAN BE DECEIVING. THOUGH PORTABLE COMPUTERS CONTINUE TO GET thinner and lighter, that doesn't mean they accomplish less than their overweight predecessors. On the contrary, the latest laptops are faster, more powerful, and far more efficient than anything we imagined ten years ago. Computers that now fit in the palm of your hand have the same capabilities of those that filled an entire room not long ago!

Manufacturers know that the more years they dedicate to research and development, the more efficient and effective the product. The same is true of our preaching. Achieving synthesis, clarity, and precision requires a great deal of time, energy, and persistence. It's not hard to be complicated, and too often complexity is mistaken for depth of thought. A sermon that is poignantly clear, however, requires far more work and understanding.

Some understand a serious effort to preach life-changing sermons as a "dumbing down" of biblical preaching. Others refer to it as "mere bottom-line preaching." They presume that preaching with an emphasis on application must necessarily be short on meaty, biblical doctrine. Their concern is that such preaching is a trade-off. Though there may be some clear direction for living life Monday through Friday, it will ultimately leave people without any theological depth or the ability to think biblically.

Such criticism is usually based on a misunderstanding of what true applicational preaching is all about. It may simply be a reaction in defense of preaching that leaves people with much to think about and nothing to act upon. Those with an interest in "theological depth" will characterize preaching to change lives as "shallow" and "simplistic." If applicational preaching is unbiblical, unfruitful, or in some way inferior to other styles, then it should be condemned as such and abandoned. But if practical application is an integral part of the preaching God expects of His spokesmen, then no amount of criticism should sway us from it. Those who truly master applicational preaching are convinced that effective applicational preaching is always supported by, built upon, and infused with an unsurpassed depth of theological insight—and they do not stop until they have injected that insight into the heart of their message.

THE GREATEST PREACHING OF ALL TIME

Naturally, Jesus was the ultimate model of a good preacher. As such, His preaching should be studied and held up as a standard for our own. Though in some respects His preaching was unique (His words were divine, and it was not a necessity that He exposit preexisting Scriptures), the goal and nature of His sermons should serve as a model for our own. If Jesus taught theological truths expecting His audience to sort out how to apply them, then we should also. In the same way, if His goal was simply to help people "think biblically" without directions for life, we should do likewise.

An objective reading of His sermons, however, reveals the highly applicational flavor of His preaching. In His first recorded sermon (Matt. 5:1–8:1), Jesus stated some of His points as general principles, but most of them are packaged in practical and highly applicational statements. Consider this sample from the first section of the Sermon on the Mount. Notice how deeply Jesus penetrated the daily lives of His audience and the manner in which He framed His instruction:

> But I say to you that whoever is angry with his brother without a cause shall be in danger of the judgment. And whoever says to his brother, "Raca!" shall be in danger of the council. But whoever says, "You fool!" shall be in danger of hell fire. Therefore if you bring your gift to the altar, and there remember that your brother has something against you, leave your gift there before the altar, and go your way. First be reconciled to your brother, and then come and offer your gift (Matt. 5:22–24).

> Agree with your adversary quickly, while you are on the way with him, lest your adversary deliver you to the judge, the judge hand you over to the officer, and you be thrown into prison. Assuredly, I say to you, you will by no means get out of there till you have paid the last penny (Matt. 5:25–26).

But I say to you that whoever looks at a woman to lust for her has already committed adultery with her in his heart (Matt. 5:28).

But I say to you, do not swear at all: neither by heaven, for it is God's throne; nor by the earth, for it is His footstool; nor by Jerusalem, for it is the city of the great King. Nor shall you swear by your head, because you cannot make one hair white or black. But let your "Yes" be "Yes," and your "No," "No." For whatever is more than these is from the evil one (Matt. 5:34–37).

But I tell you not to resist an evil person. But whoever slaps you on your right cheek, turn the other to him also. If anyone wants to sue you and take away your tunic, let him have your cloak also. And whoever compels you to go one mile, go with him two. Give to him who asks you, and from him who wants to borrow from you do not turn away (Matt. 5:39–42).

But I say to you, love your enemies, bless those who curse you, do good to those who hate you, and pray for those who spitefully use you and persecute you, that you may be sons of your Father in heaven; for He makes His sun rise on the evil and on the good, and sends rain on the just and on the unjust. For if you love those who love you, what reward have you? Do not even the tax collectors do the same? And if you greet your brethren only, what do you do more than others? Do not even the tax collectors do so? (Matt. 5:44–47).

Take heed that you do not do your charitable deeds before men, to be seen by them. Otherwise you have no reward from your Father in heaven. Therefore, when you do a charitable deed, do not sound a trumpet before you as the hypocrites do in the synagogues and in the streets, that they may have glory from men. Assuredly, I say to you, they have their reward. But when you do a charitable deed, do not let your left hand know what your right hand is doing, that your charitable deed may be in secret; and your Father who sees in secret will Himself reward you openly (Matt. 6:1–4).

But you, when you pray, go into your room, and when you have shut your door, pray to your Father who is in the secret place; and your Father who sees in secret will reward you openly. And when you pray, do not use vain repetitions as the heathen do. For they think that they will be heard for their many words. Therefore do not be like them. For your Father knows the things you have need of before you ask Him. In this manner, therefore, pray: Our Father in heaven . . . (Matt. 6:6–9a).

It is hard to imagine preaching that is much more practical or concrete than this! Christ drove the truth into the daily "real time" situations in which His audience lived. He contrasted true righteousness with the teaching of the "religious culture" they heard from every day. He used examples from the legal system of the time. He taught the people how to deal with those who were obnoxious. He instructed them how to put money in the Jewish treasury. He even gave them specific guidelines on prayer.

Some might claim that Jesus could be so specific and forthright because He is the Christ, and only God has the right to be so direct and practical. But this is not the case. While this straightforward manner characterized His preaching, He did not reserve it for His use only. Consider this preaching referral from Jesus on behalf of someone who wasn't divine. When Jesus described John the Baptist's ministry to the crowds in Galilee, He concluded His glowing endorsement with the words, "Assuredly, I say to you, among those born of women there has not risen one greater than John the Baptist" (Matt. 11:11; see also Luke 7:28). That Jesus approved of John's preaching could hardly be made more obvious, so it only makes sense that we glean from his approach. We should note whether John's sermons were highly applicational, or whether they hovered in the realm of the abstract and ethereal. Note this excerpt of John's preaching:

> Then he said to the multitudes that came out to be baptized by him, "Brood of vipers! Who warned you to flee from the wrath to come? Therefore bear fruits worthy of repentance, and do not begin to say to yourselves, 'We have Abraham as *our* father.' For I say to you that God is able to raise up children to Abraham from these stones. And even now the ax is laid to the root of the trees. Therefore every tree which does not bear good fruit is cut down and thrown into the fire." So the people asked him, saying, "What shall we do then?" He answered and said to them, "He who has two tunics, let him give to him who has none; and he who has food, let him do likewise." Then tax collectors also came to be baptized, and said to him, "Teacher, what shall we do?" And he said to them, "Collect no more than what is appointed for you." Likewise the soldiers asked him, saying, "And what shall we do?" So he said to them, "Do not intimidate anyone or accuse falsely, and be content with your wages" (Luke 3:7–14).

John clearly wasn't afraid of "bottom-line" preaching. He engaged in practical instruction that clarified how the doctrine of repentance played out in everyday life.

We need to recognize that the most effective preaching in Scripture drives truth to specific application that is tailored to the specific audience to which it is delivered. It is the kind of preaching Jesus was engaged in and

144

the kind of preaching that He lauded as great. The most fruitful preaching since the time of Jesus and John has continued to follow the model of highly applicational preaching with a practical emphasis on how truth is to be lived out. To do otherwise in our own preaching would be unwise.

APPLICATION'S DOCTRINAL ROOTS

Placing a heavy emphasis on the applicational element of biblical preaching does not deny the place of doctrine and theology in a good sermon. On the contrary! But my goal to this point has been to establish that the presentation of doctrine alone does not constitute true biblical preaching.

By the term *doctrine,* I am referring to the popular use of the term.[1] Doctrine or doctrinal preaching most commonly refers to the presentation of truths as abstract propositions as opposed to practical directives.[2] To say, "Jesus is Lord" is considered a doctrinal statement. To say, "You must give your allegiance to Jesus" is understood as an applicational statement. I contend that the former proposition, while entirely true, leaves the original intent of the truth without a voice.

Doctrine without Application?

Some people have pointed to Paul's epistles to the Romans, Ephesians, or Colossians in an effort to justify sermons with an emphasis that is totally doctrinal. They encourage purely doctrinal preaching because large sections of these books deal with doctrinal issues. For example, one preacher writes:

> As I preached my way through Colossians . . . we gradually tromped out a wide path to the truth that simply trusting Christ equips us with greater wisdom and righteousness than any counterfeit wisdom can offer. Put that way, it seems like an esoteric, impractical truth, far removed from the water cooler and van pool. But it was Paul's purpose, and therefore mine, to show just how practical this is for the believer. How freeing, simple, and safe. When we eventually arrived at the "practical" passages later in the epistle—"clothe yourself with compassion," for example—we could see not only the command but we had come to better understand the spiritual thinking that makes Christian compassion possible.[3]

While I am about to make a case for the importance of "spiritual thinking" in the preaching mosaic, I am concerned that some people, in their zeal to preach "doctrinal sermons," will consistently preach sermons so "far removed from the water cooler and the van pool" that their hearers

145

won't see the truth's relevance. True, the first section of Colossians is primarily doctrinal, but don't forget that it only takes twelve minutes to read the entire letter aloud—and that's how it was originally communicated to the Christians at Colossae (Col. 4:16).

In reality, Paul knew that the interval between the doctrinal propositions regarding Christ and the commands to be clothed with compassion were only minutes apart, not weeks or months. He wanted his hearers to understand, in one sitting, Christian "doctrine" (abstract truth) and to be clearly and specifically called to live out that doctrine (concrete truth) in their particular situations.

The Indispensable Nature of Doctrine

Let me emphasize that I firmly advocate the establishment of doctrine as the cornerstone of every sermon. It is not my intention to propagate the idea that doctrine is unimportant or obsolete. Absolutely not! It is the one and only foundation for forming applicational directives.

Let's go back to the earlier propositions: "Jesus is Lord" (a doctrinal statement), and "You must give your allegiance to Jesus" (its applicational expression). If a passage directs us to give our allegiance to Jesus, it does so on the basis of doctrine (that is, Jesus is Lord, among other truths) whether the context explicitly states it or not. But if the passage at hand presents the doctrine that "Jesus is Lord," it inherently carries with it biblical application (that is, we should give Him our allegiance, among other applications) whether or not the context explicitly states it. It would be a mistake to present a doctrine without a life application that is contextually appropriate. In the same way, I believe it is a mistake to offer life application without clearly presenting the doctrine upon which it rests.

We can see this pattern in Christ's preaching. Consider, for example, His instruction regarding oaths and swearing. He told His audience what was to be done and what was to be avoided, then gave the "doctrinal reason" that provided the rationale for the command: "But I say to you, do not swear at all: neither by heaven, for it is God's throne; nor by the earth, for it is His footstool; nor by Jerusalem, for it is the city of the great King. Nor shall you swear by your head, because you cannot make one hair white or black. But let your 'Yes' be 'Yes,' and your 'No,' 'No.' For whatever is more than these is from the evil one" (Matt. 5:34–37).

The majesty of God, Jesus' association with heaven, His special relationship to earth, His choice of Jerusalem, and man's finite nature are all truths upon which His application rests. To properly proclaim these applicational directives with the power and force that Christ intended, a sermon must explore the doctrinal foundation on which they rest. Jesus did this again with beautiful simplicity later in His sermon:

> Therefore I say to you, do not worry about your life, what you will eat or what you will drink; nor about your body, what you will put on. Is not life more than food and the body more than clothing? Look at the birds of the air, for they neither sow nor reap nor gather into barns; yet your heavenly Father feeds them. Are you not of more value than they? Which of you by worrying can add one cubit to his stature? So why do you worry about clothing? Consider the lilies of the field, how they grow: they neither toil nor spin; and yet I say to you that even Solomon in all his glory was not arrayed like one of these. Now if God so clothes the grass of the field, which today is, and tomorrow is thrown into the oven, will He not much more clothe you, O you of little faith? (Matt. 6:25–30).

This passage addresses fundamental aspects of life, *and* it is rooted in theology. The rationale for the defeat of anxiety is rooted in the eternal principles of God's sovereign, powerful care for His creation and in the primacy of human life in the creative order of God. We conclude that this practical area of life rests on the exercise of faith—faith in God, but even more immediately, in the biblical doctrine of God.

It is for this reason that some interpreters have represented Christ's practical teachings as "doctrinal preaching." C. I. Scofield observed: "[People] say just give us rules of conduct; tell us how to live. Dear friends, there is always doctrine in the background of the ethics of the Lord Jesus Christ. Jesus of Nazareth was a preacher of eternal principles; and that is doctrinal preaching."[4] So it is that we must be careful to highlight and elucidate the "doctrine" that exists in each sermonic exhortation.

Doctrinal/Applicational Preaching

It might seem odd to take what traditionally has been deemed as "highly applicational" preaching and call it "doctrinal" preaching, but that is precisely my point. True applicational preaching *always* puts doctrine on display. If it does not, then it does not supply adequate reason or basis for directing life. On the other hand, "doctrinal" preaching is not authentic preaching if it fails to drive listeners to application. Consider the great "doctrinal sections" of Scripture like those found in Philippians 2:

> [Christ] who, being in the form of God, did not consider it robbery to be equal with God, but made Himself of no reputation, taking the form of a servant, and coming in the likeness of men. And being found in appearance as a man, He humbled Himself and became obedient to the point of death, even the death of the cross. Therefore God also has highly exalted Him and given Him the name which is above every name (Phil. 2:6–9).

One could preach on the theology of this text for weeks. But it is important to note that this, perhaps the greatest Christological passage in the New Testament, was presented as the rationale for a practical application that Paul made moments earlier: "Let each of you look out not only for his own interests, but also for the interests of others. Let this mind be in you which was also in Christ Jesus, who, being in the form of God, did not consider it robbery to be equal with God" (Phil. 2:4–6).

Notice that even the "doctrinal section" of Philippians 2 culminates with a statement of practical application: "Therefore God also has highly exalted Him and given Him the name which is above every name, that at the name of Jesus every knee should bow, of those in heaven, and of those on earth, and of those under the earth, and that every tongue should confess that Jesus Christ is Lord, to the glory of God the Father" (Phil. 2:9–11).

God desires to change lives through the means of preaching, and He does so specifically through practical application drawn from biblical doctrine. Therefore, the role of doctrine as the foundation of life change must be emphasized.[5] As L. R. Scarborough wrote many years ago, "The creedless Christian, the doctrineless church, the sermon without deep-rooted convictions of the fundamentals of revealed truth, these are invertebrate, flabby, sappy, soppy, and superficial."[6] May our careful attention to the inseparable link between doctrine and application insure that our preaching never qualifies for such a stinging indictment.

THINKING DOCTRINALLY

If our preaching is to be effective, we must proclaim God's eternal truths as the only adequate catalysts for biblical application. It is inherent in good study, and it must be apparent in good preaching.[7] Through thoughtful study we uncover eternal principles, and by our transformational preaching we demonstrate their applicability to life. This requires theological thinking on our part *and* the ability to instill theological thoughts in the minds of our hearers.

It Starts with You

If doctrinal thinking is to dominate our exegesis and preaching, then we must think doctrinally. Unfortunately, our pastoral training has prepared us poorly for this work. Theological thinking is often absent in our study and our preaching because it was largely absent in our education—and the more recent your education the more likely you are to have been a victim of the shift in the focus of pastoral training. Years ago, pastoral candidates were subjected to an in-depth theological education. More recently, much of the classic doctrinal course work has been eliminated and replaced by a diversified track of ministerial, professional, and leadership training. Preparation to think doctrinally has largely given way to more "practical" courses. This has left modern preachers at a disadvantage in thinking of the eternal principles that have always made up the platform for effective ministry and transformational preaching.[8] David Wells explains:

> In the one model, theology is foundational, and in the other it is only peripheral. In the one, theological truth explains why there is a ministry at all, what it is about, and why the Church without it will shrivel and die. In the other, this reasoning is marginalized so that what shapes, explains, and drives the work of ministry arises from the needs of the modern profession.[9]

This needs-based mind-set has had an eroding effect on pulpit ministry. Many preachers abandon doctrinal thinking and drift hopelessly upon a sea of pragmatism. The more perceptive preachers will abandon ship and swim for doctrinal shores, but they will often be content to arrive safely in one piece. These will likely fail to build the necessary bridge to the lives of their parishioners. Ideally, preparation for preaching would include a heavy theological emphasis and would be accompanied by the development of skills and practice to move doctrinal thinking into contemporary settings.

For most of us, the cultivation of doctrinal thinking skills is primarily a "post-graduate" endeavor, so we must continue to foster a growing appetite for thinking theologically. We must master the process of moving from ancient contexts to eternal principles. We must learn to love thinking in abstract doctrines because we long to see those doctrines applied in a practical way to the daily lives of those to whom we are called to preach.[10]

We should evaluate critically what we read. We ought to pick up fewer best-selling paperbacks from the front racks of the Christian bookstore and instead take home more hardbacks from the Doctrine/Theology section at the back of the store. Reading theologies and doctrinal treatises should not be considered irrelevant to applicational preaching, but as foundational to it.

Be careful not to develop an appetite for doctrine that doesn't also thirst for finding its connection to the here and now. After asserting that the preacher's interest must be set on "the principles and things that are permanent," Martyn Lloyd-Jones warns us that when we enter the pulpit, "it is always our business to be contemporary; our object is to deal with the living people who are in front of us and listening to us."[11]

149

Thinking Comes Before Doing

Being contemporary in the pulpit does not mean that we leave our doctrine in the study. We must bring it with us when we preach. This is necessary not because our audience needs to be taken through the step-by-step process of discovery, but because the Bible tells us that thinking comes before doing.

The relationship between thinking and doing was highlighted by Christ in His words regarding lust and adultery (see Matt. 5:28). Since "the heart" in Jewish culture was considered to be the center of one's thinking,[12] these instructions from Proverbs are quite significant: "Above all else, guard your heart, for it is the wellspring of life" (Prov. 4:23 NIV). Christ emphasized this important truth in response to the Pharisees' criticism:

> Do you not yet understand that whatever enters the mouth goes into the stomach and is eliminated? But those things which proceed out of the mouth come from the heart, and they defile a man. For out of the heart proceed evil thoughts, murders, adulteries, fornications, thefts, false witness, blasphemies. These are the things which defile a man, but to eat with unwashed hands does not defile a man (Matt. 15:17–20).

In speaking about "the heart," Jesus also said: "A good man out of the good treasure of his heart brings forth good things, and an evil man out of the evil treasure brings forth evil things" (Matt. 12:35). Such statements show clearly that Jesus sought to address His listeners' thinking before He tried to direct their steps.

Target the Mind

We must access that storehouse within the human mind in order to bring about biblical change in people's lives. According to God's Word, the mind is not only the battlefield, but also the spoils of war for the enemy. The Bible depicts Satan as the "father of lies" (John 8:44) who completely envelops the minds of those who are alienated from God (2 Cor. 4:4) and seeks to change the minds of those who walk with God (Gen. 3:4–5). That is why Paul holds up the life that grasps the good, pleasing, and perfect will of God as one "transformed by the renewing of [the] mind" (Rom. 12:2).

We must realize that our hearers come to worship needing not just biblical direction, but divine rationale. It is up to us to show them the timeless principles that call for redirected behavior. We must call for biblical action that is predicated upon biblical thinking. As Spurgeon said, "Every promise leads to a precept, and every doctrine has its duty."[13] To preach both must always be our aim.

150

CHAPTER TWELVE

Preach Periodically About Life-changing Preaching

THE EXCITEMENT AND TEACHABILITY OF A NEW CHRISTIAN IS SO REFRESHING. IT IS a joy, and at times convicting, to listen to the inquisitive spirit of a new follower of Christ. I can remember one enthusiastic convert asking me everything from "How do I pray?" to "How much money am I supposed to pay each Sunday?" But the question that has reverberated longest in my mind is the question, "How can I get the most out of your sermons each week?"

Like most of the questions asked by the newborn Christian, we need to provide an answer to this critical question not only in the "New Believers' Class" but also in a forum where the men and women sitting under our teaching year after year can hear our answer. Jesus had a lot to say about this topic, and His instructions are still very timely in a day when we often assume far too much about the preparedness of our people to rightly hear and obey God's Word.

The average preacher has spent thousands of hours reading, attending classes, learning biblical languages, and honing skills in order to communicate the life-changing Word of God in an effective way.

The average congregation, on the other hand, has received little or no training on how to listen to and integrate the sermons they hear each week. Few books have been written to worshipers on the reception of sermons,[1] and it's a rare member of your congregation who has ever read one. There are no seminars, workshops, or conferences designed to prepare your audience on how to receive the life-changing messages you proclaim week after week. This is amazing when you consider that the Bible gives more instruction on how to receive God's truth properly than it gives on how to proclaim it properly. God is very concerned with how preachers preach. But we tend to neglect His concern with how listeners listen.

It is part of our ministry to help our people raise the bar. Unless your congregation is ready, willing, and able to embrace your sermons, even your best expositions will fail to change lives. Consider that none of our sermons can match those of Jesus, yet even His most accurate, authoritative, and persuasive sermons often fell on deaf ears. He was well aware of the tendencies and temperaments of the crowds He faced. That's why He made it a point to tell His audience, "Take heed how you hear" (Luke 8:18). Fifteen times the Gospel writers record Christ's exhortation, "To him who has ears, let him hear!" At times, Jesus even began His preaching with the imperative that could be translated, "Listen up!" (Mark 4:3).[2]

There are two sides to sermonic communication that actually changes lives. So we would be foolish to miss Christ's cue to instruct our hearers to be effective listeners. Very few people will think about their responsibility to listen well or seek to improve their listening skills. This means it is up to you, their preacher, to address the issue. Do not consider it unreasonable, then, to dedicate an entire sermon occasionally to what Richard Baxter called "the duty" of "profitable hearing."[3]

PREACHING ON PREACHING

Preaching on preaching may feel awkward. Some people in your church may feel you are engaging in a self-serving exercise. They may think you are attempting to unite a band of blind followers who will dote over every pearl that falls from your lips. Be mindful of this concern and attempt to dispel it as you preach. Remind them that all of you should be working toward the same goal—to encounter the Word as God intended.

As uncomfortable as it may sound, to preach periodically about preaching is one of the best things you can do for your church. To address how the people can take hold of the life-changing power of preaching is to address one of their most fundamental needs. As John Stott writes, "It is plain throughout [Scripture] that the health of God's people depends on their attentiveness to his Word."[4] Simply put, "A deaf church is a dead church!"[5]

Addressing the needs of your people to improve does *not* suggest that you have perfected your side of the communication process. Express your need and desire to be a better preacher. As you unveil your heart, appeal to them to become the best hearers and respondents they can be.

The point of preaching about preaching is not to relinquish the responsibility for a fruitful, life-changing encounter with your sermon; rather, it is to share that responsibility with your congregation. When both parties

152

do what God desires, the sermon has the greatest opportunity to bear fruit. On some days you will leave the pulpit with a sense that you have not done your part. But on other days the listeners will sense they have not done their part. Perhaps they will share the sentiment of F. W. Boreham: "I suppose it was largely my fault that the sermon seemed to me to be so ineffective. There are tremendous astonishments in the Christian evangel which, however badly stated, should fire my sluggish soul with wonder, and fill me with amazement. The fact that I listened so blandly shows that I have become blasé.[6]

Sermons about listening need not be frequent or protracted into a four-week series. But at least once a year expound on a passage that reminds your hearers of their responsibility. Make sure sermons with such an emphasis are preached as part of a balanced biblical diet.

THE ESSENTIALS OF "PROFITABLE HEARING"

During a recent, unprecedented, five-week break from preaching, I encountered a "new" rhythm of busy work weeks sandwiched between forty-minute sermons crafted by other preachers. Without my usual hours of preparation, study, and anticipation, Sunday mornings had an unfamiliar, eerie serenity. Over time my own level of expectancy and enthusiasm began to wane. Sitting in the pew, I found it was easy to neglect the essentials of active listening.

Following are the essentials of listening that our congregations cannot afford to neglect. They should understand their responsibilities before, during, and after the Word is actually preached to them. Your continual encouragement in these areas is the best way to keep your hearers coming back with expectant ears and responsive hearts.

Responsibilities Before the Word Is Preached

My own research shows that most people do not prepare in any significant way for church. In an average church, fewer than half of the worshipers pray for their encounter with the sermon. Less than a third pray for their pastor or his preparation. Even when the passage is clearly announced the previous week, only one in five people will take the time to read it before they come to church. Most people wake up less than two hours before the service begins, and half don't eat anything for breakfast.[7]

With grumbling stomachs and sleep in their eyes, most Christians leave church with a greater appetite for lunch than they brought for the spiritual meal the pastor just served up. But take heart. With a little effort, some faithful reminders and God's empowerment, these statistics can change dramatically.

1. Focus on Preparation

We must address our congregations with the need to come to church prepared. Spurgeon recognized this priority:

> We are told men ought not to preach without preparation. Granted. But, we add, men ought not *hear* without preparation. Which, do you think, needs the most preparation, the sower or the ground? . . . It seems to me that there is more preparation needed by the ground than by the sower, more by the hearer than by the preacher.[8]

In the words of Baxter, we must call our hearers to "remember the Lord's Day before it cometh, and prepare for it."[9] A sermon on Jesus' parable of the soils can highlight the need for well-cultivated hearts. Like Christ, we should underscore the importance of coming to church as "those who, having heard the word with a noble and good heart, keep it and bear fruit with patience" (Luke 8:15).

Help your listeners by providing the text and topic of next week's sermon and encourage them to read and study the passage in the coming week. Publish your preaching calendar in the bulletin, allowing them the time to get excited about what is coming up. Post the pending sermon information on your church's web site. Give them every opportunity and encouragement to put more effort and thought into next Sunday's message.

2. Pray for Something Significant

Our listeners must be taught to pray and trust God for a significant encounter each time they come to hear His Word. Often their minds and hearts are not aligned with God's. We must prompt them to spend more time with God in prayer, asking for His expectation to become theirs. Spurgeon was very open and direct about this need when he told his congregation, "[when] men come into these places of worship, they do not know what they want . . . and they go away, and they have no spiritual profit. How could they? What profit would a man make on chance, if he went there without a purpose?"[10]

I've discovered that an occasional reminder for the congregation to ask God for something significant will drive the number praying for the service from one-third to two-thirds. And as the percentage of praying people rises, so does their sense of anticipation.

One growing church I surveyed reported that 35 percent of its people prayed for the service. Thirty-five percent also said they came to the service with "a very high expectation for the sermon." But in another growing church, where 61 percent of the people said they prayed for the upcoming service, 66 percent of the congregation said they came to church with "a very high expectation for the sermon." The difference between the two is simple and dramatic. Since most people leave with their spiritual expectations realized, it's important to emphasize the need for the congregation to pray for its own spiritual profit.

3. Pray for the Preacher

You can help your hearers prepare for the sermon by encouraging them to pray not only for themselves, but also for you. As Gardiner Spring wrote in his *Plea to Pray for Pastors* some two hundred years ago:

> If a people are looking for rich sermons from their minister, their prayers must supply him with the needed material; if they seek for faithful sermons, their prayers must urge him . . . If God's people are going to expect powerful and successful sermons, their prayers must make him a blessing to the souls of men. Would they have him come to them in the fullness of the blessing of the Gospel of peace . . . ? If so, their prayers must urge him to pray. . . . It is in their own closets that the people of God most effectively challenge their beloved ministers to take heed to the ministry they have received from the Lord Jesus. . . . When the churches cease to pray for ministers, ministers will no longer be a blessing to the churches.[11]

Be bold and ask your congregation in a spirit of humility to pray for you and your preaching (see chapter 6). This requires nothing more than reminding them of the oft-repeated appeal of the first-century preachers to "pray for us" (Col. 4:3; 1 Thess. 5:25; 2 Thess. 3:1; Heb. 13:18). General requests will bring general prayers, so be as specific as you can in order to enlist your congregation as true colaborers in the Lord's work.

4. Schedule Around Church

"God's household, the church of the living God, the pillar and foundation of the truth" (1 Tim. 3:15b NIV), certainly should be given a high priority in every Christian's schedule. Scripture requires that we "not forsake the assembling of ourselves together" (Heb. 10:25), so we can remind our people to plan their weekends around the gathering of "God's household."

Emphasize the importance of weekly attendance, punctuality, and practical planning on Sunday mornings. Challenge them to think counter-culturally about Sunday mornings! While the rest of the world sleeps in and ratchets back on the first day of the week, we need to build in a value that declares Sunday morning the most important time of the week. Encourage them to wake up earlier and plan a real breakfast. Make it clear that getting ready for church has greater implications for their lives than getting ready for work or class any other day of the week.

Their obedience to your instruction in this area will impact their Saturday evening plans, weekend getaways, and Sunday morning routines—and it should motivate us even more to give our best effort when they arrive with great expectations on Sundays. Asking them to sacrifice in order to attend services provides a built-in accountability and places the responsibility squarely upon us to make the preaching and worship all it deserves to be.

Responsibilities During the Preaching of the Word

The most critical moments in the process of preaching to change lives are those in and around the preaching event itself. This means we must instruct our listeners on how to maximize the values of these crucial minutes.

1. Worship

Songs of worship and praise traditionally precede our preaching, and they serve as an important prelude to the proper reception of God's Word. Their value should not be underestimated. On the contrary, consider preaching on the necessity of engaging our total selves in worship, prayer, and Scripture reading before the message.

But be careful not to separate these events. Preaching, in a very real sense, is an extension of this engagement in worship. As Don Whitney points out, "Reverently and responsively listening to God's Word preached is one of the highest forms of honoring and worshiping God."[12] If your listeners have not honored God during the other elements of worship, they are not likely to give proper honor to His Word. But when a church honors God through every element of the service, your sermon is apt to be received (and responded to) as a natural by-product of meaningful worship.

2. Think

Your listeners are responsible, before God, to think as you preach. They should carefully evaluate and process all that is expounded from the pulpit (1 Cor. 14:29). Remind them of their obligation to think, and encourage them to do so by providing thought-provoking sermons.

While guiding them in critical thinking skills, we must be careful not to propagate critical spirits. Jay Adams reinforces the biblical call to be "positively biased toward the message of Scripture and its messenger."[13] This is in keeping with the balanced praise accorded those who "accepted" or "welcomed" the preaching of Paul as the "word of God" (1 Thess. 2:13), and those who "searched the Scriptures daily to find out" the truthfulness of Paul's preaching (Acts 17:11).

I was surprised by the responses I received when I preached on this important element of "thinking" and "critically evaluating" my weekly sermons. Some people said that in all their years of listening to preaching they

156

had never sensed "permission" from the preacher to think critically about what he says. Unlocking this door for them should not be a threat to the preacher, but it should be of mutual benefit to him and his hearers.

3. Take Notes

I am firmly convinced that taking notes, even in the form of a few simple summary statements, can greatly enhance the impact of a sermon on a listener. The statistics on recall alone should convince the average pastor to take advantage of this medium. Certainly those worshipers who take notes are more likely to remember the sermon and its implications longer than those who do not.

My research confirms this. In one church where the pastor encourages note-taking, 85 percent of the congregation said that they "usually do." A second church, with a strong pulpit and growing membership, does not promote note-taking. There, only 2 percent reported that they "normally take notes." No wonder only 22 percent of this church body said it could still recall the main points of the sermon by the following Friday. In the church that encouraged note-taking, 53 percent said they could still recall the sermon points by the end of the week.

Note-taking can also help our parishioners engage in what Adams calls "aggressive listening."[14] Having them unravel the truth through the tip of a pen can heighten their concern and their capacity to grasp what is being said. It makes people work a bit harder to capture, in summary fashion, the gist of each scriptural principle being presented.

You may need to add a word of caution for those few in your congregation who carry note-taking to an extreme. They may be prone to take copious notes on every facet and nuance of the entire sermon, even bordering on transcription. While this may seem flattering to you, it is likely to defeat the higher purpose. Provide them with some common sense parameters that will guide them in capturing the *primary* points, principles, and applications that you want them to hold on to through the week, and beyond!

4. Use Your Bibles

Computer programs that display the preaching portion and its cross-references on big screens during the preaching event are quite popular in the contemporary church. There may be an advantage to using such tools to highlight primary points. But I have found that keeping my listeners turning in their own Bibles proves invaluable in reinforcing the truths being presented.

Encourage your listeners to bring their Bibles. Promote their inspection of the texts you are preaching on. Turning to passages and orienting them to the texts in their own Bibles is another point of engagement in

157

the sermon. Though this is passé in some circles, a recent survey in my own church revealed 99 percent of the respondents "usually follow along in the Bible when the pastor refers to a verse of Scripture" because they are encouraged to do so.

5. Fight Distractions

Warn your people of the spiritual battle that is going on during the preaching of God's Word. Let them know that they are the targets of the enemy's diversions. In His parable of the four soils, Jesus made it clear that Satan loves to "snatch away" what is being sown as you preach His Word (Matt. 13:19).

Certainly one of Satan's favorite tactics is to cause distractions during the sermon. While you and the church leaders should do all you can to keep down distractions, you must instruct your congregation to take a defensive posture toward threats to their understanding of each sermon. Counter Satan's ploys by having them choose where and with whom they sit. Let them know that sitting "front and center" tends to yield better comprehension in any public setting. Eye contact with the preacher and with the Word should be key elements of the interactive process. Encourage parents to use the children's program and the church nursery for their child-care needs. Minds and hearts that wander during these critical minutes may miss a life-changing biblical concept—so they must discipline themselves to keep their minds on the sermon.

Responsibilities After the Word Is Preached

The proving ground for sermons that change lives is on the other side of the final "amen"; therefore, you must remind your hearers of their after-the-sermon responsibilities. Every sermon should emphasize *specific* responsibilities attached to that particular sermon, but consider a periodic sermon that emphasizes the *general* responsibilities of each hearer after every sermon.

1. Review

The Bible promotes the nobility of each believer personally reviewing the message that was preached (Acts 17:11; 1 Cor. 14:29). We as preachers should do this as well. We ought to encourage the church in every possible way to reexamine the texts and contexts of each sermon we preach.

Sermon notes are important tools in the review process, so we have another good reason to promote their use. Encourage your congregation to make their notes a platform for deeper study and contemplation. Highlight the value of new insights and understanding that result from the reappraisal and reevaluation of truth. Emphasize the fact that your hours of study and your message have exposed only the tip of the iceberg! Share

158

your dilemma of having to distill a truckload of great biblical information and application into a presentation of less than an hour, and encourage them to dig deeper on their own.

The pattern of Proverbs 2:1–11 is one we can apply in this context. In this passage, Solomon instructed "his son" to contemplate the words he had been taught. Notice how he promoted reflection on "his words" as a platform and catalyst for the Lord to impart wisdom to the student:

> My son, if you receive my words,
> And treasure my commands within you,
> So that you incline your ear to wisdom,
> And apply your heart to understanding;
> Yes, if you cry out for discernment,
> And lift up your voice for understanding,
> If you seek her as silver,
> And search for her as for hidden treasures;
> Then you will understand the fear of the LORD,
> And find the knowledge of God.
> For the LORD gives wisdom;
> From His mouth come knowledge and understanding;
> He stores up sound wisdom for the upright;
> He is a shield to those who walk uprightly;
> He guards the paths of justice,
> And preserves the way of His saints.
> Then you will understand righteousness and justice,
> Equity and every good path.
> When wisdom enters your heart,
> And knowledge is pleasant to your soul,
> Discretion will preserve you;
> Understanding will keep you (Prov. 2:1–11).

2. Retell

Few things will instill truth in the hearts and minds of your congregation like retelling truths that have been taught. As Richard Baxter suggests, retelling yourself the sermon is a good place to start: "Chew the cud . . . when you come home in secret, and by meditation preach it over to yourselves. If it were coldly delivered by the preacher, . . . [consider] the great weight of the matter, and preach it more earnestly over to your own hearts."15

Encourage your people to share your message with others. Promote family devotions and group studies that reexamine the passage recently preached (more on this in chapter 14). Challenge your hearers to teach other persons what they were taught the previous week.

Create the feeling that each person who hears God's truth is entrusted with something worthy of passing on to others. As Paul wrote to Timothy,

"The things that you have heard from me among many witnesses, commit these to faithful men who will be able to teach others also" (2 Tim. 2:2).

3. Take Action

As I have frequently underscored throughout this book, preaching has not fulfilled its purpose until the truths of the sermon are acted upon by the hearer. That action may be a changed belief, a changed behavior, or a changed attitude. Such changes are empowered by the Holy Spirit and are consciously and purposefully made by those people who are indwelt by Him. We must call those who hear us preach to "be doers of the word, and not hearers only" (James 1:22).

SUGGESTED SERMONS ON PREACHING

The passages referenced throughout the preceding points can provide biblical targets for exposition when preaching on preaching. Those passages would provide years of preaching material if you should decide to preach on preaching once a year as suggested. You may choose to emphasize biblical preaching by presenting these messages consecutively in a series stretching over a period of weeks. Either way, allow me to suggest four powerful passages of Scripture that will underscore the Christian's responsibilities toward biblical preaching.

1 Peter 2:2–3

"As newborn babes, desire the pure milk of the word, that you may grow thereby, if indeed you have tasted that the Lord is gracious."

Establishing the context is key in this sermon. The verses that precede the passage must be allowed to define the original forum for the feeding (1:24, "this is the word which by the gospel was preached to you"). The use of "babies" and "milk" in 2:2 does not conjure images of Christians laboring over their Bibles in their "quiet times." Rather, your hearers need to understand that these were people who were gathered in order to listen to preaching. At the very least, this passage challenges our listeners (1) to crave biblical preaching; (2) to make sure they crave a "pure" meal; and (3) to remember the past results of biblical preaching as an inspiration to thirst for more.

1 Thessalonians 2:13

"For this reason we also thank God without ceasing, because when you received the word of God which you heard from us, you welcomed it not as the word of men, but as it is in truth, the word of God, which also effectively works in you who believe."

160

This text presents the attitude toward biblical preaching that God desires to see in our churches. It can be an effective sermon for instructing your parishioners in the attentive, humble, and wholehearted reception of the message.

Acts 17:10–12

"Then the brethren immediately sent Paul and Silas away by night to Berea. When they arrived, they went into the synagogue of the Jews. These were more fair-minded than those in Thessalonica, in that they received the word with all readiness, and searched the Scriptures daily to find out whether these things were so. Therefore many of them believed, and also not a few of the Greeks, prominent women as well as men."

This text provides worshipers with the important balance between a positive bias and discernment. This sermon can direct your hearers (1) to carefully judge every sermon; (2) to show caution and not allow their critical thinking to digress into a critical spirit; and (3) to allow the biblical sermon to judge them.

James 1:21–25

"Therefore lay aside all filthiness and overflow of wickedness, and receive with meekness the implanted word, which is able to save your souls. But be doers of the word, and not hearers only, deceiving yourselves. For if anyone is a hearer of the word and not a doer, he is like a man observing his natural face in a mirror; for he observes himself, goes away, and immediately forgets what kind of man he was. But he who looks into the perfect law of liberty and continues in it, and is not a forgetful hearer but a doer of the work, this one will be blessed in what he does."

This classic text on "profitable hearing" will yield a wealth of insight regarding God's desire for all who listen to His Word. At the minimum we would be wise (1) to remind our listeners that God's intention is to change their lives with biblical preaching; (2) to warn them of the self-deception of learning without growing; and (3) to direct them to live out every sermon they hear in a purposeful way.

PART
FOUR
FOLLOW
THROUGH
TO CHANGE
LIVES

CHAPTER THIRTEEN

Cultivate a Culture of Commitments and Accountability

NEVER UNDERESTIMATE THE PRIVILEGE OF PREACHING TO PEOPLE YOU KNOW AND shepherd. Guest preachers, radio pastors, and conference speakers may have greater preaching gifts. But as the local pastor-teachers, we still have significant advantages over them. Our personal relationships, shared history, and local insights help to make our biblical appeals more effective.[1] But perhaps the greatest advantage we have as community leaders is our ability to help shape the culture in which our sermons are received.

The prophet Ezekiel struggled to preach in a climate of feigned devotion. He was a capable communicator of truth, but the prevailing religious hypocrisy dashed his hopes of seeing his hearers transformed. Notice God's commentary on Ezekiel's preaching ministry:

> My people come to you, as they usually do, and sit before you to listen to your words, but they do not put them into practice. With their mouths they express devotion, but their hearts are greedy for unjust gain. Indeed, to them you are nothing more than one who sings love songs with a beautiful voice and plays an instrument well, for they hear your words but do not put them into practice (Ezek. 33:31–32 NIV).

Fortunately, our preaching ministry, unlike Ezekiel's, is not conducted on a national stage over which we have little administrative control. In fact, we can assume an active leadership role in our preaching forum that can influence profoundly how our sermons are heard and lived out.

I know a pastor who has high expectations for his staff's physical health. Not only does he run ten miles a day, he also expects his staff to maintain a rigorous exercise regimen. He has lunch meetings over a table of healthy foods, encourages afternoon workouts, and lauds even the smallest victory in his staff's quest for good health.

While I don't share his passion (nor did I divulge our penchant for pepperoni pizzas at staff meetings), I did learn something important from the effective reshaping of the culture of his church. His high expectations of those around him resulted in a staff with perhaps the lowest body-to-fat ratio in the country! The celebration of victories, the tools, and support that are constantly flowing from this leader have made a marked difference in his team's physical health.

Of course, far more important is our effect upon our team's spiritual health. The expectations you uphold for your leaders *and* laypeople have the same potential to significantly impact their lives. The ingredients won't be workouts and brussels spouts, but they will include the encouragement to regular commitments and expectation of personal accountability.

CONSIDER YOUR CHURCH CULTURE

Begin by assessing your current church culture. Ask yourself questions like these: Is there a high or low level of commitment throughout the church? Are people usually dependable or unreliable? Is there a common expectation of excellence or an air of mediocrity? Are they basically private people, or do they value openness? When they are open with one another, are they transparent and honest, or is there a protective gloss over their lives? Would God say they possess humble hearts, or is there underlying pride and arrogance? How entangled are they in materialism? How highly do they value their comfort and convenience? Do their tangible expressions of love generally stay within their family units, or do they stretch to sacrifice for non-family members? Are they regularly involved in sharing the gospel with others, or do you sense that evangelism is a rare and unnatural practice for them? Do they regularly pray about reaching the world for Christ, or is missions simply a bulletin board and a map?

The church to which I preach each week is far from perfect, yet there is no place where my sermons are more effective. Familiarity with the congregation and years shaping the church culture are the reasons for this. For the past fifteen years, I have worked to come up with the answers to the preceding questions. And with God's help I have taken that information and attempted to improve the culture in which I preach. Though it is not yet optimized, it is improving—and as it improves, my sermons carry an increasing potential for change in people's lives. I attempt constantly to make the culture better, not only through the sermons and tailored application, but also through programming, staffing, and personal influence as a shepherd.

On several occasions I have preached the same sermon in a different setting just after preaching it to my own congregation. The text, sermon, and illustrations were the same, but the results were dramatically different. The sermon did not take hold and change lives in the foreign environment like it did in my home church. The difference was far more than the listeners' familiarity or rapport with the preacher. The core distinction was that the original message was crafted and aimed at a congregation I knew well, but was now being delivered to unknown faces living in an "unknown" culture. The sermon fell flat because I assumed certain values in these other hearers that did not exist.

To some degree, you may be making a similar assumption in your own preaching ministry. Week after week you may be delivering messages that would profoundly impact a congregation—but not necessarily your own! Before you go searching for a new congregation, consider using your leadership influence to optimize the culture in which your sermons are delivered. To do so, you must nurture two primary elements in the corporate life of your hearers.

HEIGHTEN THE VALUE OF COMMITMENT

The first element we need to foster is commitment! In all of our preaching, we should ask for a decision with all its accompanying ramifications. We should challenge each person in our congregation to commit to do what God's Word is calling for in every sermon we preach.

The Sunday Illusion

A big part of our problem stems from a common misconception that the *congregation's* responsiveness to the sermon translates into a response in each *individual life*. But as Phillips Brooks points out, our assembled congregation takes on a life of its own. Meanwhile, we go on our way thinking they will do as individuals what they appear to have embraced as a corporate body.[2] How many times have you preached a sermon and sensed it was being eagerly accepted, only to find it yielded sparse results?

This is disheartening. But preaching to change lives is not for the fainthearted. Phillip Brooks responded to the charge that lawyers are better at persuasion than preachers because they can secure a genuine and lasting decision in far less time:

167

> The fallacy is obvious. We are like lawyers pleading before a jury which in the first place feels itself under no compulsion to decide at all; and in the second place, if it decides as we are urging it, must change its life, break off its habits, and make new ones, which it does not like to contemplate. There is no likeness between it and that body of twelve men who cannot go home till they decide one way or the other, and who have no selfish interest to bias their decision. No wonder that our jury listens to us as long as it pleases, perhaps trembles a little when we are most true and powerful, and then like Felix, who was both judge and jury to St. Paul, shuts up the court, and departs with only the dimmest feeling of responsibility, saying, "Go thy way for this time. I will hear thee again of this matter."[3]

The illusionary Sunday commitment is evident in the pastoral counseling office. Biblical counseling, rightly done, is much like delivering a biblical sermon one-on-one. Passages are expounded, truth is presented, and a commitment is called for. But the same person who nodded in agreement on Sunday will fight the logic, the implications, and the commitment to which you are now calling him in person. In the isolation of an office, with the challenges and personal cost clearly in view, the commitment to change takes on a different perspective.

Securing a commitment to change in keeping with God's Word is quite different from garnering the nods, encouragement, and hearty approvals of our people in the church lobby.

Ways to Value Commitment

A leader should always underscore the importance of godly commitments and biblical resolve, placing a high value on a person's decision to do right. Here are a few practical suggestions to move your congregation toward the desired goal.

Promote Formal Membership

Committing oneself to membership in a local church has fallen into disrepute in many modern circles. People claim that church leaders have "no right" to call for something that isn't specifically spelled out in the Bible. Of course, such objections aren't heard as long as the requests of leadership fit nicely into the comfortable expectations of parishioners. But the real issue is not "the right" of the church leaders to structure church life in an optimal way (though Heb. 13:17 calls for obedience when they do). The real issue coloring the thinking of reluctant church-joiners is our society's aversion to commitment.

Getting people to commit to *anything* is increasingly difficult these days. Folks are leery about signing on the dotted line. They ask, "What's their angle?" "What will it cost me?" "Is it really necessary?" Our people have become conditioned to ask these questions when challenged to make the most benign of commitments. Therefore, we should help Christians expect "commitment" as normative in God's way of doing things. Promoting formal church membership is a good place to start.

Some people have labored to defend the advantages of church membership,[4] and others have even sought to establish its biblical warrant.[5] But my point is that church leaders should use their authority as leaders to characterize the church by commitments from the outset. Let people see the value that your church places on making good and appropriate resolves. This does not mean you should "erect artificial or unbiblical barriers to your fellowship."[6] It simply means that you seek to formalize the connection to a local body by securing a commitment. You may even find it advantageous to call your members to renew their commitments to the church once a year. Some churches do this by having their members sign a "covenant renewal" at the beginning of each new year.

Whether annual or initial, we would be wise not to shy away from this kind of commitment to the fellowship. By embracing it unapologetically, we can set the tone in our church culture for the weekly exercise of personal and biblical commitments.

Reward Faithful Service

We can bolster the community-wide value of promises kept by recognizing and rewarding faithful service within the church on a regular basis.

When our church was smaller, we would recognize the consistency and dependability of volunteer servants in the church in a public way. During a weekend service we would call them up to the front, present them with a small gift of appreciation, and commend their commitment to the body. We did this for years. When a few naysayers objected to this procedure as "exalting people" or "giving glory to men," I would remind them of the pattern set forth in Scripture.

The Bible assures us that "God is not unjust to forget your work and labor of love which you have shown toward His name, in that you have ministered to the saints, and do minister" (Heb. 6:10). Having a God who shows His pleasure with faithfulness by the recurring biblical affirmation, "Well done good and faithful servant, you have been trustworthy" (Luke 19:17; Matt. 25:21, 23 NIV) should convince us that a pledge fulfilled is worthy of recognition.

Celebrate the Marriage Covenant

The commitment of marriage should be held in the highest honor in our churches, and it should be an obvious target for our praise. Without detracting from the commitment to singleness (1 Cor. 7:32–38; 1 Tim. 5:11–12), we should always seek to affirm the vows of marriage.

We can do so through the appropriate recognition of anniversaries and long-lasting marital relationships in our churches. It can also be done by the sobriety we bring to premarital preparation classes and counseling in our churches. At every turn, the promises kept in this fundamental commitment to relationships should be heartily celebrated.

Provide Opportunities for Formal Commitments

If commitments to do good are to become the normative results of our sermons, then we ought to supply numerous opportunities to engage in them. From the simplest church program to the most demanding missions opportunity, the requirements for participation ought to be clearly defined. The standards and terms should be well thought out and plainly presented. Both child care worker and prospective missionary should count the cost involved.

The goal of this careful clarification is not to discourage participation, but to define it. This reduces the risk of confusion and also separates serious servants from the "dabblers." Some people listen to our sermons and say to themselves, "That sounds like a pretty good idea; I might give that a try and see how it goes." We certainly don't want selective obedience or half-hearted efforts in response to our sermons, nor do we want to encourage it in other areas of church life. Our hope is that "dabbling in good" will be replaced by "resolving to do good."

The church can also be a forum for formalizing unconventional commitments that extend beyond "church life." I recently witnessed a weekend service that involved teens and preteens vowing before the congregation to be obedient to their parents. Each young person stepped up to the microphone with a prepared statement and vowed his or her loyalty to mom and dad. Through that service we were reminded that God's Word requires a serious response.

Working to increase opportunities and encourage participation in formalized commitments throughout our church culture will improve the viability and effectiveness of the sermons we preach.

FOSTER A CLIMATE OF ACCOUNTABILITY

Commitment-making should be part of every Christian community, but commitments can turn into fuel for hypocrisy without an emphasis on keeping the promises made. This is why it is necessary to emphasize the counterpart to commitment—personal accountability.

Solomon warns, "When you make a vow to God, do not delay in fulfilling it. He has no pleasure in fools; fulfill your vow" (Eccl. 5:4 NIV). Broken vows were epidemic among the Pharisees, causing Jesus to recite the words of Isaiah 29, "These people come near to me with their mouth and honor me with their lips, but their hearts are far from me" (Isa. 29:13a; Matt. 15:8; Mark 7:6).

We cannot afford to create a culture of commitment-making without fostering a climate of accountability at the same time. When people make promises to do right, they should be held responsible for keeping them.

The Case for Accountability

Some people object to any form of accountability, because they believe their Christianity is "a highly personal matter." By personal, they mean private. By private, they mean their affairs are no one else's business.

Such Christianity is entirely foreign to the New Testament. The modern church has peddled phrases and ideas that frame Christianity as entirely "individual" and "personal" and has made a habit of calling for commitments "with every head bowed and every eye closed." But the community of believers in the early church understood that one's spiritual journey was never intended to be a private affair.

God places a high value on openness—so high that He replaced the autonomy and independence of the religious hierarchy with mutual support and interdependence. The victories and defeats of one person were to be felt by his Christian associates. This weaving together of lives is one implication of the New Testament description of the church as a "body." The apostle Paul wrote, "The members should have the same care for one another. And if one members suffers, all the members suffer with it; or if one member is honored, all the members rejoice with it" (1 Cor. 12:25b–26).

Although we are drawn to foster all sorts of pretense and our pride tempts us to isolation, Paul calls us to fight the conceit of a "private spirituality." He exhorts Christians to "rejoice with those who rejoice; mourn with those who mourn. Live in harmony with one another. Do not be proud, but be willing to associate with people of low position. Do not be conceited" (Rom. 12:15–16 NIV). James was even more direct. He addressed the most difficult aspect of spiritual honesty and implored those who were struggling with sin to "confess your trespasses to one another, and pray for one another" (James 5:16a).

Not only must we understand the biblical case for authentic Christian accountability; we must also present that case regularly. We must confront the priority so often given to personal independence and spiritual privacy. If we do not, we will have little hope of promoting the kind of mutual accountability in our churches which is such an important component of personal response to biblical exposition.

How to Encourage Accountability

Encouraging appropriate forums of mutual accountability throughout the congregation is not an easy task. But if it is to become the norm, it must be modeled by the church leadership.

Be Accountable Yourself

To promote this value with integrity, you need to hold to it yourself. As preachers, we may be tempted to apply some sort of exemption to ourselves in this regard, but the Bible does not allow for one.

A regular time of personal accountability, when temptations are honestly discussed and sins are openly confessed, can keep you from qualifying for the sobering directive given to the elders of the church in 1 Timothy: "Those who are sinning rebuke in the presence of all, that the rest also may fear" (1 Tim. 5:20). Take special note of the next verse: "I charge you before God and the Lord Jesus Christ and the elect angels that you observe these things without prejudice, doing nothing with partiality" (1 Tim. 5:21).

Because you are a pastor, you might think of several compelling reasons for keeping your struggles to yourself. Don't fool yourself. You have an equal if not greater obligation to be personally accountable for the commitments you've made in your Christian life.

Set the pace. Don't hide the fact that you regularly submit yourself to scrutinizing accountability. Make it clear that you don't believe in a double standard when it comes to being held responsible to do what you have vowed.

Keep Leaders Accountable for Accountability

It is not possible to be involved personally in every leader's accountability. But you should at least keep all church leaders accountable for being accountable. Accountability should be a part of your leadership standards for elders, deacons, teachers, and ministry leaders. Those in leadership positions ought to lead the way in their respective spheres of influence.

As a leader among leaders, speak to your staff regularly about the importance of having others hold them responsible for maintaining their commitments. Set up networks and opportunities to assist in this. Encourage them to create and maintain accountability partnerships and accountability groups in their own ministries.

Practice Church Discipline

Church discipline is nothing more than accountability on the broadest scale. When Christians are unfaithful and unrepentant, the Bible calls church leaders to be faithful in their duty to hold them accountable. Much

172

has been written about the practical implementation of church discipline,[7] yet many church leaders still shun this difficult task.

Jesus didn't leave any loopholes in His dissertation on discipline. He called His followers to point out a brother's sin: "If your brother sins against you, go and show him his fault" (Matt. 18:15a). If the sin was not resolved, the circle was widened to include others in the community: "But if he will not hear, take with you one or two more" (Matt. 18:16a). If he still remained unrepentant, Jesus said, "Tell it to the church" (Matt. 18:17a).

Those who have engaged in this biblical practice testify that few things have bolstered the congregation's value of commitment and accountability so profoundly. In time they will understand that church discipline is not mean or combative, nor is it optional. Rather, its loving practice is the way to a healthy body.

COUNT THE COST OF RAISING THE BAR

Some pastors may fear a mass exodus if they push for costly commitments and honest accountability in their congregation. Yet, as the Book of Acts demonstrates, the highest standards of commitment and accountability do not deter growth, but they often stimulate it. Consider the response of the early church on the heels of the most severe case of church discipline on record—the death of Ananias and Sapphira:

> So great fear came upon all the church and upon all who heard these things. And through the hands of the apostles many signs and wonders were done among the people. And they were all with one accord in Solomon's Porch. Yet none of the rest dared join them, but the people esteemed them highly. And believers were increasingly added to the Lord, multitudes of both men and women (Acts 5:11–14).

Though a healthy fear accompanied such a high standard and the congregation at large was not signing up for dinner with the apostles, the numbers of those joining the church was constantly increasing. The standard was raised, yet God drew more and more people to the church—admittedly, a certain kind of people.

Raising the bar of commitment and accountability will definitely turn some people off. Many expect something quite different from their "church experience." Today, more than ever, people want a church (and a god) that doesn't expect much from them. When encouraged to change in these areas, they may grumble that things aren't as comfortable as they used to be. Some people may even choose to leave for a more accommodating religious experience. Brace yourself—it's bound to happen.

Whenever we call people to press on to a higher level of godliness, we are bound to incur some opposition. As Jesus said, we ought to be concerned if we *don't* incur it: "Woe to you when all men speak well of you, for so did their fathers to the false prophets" (Luke 6:26).

If we only affirm our people's present standard of Christian living, we will ensure for ourselves a certain kind of popularity. Spurgeon reminds us that "a minister flings his soul away if he spends his energies in the attempt to please his congregation."[8] We work for their good, not for their pleasure and comfort. Pushing for transformation is risky business.[9] In the short run, it may reduce your Sunday attendance, costing you a handful of casual attendees and seekers of convenient Christianity. It may even cost you a leader or two. But be encouraged. Promoting a culture that is responsive and submissive to the voice of God is always worth it.

Among the benefits, it will streamline your ministry and keep you from chasing the latest ecclesiastical fads. It will also keep you focused on what is truly important.[10] Above all, it will ultimately produce a body of Christians whom God is eager to meet in a profound way Sunday after Sunday.

> Heaven is my throne,
>   and the earth is my footstool.
> Where is the house you will build for me?
>   Where will my resting place be?
> Has not my hand made all these things,
>   and so they came into being?"
>   declares the LORD.
> This is the one I esteem:
>   he who is humble and contrite in spirit,
>   and trembles at my word (Isa. 66:1–2 NIV).

CHAPTER FOURTEEN

Provide Tools to Help Your Audience Make Specific Changes

As Jesus was preaching out in the Judean countryside, a woman interrupted with an exuberant compliment: "Blessed is the mother who gave you birth and nursed you" (Luke 11:27 NIV). While one might expect Jesus to say, "Thank you," he surprised everyone by turning the crowd's attention to the place where ultimate blessings are found. Instead of affirming the gratification that might come from having raised a skilled expositor, he directed their focus to the blessings that come to those who obediently *respond* to exposited truth. Jesus said, "Blessed rather are those who hear the word and obey it" (Luke 11:28 NIV).

Jesus was passionate in his desire to elicit obedient and practical responses to his sermons. We must have that same passion. While God may work *in* our listeners as we preach, he wants to work *through* them as they fulfill their respective roles in their families, neighborhoods and workplaces. When the sermon is over, their opportunities for life-change begin. We must do all that we can to assist our people in acting upon the truth we dispense. Therefore, it behooves us to design and supply tools that will assist them in this process. Providing your congregation with a few useful aids for application is well worth your time and effort. Here are a few basic ideas.

My five-year old son loves to draw. Of course, he hasn't won any art scholarships yet, but he is learning to master the basics. Once he successfully draws a particular form or shape, whether a tree, a plane, or a house, he never forgets how to do it again. Like most budding artists, though, his greatest struggle is producing that elusive first draft!

When he asked for help in drawing a car or a boat for the first time, I would sketch one out for him (as best I could!), then give him a blank piece of paper and have him re-produce my effort. This didn't always go so well. The copy rarely resembled the original.

I soon discovered that his proficiency spiked when I directly assisted him as he created his first sketch. With a little practice I learned to plot an impromptu dot-to-dot template of the requested object. Now, as his little hand carefully drags that pen from one coordinate to the next, my simple guideline is usually all he needs to add a new image to his artistic repertoire.

We should never minimize the importance of providing templates for our listeners as they move from being hearers of the Word to doers of the Word. Whether it's acquiring the truths from the sermon or applying them to their lives, with a little practice we can learn to plot out guidelines that will accelerate their proficiency in living the truth.

We must do all we can to help our people act on the truth we proclaim. We should design and supply tools to assist them in this process. Providing your congregation with a few useful aids for application is well worth your time and effort. Following are a few basic ideas.

WORKSHEETS

Almost 90 percent of those who take notes during a sermon say the practice helps them to ingest the sermon.[1] While a great teaching aid, the congregant's notes may be most effective *after* the sermon is completed. If you carefully design your note sheet you may find that it can be transformed into a worksheet from which they will review, rework and actually digest the sermon. It will teach long after you have stopped!

A few simple adjustments to the typical note page significantly bolstered the long-term usability of my congregation's sermon notes. After redesigning my page, their frequent review of preaching notes rose from 36 percent to 55 percent.[2] With the old format, which allowed limited space to write on the bulletin proper, 41 percent confessed to discarding their notes after only a couple of weeks. Now, 72 percent of the them say that they file them for later reference with some thought given to their reuse and retrieval—and over half say they have a filing *system* for their collection of preaching notes.

The changes I implemented were minor, but very productive. We printed the worksheet on 8½ by 11 inch paper instead of the previous half sheet. We found that it was worth a crease in the middle of the page and the extra expense if the page actually fit a file folder or a notebook. I also began to print them on three-hole punched paper, which encouraged the creation of notebooks for easy retrieval of notes from the biblical books that we studied.

At the top of each worksheet I added pertinent filing information. Along with the title and subtitle, I added (1) the preaching text; (2) the subject

176

the sermon addresses; (3) the series which the message is part of; and (4) the local information, comprised of the place, date, and preacher. This improved their filing system for later access and retrieval.

The result is a worksheet that not only prompts each main point, but also provides information that encourages the review and recovery of the notes when a situation calls for them. (See figure 14.1.)

Figure 14.1
Sample Worksheet

Text: 2 Samuel 9:1-13   Pacific Coast Church
Topic: Kindness, Grace, Relationships   November 9, 2003
Series: Book of 2 Samuel

Radical Kindness
The Unique Love of People Who Know God's Grace

1. Love _____(w.1–3a)

2. Don't _____(w.3b–8)

3. Boldly _____(w.9–13)

These elements, along with a regular exhortation to reexamine their notes, have helped make the information usable not simply for days or weeks, but for years to come!

SPECIFIC APPLICATION QUESTIONS

A second way to encourage the implementation of sermon content is the use of weekly application questions. I can take the application only so far in my 40-minute sermon, so the extra application questions help move the content of the sermon further into the specific realm of one's daily life. Long after I turn off the microphone, a set of carefully worded questions can prompt action in the situations, relationships and personal contexts of my hearers.

Printing the application questions on the backside of the worksheet keeps the scriptural basis contiguous to the applicational thrust. It is also important to leave enough blank space between questions for people to write a brief answer for each. I attempt to stay within the parameter of the sermon, but often provide a few references or a sidebar to help augment the information that I am calling on them to apply.

Don't make these questions a postscript to your sermon preparation. I encourage you to start formulating them early in your study. As you work through the passage, jot down any applicational thoughts or questions not included in your sermon yet appropriate for a one-on-one discussion.

Take note of the kinds of applications that require specific information. For instance, when preaching about loving those who are difficult to love, you can direct the focus of your congregants in many different directions. One person may focus on a coworker and another on their boss at work. Someone else may be thinking of a family member, spouse, or a leader in the church. All of these situations are handled with the same set of principles, yet each with a different strategy.

Herein lies the beauty of the worksheet. An initial application question can guide the listener of your sermon to a specific strategy in his or her own study or in a study group. Further identifying the person who is hard to love and his relationship to the hearer is something that cannot be fully explored in the sermon setting, but is easily done on a worksheet.

By the end of your study time you will very likely have created more questions than you can possibly use, so pick the best six or seven for the back of the worksheet.

Here are some examples from a sermon I presented from Colossians 3:22–23 regarding Christians under authority in the workplace. The text reads, "Bondservants, obey in all things your masters according to the flesh, not with eyeservice, as men-pleasers, but in sincerity of heart, fearing God. And whatever you do, do it heartily, as to the Lord and not to men." (See figure 14.2.)

178

Figure 14.2
Sample Application Questions

- How would you rate your aptitude and competence as a worker?

- How do you think your boss (or those who evaluate your work) would characterize your work ethic?

- How would you describe your attitude toward your boss (or those you answer to in your daily work)?

- Read Ephesians 6:5. What specific changes need to be made in your life and behavior so that your response to your boss (or those you answer to) is more like the response that you would give Christ?

- What difference would it make in your work if you knew that Jesus Christ was the "customer" or beneficiary of the products or services you render?

- In what measurable way can you raise the standard of excellence in the work that you will perform this week?

- Read Proverbs 24:30–31; 18:9; and 2 Thessalonians 3:11–13. Write out a prayer confessing any residual laziness in your life and commit yourself afresh to diligent and faithful work in the coming weeks.

READING LISTS

Prompting your congregation to read good Christian material is another way to facilitate their application of your sermons. And since you just concluded a week of study which included the reading of books, articles and other materials, you know exactly which writings might be most helpful.

After being habitually asked to provide titles of good resources for further study, I decided to print weekly reading lists for my congregation. Doing so broadcasts the high value of reading, and it reminds my listeners of the priority that Christians have always placed on reading.[3] Notice the apostle Paul's urgent request of Timothy to bring his "books" and "parchments" so that he could continue his practice of reading while imprisoned (2 Tim. 4:13).

If congregants don't receive encouragement to invest in reading from their pastors, they likely won't receive it at all. While we must always promote the Bible as the unsurpassed priority on every Christian's reading list, we also need to present other profitable works for our hearers' edification. There is even great advantage in providing titles of books and articles you *did not*

179

consult that week, yet know will answer the questions your sermon raised but could not necessarily address.

The immediate goal of a weekly reading list is to help the hearer implement the sermon you just preached. Your long-range goal will be to foster a love for reading that will add to the overall maturity and spiritual development of your church in general. As Tozer lamented, "To enjoy a great religious book requires a degree of consecration to God and detachment from the world that few modern Christians have."[4] We would be wise shepherds to raise up a congregation of readers.

Figure 14.3 is an example of a reading list provided for a sermon from Romans 10:1–15. The sermon was intended to move our people, with all their objections, to have a greater concern for the lost and a passion for evangelism. These were the resources I provided to help them in this area. (See figure 14.3.)

Figure 14.3
Sample Reading List

Beckwith, Frank and Greg Koukl. *Relativism: Feet Firmly Planted in Mid-Air.* Grand Rapids: Baker Books, 1998.

House, Paul and Gregory Thornbury. *Who Will Be Saved? Defending the Biblical Understanding of God, Salvation and Evangelism.* Wheaton: Crossway, 2000.

Johnstone, Patrick and Jason Mandryk. *Operation World:* 21st Century Edition. Waynesboro: Paternoster, 2001.

Lutzer, Erwin. *Christ Among Other Gods.* Chicago: Moody Press, 1994.

Metzger, Will. *Tell the Truth: The Whole Gospel to the Whole Person by Whole People.* Downers Grove: InterVarsity Press, 1984.

Nash, Ronald. *Is Jesus the Only Savior?* Grand Rapids: Zondervan, 1994.

Peterson, Robert. *Hell on Trial: The Case for Eternal Punishment.* Phillipsburg, N.J.: P & R Publishing, 1995.

Ryken, Philip. *Is Jesus the Only Way?* Wheaton: Crossway Books, 2000.

Thomas, Robert. "Jesus' View of Eternal Punishment," in *The Master's Seminary Journal* vol. 9, no. 2 (Fall 1998): 147–67.

Zacharias, Ravi. *Jesus Among Other Gods: The Absolute Claims of the Christian Message.* Nashville: Word Publishing, 2000.

In order to emphasize that Scripture reading is always to be valued above other books, I also provide a Bible reading guide for each day of the week following the sermon. This guide doesn't always directly relate to the sermon, but it will lead our people through the entire Bible one time each year. (See figure 14.4.)

Figure 14.4

Our church is reading through the Bible in a year. Here is this week's schedule.

Sunday	Jer. 41–42 & 1 Thess. 4
Monday	Jer. 43–44 & 1 Thess. 5
Tuesday	Jer. 45–46 & 2 Thess. 1
Wednesday	Jer. 47–48 & 2 Thess. 2
Thursday	Jer. 49–50 & 2 Thess. 3
Friday	Jer. 51–52 & 1 Tim. 1
Saturday	Lam. 1–2 & 1 Tim. 2

Along with the reading list and the Bible reading guide, the backside of the weekly worksheet contains the application questions with an explanatory introduction. Figure 14.5 provides an example of application questions from a sermon on Colossians 3:21 about parenting, with a heavy emphasis on the context of the family found in verses 18 through 20. (See figure 14.5.)

Figure 14.5 Sample Backside of Worksheet

Application Questions

These questions are provided for your further study and application of today's message. Thoughtfully writing out the answers to these questions will help to drive home the point of today's message. It is also helpful to discuss your answers with others. This can take place with friends, your family, accountability partners, or ministry groups within the church. For more information about groups at PCC that use these questions as the basis for their weekly discussion, please call the church office at (949) 489-2600.

1. Describe your mom and dad's relationship with each other when you were growing up.

   What good and/or bad traits, habits or characteristics do you think have become a part of your life because you have followed the example of your parents' relationship with one another?

2. If you are married, what specific and measurable steps can you take to nurture and strengthen your marriage?

3. If you have children, what do you think they have learned (or are learning) about obedience and respect for authority from watching you?

   What can you do to become a better model of respect and obedience?

4. How well do your children obey your parental instructions?

   How well do they respond to other authority figures in their lives?

5. Write out a prayer that expresses your desire to see God elevate the value of obedience and respect in your home.

We are reading through the Bible in a year! Here is this week's schedule.
Sunday
  Is.9-10 & 1Cor.4
Monday
  Is.11-12 & 1Cor.5
Tuesday
  Is.13-14 & 1Cor.6
Wednesday
  Is.15-16 & 1Cor.7
Thursday
  Is.17-18 & 1Cor.8
Friday
  Is.19-20 & 1Cor.9
Saturday
  Is.21-22 & 1Cor.10

Here are some resources which may help lead your children toward a life of obedience.

Gundersen, Dennis. *Your Child's Profession of Faith.* Amityville, NY: Calvary Press, 1994.
MacArthur, John. *Successful Christian Parenting: Raising Your Child with Care, Compassion, and Common Sense.* Nashville: Word Publishing, 1998.
Priolo, Lou. *The Heart of Anger: Practical Help for the Prevention & Cure of Anger in Children.* Amityville, NY: Calvary Press, 1997.
Tripp, Tedd. *Shepherding a Child's Heart.* Wapwallopen, PA: Shepherd Press, 1995.
Turansky, Scott and Joanne Miller. *Say Good-bye to Whining, Complaining and Bad Attitudes in You and Your Kids.* Colorado Springs: Waterbrook Press, 2000.

A BOOKSTORE

Hand in hand with a pastoral emphasis on reading good books is making them available to the congregation on the church campus. While many churches have established lending libraries, most churches cannot provide their congregation with a growing number of sought-after titles to borrow. Your church library probably contains many Christian classics, but chances are it will not accommodate the interest your reading lists will generate.

For this reason, a church should establish a small bookstore that stocks the books you recommend, as well as those promoted by church leaders and church ministries. Some leaders are reluctant to charge for books, but consider what our congregants spend each week on trivial matters alone! That amount could easily purchase a life-changing book or two. Assure those with concerns that the bookstore will not become a cash cow—your goal is only to break-even financially.

The church budget may be able to seed some money for the initiation of this project. You will find that there are book distributors who are very happy to assist churches in this endeavor.[5] A lay-leader could manage the bookstore and stock it with titles that will augment your weekly sermons. With such low overhead, a church bookstore ministry should be able to offer an increasing number of titles at very good prices.

CASSETTE TAPES AND DIGITAL AUDIO

There is no better way to "review" a message than to hear it again and again. Many have testified that the power of a challenging sermon has taken root in their lives only after they've had exposure to it for a second or third time—so give them opportunity to do so.

Any technology that reproduces the sermon can tremendously benefit your congregants as they seek to follow through on the truth that you have expounded. It would make sense, then, that anything that gives a sermon a longer life and a reiterative voice should be enthusiastically embraced. Imagine the Apostle Paul having access to the kinds of technology at our disposal today. Do you think he would encourage its use among the churches of Asia Minor? No doubt such innovations would have been fully utilized by those early Christians zealous to see God's word "grow and multiply" (Acts 12:24).

A well-managed tape and digital audio ministry can be invaluable, and its worth grows exponentially if the sermon tapes are available to congregants upon the conclusion of the service. Making tapes or CDs available right after the service, when residual interest from the freshly heard sermon is highest, increases the possibility that people will grab one for review on their way to the car.

Providing this timely service will require a small, well-trained team. Someone removes the master tape or CD from the recording deck after the last word of your sermon. From there, it's transferred to a duplication deck which is waiting along with pre-labeled media. These copies are immediately taken to a high-traffic area for distribution.

The quantity price on materials makes the unit price minimal.[6] Even if the church recoups equipment costs or saves for new or better equipment, the cost per unit can usually be kept to a few dollars. This is money well-spent if the media prompts people to carefully review and reconsider the Scripture you have faithfully expounded.

Once the sermon has been recorded it is no trouble for a technologically savvy volunteer to make the sermon available over the internet in some digital audio format. These sermons can be uploaded on Sunday afternoon and made available to those who frequent your church website. A great advantage of this technology is that your sermons can be reviewed and relived at no cost to the user.

APPLICATION GROUPS

The small group meeting is another significant tool that can be used to prompt God's people to become doers of the Word. I am not referring to the kind of small group that gathers people in a circle to ask what a passage of Scripture *means*. I am talking about a group of Christians that gathers around the passage expounded the previous Sunday to decide how they will specifically *apply* it. Most small groups desire more Bible *knowledge*. What most Christians need is more biblical *application* of what they already know!

This need was underscored by the preacher who assumed the pulpit duties at a new church and continued to preach the same sermon over and over and over again. After a few weeks he was confronted by some of the congregants who asked him why he kept preaching the exact sermon each Sunday. He simply replied, "When you start living that one, I'll move on to the next one."

It is hard to deny that most of us suffer from biblical indigestion—we know far more than we are currently putting into practice! But that will quickly change when groups gather for the purpose of biblical application. Replacing study groups with a set of small groups that focus exclusively on application will provide your church with some needed relief.

This idea is not a new one. In the wake of the Protestant Reformation, Pietist leader, Philip Jacob Spener, promoted the idea of application groups. One church historian describes their practice:

184

> Spener sought a way to renew the church from the inside out. In his thinking, one could begin in a small way and with a few people and watch the "practice of theology" bear fruit. What emerged was . . . a small group of people who met to discuss the Sunday sermon and to make application to their lives.[7]

Following his three-hundred-year-old cue, we ought to create groups in our churches that seek to apply what has already been preached. These groups should secure commitments from their participants and utilize this weekly forum for the purpose of regular accountability.

Begin by training a team of mature leaders who will host the small group meetings and focus the group's conversation on application. As they learn the dynamics of directing applicational discussion, they can utilize the sermon application questions that you have crafted as their guide.

Those who attend these groups in our church receive the biggest blessing from the weekly sermons since the truth of each sermon is so extensively discussed and applied. Their anticipation of these meetings changes the way they listen to each message. They know there will be a personal discussion about the truth of the passage and its demands upon their own lives. They understand, in the most profound way, that the preaching of God's Word is not for their entertainment, or solely for increased knowledge. More than others, participants in these groups recognize that God intends every sermon to change their lives!

CHAPTER FIFTEEN

Personally Model the Changes from Last Week's Sermon

THOUGH FEW DARE TO ARTICULATE IT, MOST CHRISTIANS LIVE BY THE MOTTO, "Do as I say, not as I do." Christians find it comfortable and spiritually pious to point people to the message of Christ while at the same time sheepishly downplaying their own role as messengers.

They deflect their own shortcomings with phrases like, "Don't look at me; I'm just a fellow beggar looking for bread." In so doing they do not realize their "humble" justification does not add to the message, it detracts from it. Other popular mantras such as, "We're not perfect, just forgiven" and "Don't look at me, just keep looking at Him," may be well-meaning, but they surely are not well-grounded in Scripture. These all fail to recognize that God wants more than proclamation—he wants *transformation* in the life of the messenger, as well as in the life of the listener.

While such sentiments have an appearance of wisdom, they are disastrous if adopted by those who preach God's Word. Beyond expositors of His Word, God clearly calls us to be a living illustration of it. Pastor Timothy is instructed, "be an example to the believers in word, in conduct, in love, in spirit, in faith, in purity" (1 Tim. 4:12b). Pastor Titus is told, "In everything set them an example by doing what is good. In your teaching show integrity" (Titus 2:7 NIV).

On my first visit to Jerusalem I had an insatiable appetite for exploring the old city. One afternoon a fellow traveler and I ventured out to see all that we could see. However, political tensions in the Middle East were particularly high at the time, and we soon realized there were parts of the city where we definitely were *not* welcome. School kids began to throw things at us under the approving, angry glare of their parents.

Suddenly we knew our intrepid tour was over, and we longed to be back in the safety of our hotel, enjoying an early dinner. The problem was, we weren't sure how to get there! The twisted maze of narrow roads seemed to defy our sense of direction, and our tour maps offered us little assistance. Finally, a weathered man leaning against an old stone wall saw our bewildered looks and calmly said, "I'll take you were you need to go—for twenty-five shekels!"

Assessing our predicament, we looked deeply into his eyes, hoping we were dealing with an entrepreneur and not a thug. Within moments we had decided to hire our own tour guide. As it turned out, his knowledge of the locale and his personal integrity were worth all the shekels we were carrying!

We often underestimate the challenges our congregants face as they attempt to navigate the Christian life in a non-Christian world. This life is not lived on traveler-friendly highways with well-marked road signs. Our hearers need more than mere directions, and we need to be more than cartographers. We must be the insightful guides God called us to be, men of knowledge and integrity who *lead* them along the way.

While we may not enjoy the tension caused by living in a spiritual fishbowl, it is a part of our job description—and God didn't put it in fine print. He tells Christians to look to their messengers for a living template of how to live the Christian life. "Remember your leaders, who spoke the word of God to you. Consider the outcome of their way of life and imitate their faith" (Heb. 13:7 NIV). This is why the apostle Paul unabashedly challenged his hearers to watch his life:

Imitate me, just as I also imitate Christ (1 Cor. 11:1).

Therefore I urge you, imitate me (1 Cor. 4:16).

Brethren, join in following my example (Phil. 3:17a).

The things which you learned and received and heard and saw in me, these do (Phil. 4:9a).

For you yourselves know how you ought to follow us (2 Thess. 3:7a).

While preachers are to be the pacesetters of application, the Bible does not presume that preachers will be perfect or infallible guides. The apostles were equally bold in admitting their imperfection (1 Tim. 1:15–16; Luke 5:8; John 21; Phil. 3:12–14; 2 Cor. 3:5). We too have feet of clay, yet we must turn the tide of false humility, refusing to relinquish our responsibility to model the truth we preach.

188

Is your congregation confident that you practice what you preach? Do they see your life as a "how-to" manual of the truths you expound? We cannot afford to fail in this regard. In the words of Haddon Robinson:

> Preachers . . . have to be more than "fellow strugglers." No one is helped by "you're a loser; I'm a loser; let's keep losing together." People want to believe you have taken your own advice and, while you've not arrived, you're on the way. You'll never learn to be a .300 hitter by watching three .100 hitters. You study a .325 hitter. Although he will occasionally strike out, he knows how to hit.[1]

THE MODERN LEADERSHIP CRISIS

Howard Hendricks claims, "credible and trustworthy leaders are fast becoming an endangered species."[2] To "do as I say *and as I do*" is a fleeting model of leadership. The religious scandals of the past twenty years have convinced many that the integrity of the church ranks alongside that of marketplace traders and politicians. This presents a new challenge for the church, as Warren Wiersbe observes:

> The church has grown accustomed to hearing people question the *message* of the gospel, because that message is foolishness to the lost. But today the situation is embarrassingly reversed, for now the *messenger* is suspect. Both the ministry and the message of the church have lost credibility before a watching world.[3]

Rather than running up the white flag, we need to realize there is no better time than ours for a renewed emphasis on pastoral integrity. Though our society says it cares little if its leaders are people of integrity (as long as its felt needs are met) God knows that the *real need* of the hour is leadership that practices what it preaches. Now more than ever pastors must be more than capable managers and effective communicators. We must be "shepherds" who are "eager" to serve as "examples to the flock" (1 Pet. 5:2–3). As James Stewart pointed out, "Christ has chosen you for [a vocation] which more than any other calling in the world depends upon the quality of life and the total witness of [your] character."[4]

This modern leadership crisis may seem like an insurmountable problem for one preacher to solve—but for your congregation, one is all it takes. They need only one preacher who truly practices what he preaches in order to restore leadership integrity in their corner of Christendom. Do not, therefore, underestimate the influential power of your integrity.

The famed nineteenth-century British preacher, F. W. Robertson, was soberly reminded of this truth when he visited one of his parishioners. The

189

man, who was busily maintaining his shop, stopped and pointed to a picture of Robertson on his wall. The shopkeeper explained that whenever he was tempted to sell someone shoddy goods he looked at Robertson's picture to find strength to do what was right.[5]

Now more than ever, congregations are in need of a pastor who will eagerly serve as a living example of the preaching they hear from week to week.

PURPOSEFULLY PRACTICE WHAT YOU PREACH

Without being ostentatious, it is important that we live out Sunday's application in a way that *can be seen* by others. Paul regularly extended himself beyond what was convenient in order to provide an example of his sermons in action. By financially supporting himself as he preached, Paul could authoritatively address an existing problem in the Thessalonian congregation regarding the Christian's work ethic and the need to "labor for one's daily bread" (1 Thess. 4:11–12; 5:12, 14; 2 Thess. 3:10–13). Between sermons, he made an effort to model this truth. He testifies:

> For you yourselves know how you ought to follow our example. We were not idle when we were with you, nor did we eat anyone's food without paying for it. On the contrary, we worked night and day, laboring and toiling so that we would not be a burden to any of you. We did this, not because we do not have the right to such help, but in order to make ourselves a model for you to follow (2 Thess. 3:7–9).

Costly Choices

Like Paul, we must attempt to become an applicational template of our own sermons. We, too, must be willing to sacrifice our own comfort and convenience in order to lay down a pattern of behavior called for in our preaching texts.

I was recently faced with this challenge one Sunday evening after preaching seven times in two days. I was exhausted and more than ready to dash home, eat, and fall into bed. As I imagined the bliss of solitude, the challenge of my own sermon was too fresh to ignore. I had just finished speaking on the command to be like Christ and "not please ourselves." I spoke of sacrificially edifying our neighbor "for his good" (Rom. 15:1–3)—and here I was determined to focus on my own welfare.

As I walked from the platform, I momentarily grappled with all the seemingly legitimate reasons I had to exempt myself from any tangible application of the message—at least for this one evening! "I've done my part," I argued, "let them pick it up from here." But I knew that to truly practice what I had just preached, and to provide a pattern for others to follow, I needed to set aside my personal agenda. By God's grace, I invited four fairly new members over to my home for a visit.

God kindly sustained my strength as I attempted to build their faith and meet needs through our conversation around the coffee table. I didn't realize the impact of my decision until the couples said their good-byes on my front porch. Our new friends were deeply grateful for our simple act of hospitality that night. Throughout that week, I heard how they were actively sharing the impact of the invitation into our home that Sunday evening. I soon realized that this "addendum" to the sermon stirred an infectious commitment to hospitality that a sermon alone could not.

The Need for Improvement

Unfortunately, not every example is as glowing. How many times have I preached on kindness or compassion, only to invalidate its proper application within the hour with an insensitive remark or a sarcastic comment? It's easy to speak of commitment, forgiveness, or harmony in marriage, only to prove in the days that follow that the sermon had never really taken root in my own life.

This is an ever-present peril of preaching. As one pastor put it, "We're not forced to [talk beyond what we actually walk], but we're tempted to; there's always the opportunity, so we usually do."[6] We must repent whenever we get caught in this trap, then start with an honest evaluation of your own applicational batting average. What kind of disciple are *you*? Recall your last five sermons and carefully consider how well you have put those truths into practice. Can your family, close friends, and congregation see that you have diligently applied these truths? Have your "life-changing sermons" changed *your* life?

Don't stop there. Ask God for an honest appraisal. With the psalmist, ask God to search you and know your heart (Ps. 139:23), to examine your preaching, and reveal any personal failures in this area. May we learn to loathe the state of affairs that Baxter poignantly describes:

> [I]t is too common with us to expect that from our people, which we do little or nothing in ourselves. What pains do we take to humble them, while we ourselves are unhumbled! How hard do we expostulate with them to wring out of them a few penitential tears, (and all too little) while yet our own eyes are dry! Alas! how we set them an example of hard-heartedness, while we are endeavoring by our words to melt and mollify them. Oh, if we did but study half as much to affect and amend our own hearts, as we do those of our hearers, it would not be with many of us as it is![7]

When words like these penetrate our heart, may they also drive us into the liberating reality of confession, repentance, forgiveness and resolve. Once there, we will soon realize that to effectively and consistently serve as an example to the flock we must get serious about being personally accessible.

PERSONAL ACCESSIBILITY

When asked what integrity looks like, Howard Hendricks responded, "It is best defined and illustrated in a person's life—convincingly transmitted through what others see, hear, and feel in the heartbeat of a lifestyle."[8] Unfortunately, modern-day pastors tend to spend less and less of their time with their lifestyles showing.

I have been to many pastors' conferences and seminars where the well-meaning lecturer directed preachers to find as much "relief" from their congregations as possible. They encouraged pastors to find as many friends, hobbies, and associations outside of the environs of their church as possible. After all, spending too much time establishing true comrades and confidants within the local body only saddles the pastor with undue burdens and excessive complications. Pastors are taught to screen their calls, curtail their schedules, and insulate themselves and their families from those they shepherd. One pastor glibly confessed that he did not visit people in his congregation or even dine out with them because that kind of "hobnobbing" would cripple his pulpit ministry.[9]

If the goals of ministry were self-promotion or self-preservation, and not the transformation of people's lives, this would be a terrific strategy. Jesus' strategy, on the other hand, involved consistent contact and personal accessibility, and there is no more effective way to teach, train, and disciple Christians than His. Granted, Christ sought short respites of solitude (Mark 1:35; Matt. 14:23; Luke 5:16), but those hours were the exception, and not the rule. His primary concern was to couple his preaching with truth incarnate.

Oswald Sanders contrasts this Christ-like virtue in the ministry of the apostle Paul to many forms of worldly leadership:

> There are men like General Charles de Gaulle whose greatness is the greatness of isolation. On the contrary, Paul's greatness and successful leadership lay in no small measure in this ability to capture and to hold the intense love and loyalty of the friends with whom he freely mixed.[10]

I sympathize the temptation to isolate yourself, especially in a growing church where demands seem limitless. But we must consider the cost of removing from our hearers what they can "see, hear, and feel in the heartbeat of our lifestyle." We should ask God to fill our hearts with a love for his people as they progress in Christ (Phil. 1:25), so that we can honestly echo the words of the Apostle when he wrote, "We loved you so much that we were delighted to share with you not only the gospel of God but our lives as well" (1 Thess. 2:8 NIV).

Meals

Sharing our lives as well as our sermons must be intentional. We must recognize that if we are to become models of what we preach we must make room in our schedules to do so. One of the effective means by which to share our lives is simply "taking our meals together" (Acts 2:46). There is something disarming about eating with one another. The real person usually emerges between the bites of a sandwich and the spilling of coffee on our trousers. While we pastors view this as a great way to learn about the people in our church, we must see that it works both ways—in this context the congregants are given equal opportunity to observe the speech, values, and conduct of their pastor. If we are commanded to set the example in such things (1 Tim. 4:12), then sharing a meal can be one practical and efficient way to do this.

I say "efficient" because we will all take time this week to eat anyway. So at least from a time standpoint, calling a parishioner to join you for lunch can hardly be seen as "an undue burden." While we might not relish the thought of putting our lifestyle on display for half of our meals, we cannot deny that freely sharing our lives with our people is an appropriate expression of pastoral love.

Their Homes

Visiting congregants in their homes has been a traditional pastoral responsibility that carries its own inherent challenges along with its intended encouragement. When our lives are viewed in a context outside of the pulpit, we have the opportunity to show our Christianity in action. The visit itself, the unscripted words we speak and the chance for informal interaction, provides a forum for people to see how deeply truth permeates their pastor's life.

In regard to home visits, one pastoral candidate boldly informed the interview committee, "You can have my head or you can have my feet, but you can't have both." While I appreciate his priority of study and preaching, we should not see pastoral visitation as beyond the purview of effective preaching. On the contrary. Truly effective preaching seems to imply it. Notice Paul's testimony at one of his most effective preaching posts: "I kept back nothing that was helpful, but proclaimed it to you, and taught you publicly and from house to house" (Acts 20:20). If our proclamation is to be as "helpful" as Paul's, we must be willing to teach our flock, not only in public settings behind lecterns and pulpits, but in the personal settings of living rooms and around dinner tables.

Your Home

Sharing your life from house to house allows your hearers to peer into your character, but few things provide a more honest look into your life than entertaining your listeners in *your* home.

Ironically, those who are opposed to such personal openness exempt themselves from the high privilege of pastoral ministry. Both 1 Timothy 3:2 and Titus 1:8 require pastors to be "hospitable." Admittedly, the word is not limited to the act of having parishioners in the preacher's home, but it arguably includes it.[11]

If we fear that acts of hospitality may expose an embarrassing gap between the pulpit and the parsonage, perhaps we should question our own integrity and our qualifications to preach.

Counseling

We powerfully demonstrate our commitment to "bear one another's burdens" (Gal. 6:2) when we open part of our schedule to those asking for help. Regardless of the size of our ministries and the busyness of our days, we should always demonstrate our concern for the flock by being accessible for biblical counseling. Of course, parameters must be constructed to keep our priority on prayer and the Word (Acts 6:2), but such priorities do not necessitate the exclusion of our personal involvement in the trials of others.

It is easier and much less complicated to delegate your counseling responsibilities, but resist the temptation to delegate all of it. Besides giving insights into hearers' lives, time in the counseling arena will inevitably model something of our Christianity that our sermons can't possibly convey.

Recreation

Congregants are accustomed to seeing their pastor at work, but rarely are they able to glean from his life while at play. Most pastors feel their times of refreshment and recuperation ought to be a private endeavor. Granted, we must be free to get away with our family or inner circle of closest friends (Mark 6:31), but we would be wise to consider some of our ministry breaks as opportunities for modeling truth.

I discovered the value of shared recreational time amid my evangelistic efforts. It seems natural to me to share the gospel with a non-Christian in the context of a sports arena, the golf course, or the gym. In doing so I not only have the opportunity to punctuate the entire experience with conversation about Christ, but I also gain trust and credibility as the lost person studies my character in those "real life" settings.

What aids in evangelism, in this case, also aids in our preaching. As we invite our hearers to join us for outings, trips, and sporting events, we have the chance to model the applications we advocate each week.

LONGEVITY IN THE PULPIT

There is a counterproductive trend in the modern pastorate that undermines much of the message we have preached. It is reported that the average pastor remains in a given church for only four or five years.[12] A mere six percent stay in the same church for over twenty years.[13] Statistics like these shout loudly and clearly that the commitment of most pastors to their people is neither lasting nor believable.

I sympathetically concede that there are some situations that dictate a parting of ways. But much like divorce, a pastor should treat the breaking up of families, be they biological or spiritual, as a grievous exception.

It is hard to miss the implied contradiction of pulpit ministries that last only a few years at a time. In our preaching, we regularly call for commitment, loyalty, and fidelity. We counsel fractious parties to work out lasting solutions. We insist that disillusioned couples hang in there. We ask Christians to be available for one another because their mutual support is indispensable. Then, when the ministerial going gets tough, *we're the ones* who pack up our books and move on to the next congregation. It's no wonder so many congregations have so little confidence in the character and integrity of their preachers! After being dumped by pastor after pastor, most congregations flinch at fresh pastoral calls to "commitment."

Church planters and missionaries like the apostle Paul knew their stay in a given church was temporary, but so did their congregations. Though the local people always preferred they stay (Acts 20:36–38), the church planter's ultimate concern was to get the church established, then hand it off to the enduring oversight of local pastor-teachers (Acts 20:28–32; Titus 1:5).

The trust gained through the longevity of those shepherds who remain to tend their flocks is significant. Some have recognized this and have written to persuade other pastors to practice the loyalty they preach in spite of their trials and problems.[14] Since our churches are made up of so many who come from broken homes, have experienced fickle relationships, divorced parents, unstable jobs, and transient associations, the pastor who perseveres in his church for twenty, thirty, or forty years, will naturally become their greatest template for consistency in the Christian life.

Our hearers will struggle in this world to find tangible examples of what it means to be a "doer of the word" unless today's pastors begin to actively model the application of the Christianity they proclaim. Christ intended that we set the pace. By God's grace may He enable us to do so with everincreasing success.

APPENDIX 1
PRAYER GUIDE FOR PREACHING

Pray for the Crafting of the Sermon

1. Pray that the message you are preparing would be an evident part of your own life.

2. Pray for the protection of your sermon preparation time.

3. Pray that you will be given grace and illumination to rightly divide His Word.

4. Pray that the words you choose to frame your outline would be effective tools for the Holy Spirit to employ.

5. Pray that you would have insight into the needs of your audience as they relate to the sermon you are preparing.

Pray for the Delivery of the Sermon

1. Pray that people will attend the preaching event.

2. Pray that your audience will arrive in the right frame of mind.

3. Pray that God will guard against preaching distractions.

4. Pray for clarity in your vocabulary.

5. Pray that God will give your audience understanding.

6. Ask God for the most effective and fruitful sermon you have ever preached.

Pray for the Response to the Sermon

1. Pray that people will put the sermon into practice.

2. Pray that the sermon will not be compartmentalized.

3. Pray that the application of the sermon will be contagious.

4. Pray that the sermon itself will be repeatedly "delivered."

APPENDIX 2
A SAMPLE "MESSAGE PREP" PRAYER TEAM SCHEDULE

Time Period	Stage of Prep	Person Praying	Email Address
Tuesday 8:00 AM	Study of Text	Mary Johnson	maryj@abc.com
Tuesday 9:00 AM	Study of Text	Bill Smith	Billsmith@xyz.net
Tuesday 10:00 AM	Study of Text	Jane Martin	jhm@efg.org
Tuesday 11:00 AM	Word Studies	Jim Anderson	Janderson@hijk.com
Thursday 1:00 PM	Commentaries	Kathy Jones	Kjones@lmno.net
Thursday 2:00 PM	Commentaries	Bob Williams	bkw@pqr.org
Thursday 3:00 PM	Commentaries	Lori Davis	Loridavis@stu.com
Thursday 4:00 PM	Commentaries	Jeff Taylor	Jtaylor@vwx.net
Friday 8:00 AM	Study Significance	Sarah Miller	Millers12@abc.org
Friday 9:00 AM	Study Significance	Mike Brown	mkb@xyz.net
Friday 10:00 AM	Study Significance	Christy Harris	charris@efg.org
Friday 11:00 AM	Study Significance	Mark Moore	Mark374@hijk.com
Friday 1:00 PM	Craft Outline	Carol Garcia	ckg@lmno.net
Friday 2:00 PM	Craft Outline	Dan Robinson	Drobinson@abc.com
Friday 3:00 PM	Prepare Handouts	Barb Clark	barbc@xyz.net
Saturday 8:00 AM	Refine Content	Tony Lewis	Tklewis@pqr.org
Saturday 9:00 AM	Prep Illustrations	Betty Walker	Bwalker@vwx.net
Saturday 10:00 AM	Intro & Conclusion	Greg Hall	ghall@stu.com

APPENDIX 3
PREACHING EVALUATION FORM

Speaker: _____ Evaluator: _____

Date: _____ Sermon Title: _____

Text: _____ Occasion: _____

Place: _____ Start Time: _____

End Time: _____ Total Time: _____

CONTENT OF THE MESSAGE

Introduction

Did it grab my attention?	1	2	3	4	5	6	7	8	9	10
Did he give me a reason to listen?	1	2	3	4	5	6	7	8	9	10
Did he read the Scripture clearly?	1	2	3	4	5	6	7	8	9	10

The Preaching Point

Was a clear point to the message presented?	1	2	3	4	5	6	7	8	9	10
Was the point important?	1	2	3	4	5	6	7	8	9	10

The Body of the Message

What were the major points of the outline?

What illustrations were used?

How clear were the points? 1 2 3 4 5 6 7 8 9 10

Were the transitions smooth? 1 2 3 4 5 6 7 8 9 10

How well did he explain the points? 1 2 3 4 5 6 7 8 9 10

How well did he prove the points? 1 2 3 4 5 6 7 8 9 10

How well did he apply the points? 1 2 3 4 5 6 7 8 9 10

Was the application relevant? 1 2 3 4 5 6 7 8 9 10

Was the message tactful? 1 2 3 4 5 6 7 8 9 10

Was the message clearly rooted in Scripture? 1 2 3 4 5 6 7 8 9 10

Did the illustrations enhance the points? 1 2 3 4 5 6 7 8 9 10

Was the message interesting? 1 2 3 4 5 6 7 8 9 10

Were Christological truths clearly presented? 1 2 3 4 5 6 7 8 9 10

Conclusion

How well did he summarize the message? 1 2 3 4 5 6 7 8 9 10

How clearly did he restate the preaching point? 1 2 3 4 5 6 7 8 9 10

Did he end with a punch? 1 2 3 4 5 6 7 8 9 10

DELIVERY OF THE MESSAGE

Audience Response

How well did he relate to the audience? 1 2 3 4 5 6 7 8 9 10

Did he have the material mastered? 1 2 3 4 5 6 7 8 9 10

Did he stay in control? 1 2 3 4 5 6 7 8 9 10

Did he have thorough, well-balanced eye contact? 1 2 3 4 5 6 7 8 9 10

Voice Quality

How was the volume of his voice? 1 2 3 4 5 6 7 8 9 10

How well did he articulate his words? 1 2 3 4 5 6 7 8 9 10

How fluent was he? ("uhs," "ums") 1 2 3 4 5 6 7 8 9 10

Did he use effective inflections? | 1 | 2 | 3 | 4 | 5 | 6 | 7 | 8 | 9 | 10
Did he use a powerful vocabulary? | 1 | 2 | 3 | 4 | 5 | 6 | 7 | 8 | 9 | 10

Body Language

Did he have good gestures? | 1 | 2 | 3 | 4 | 5 | 6 | 7 | 8 | 9 | 10
How was his posture? | 1 | 2 | 3 | 4 | 5 | 6 | 7 | 8 | 9 | 10
Was he animated? | 1 | 2 | 3 | 4 | 5 | 6 | 7 | 8 | 9 | 10

COMMENTS

How effective do you think this sermon will be at prompting people to become doers of the Word?

What were the most effective or "life-changing" aspects of this message?

How might this sermon be improved?

ENDNOTES

INTRODUCTION

1 This phrase is attributed to Christ in fourteen passages in the New Testament: Matthew 11:15; 13:9; 13:43; Mark 4:9; 4:23; Luke 8:8; 14:35; Revelation 2:7; 2:11; 2:17; 2:29; 3:6; 3:13; 3:22.

2 This one, among many examples of Jesus' expectation that His listeners put His words into practice. See Matthew 7:21; 12:50; Luke 10:37; Luke 11:28; John 13:17.

3 A. W. Tozer, *The Best of A. W. Tozer,* comp. Warren W. Wiersbe (Grand Rapids: Baker Book House, 1978), 140–41.

4 A 1999 Gallup poll reveals that "In a typical week during 1998, two in five adults (40 percent) attended church or synagogue, a figure that has remained remarkably consistent since the early 1960s." George Gallup, Jr. and D. Michael Lindsay, *Surveying the Religious Landscape: Trends in US Beliefs* (Harrisburg, Pa.: Morehouse Publishing, 1999), 14.

5 107 *Barna Research Group. "Christians Are More Likely to Experience Divorce Than Are Non-Christians." http://www.barna.org/cgi-bin/PagePressRelease.asp?PressReleaseID=39 (15 Jul. 2001).*

6 108 *Glen T. Stanton. Focus on the Family. "Divorce: Bible-Belt Style" http://www.family.org/cforum/citizenmag/coverstory/a0011624.html (23 Jul. 2001)*

7 *The Alan Guttmacher Institute. "Abortion Common Among All Women." www.agi-usa.org/pubs/archives/prabort2.html (18 Jul. 2001)*

8 *Focus on the Family. "Zogby Survey Reveals a Growing Percentage of Those Seeking Sexual Fulfillment on the Internet." http://www.pureintimacy.org/news/a0000031.html (19 Jul.2001)*

9 J. I. Packer in Dick Lucas, et. al. *Preaching the Living Word: Addresses from the Evangelical Ministry Assembly* (Great Britain: Christian Focus Publications, 1999), 31.

10 John A. Broadus, *On the Preparation and Delivery of Sermons,* 4th ed., revised by Vernon L. Stanfield (San Francisco: HarperCollins Publishers, 1979), 165.

11 Ibid.

12 Packer in Lucas, 31

13 Bryan Chapell, *Christ-centered Preaching* (Grand Rapids: Baker Books, 1994), p.45.

14 Several good books give a complete step-by-step overview of sermon construction. For example, see Haddon Robinson, *Biblical Preaching: The Development and Delivery of Expository Messages, Second Edition* (Grand Rapids: Baker Book House, 2001); Bryan Chapell, *Christ-centered Preaching: Redeeming the Expository Sermon* (Grand Rapids: Baker Books, 1994).

15 Robinson, *Biblical Preaching,* 89. Walt Kaiser adds, "The jump from the 'then' of the original text to the 'now' of the modern audience has received so little attention in our evangelical training centers and pulpit practice that our best efforts are being crippled" (Walter C. Kaiser, Jr., *Toward an Exegetical Theology: Biblical Exegesis for Preaching and Teaching* [Grand Rapids: Baker Book House, 1981], 202.) Kaiser

revealed his concerns regarding the pastor's lack of preparedness for true preaching at the outset of his work in stating, "a gap of crisis proportions exists between the steps generally outlined in most seminary or biblical training classes in exegesis and the hard realities most pastors face every week as they prepare their sermons. Nowhere in the total curriculum of theological studies has the student been more deserted and left to his own devices than in bridging the yawning chasm between understanding the content of Scripture as it was given in the past and proclaiming it with such relevance in the present as to produce faith, life, and bona fide works" (ibid, 18). McQuilkin agrees: "At that most crucial point of all biblical studies, what God intends us to *be* and *do*, we stammer and improvise and go astray. We train theology students in criticism, exegesis, doctrine, and methods of preaching and counseling but offer few if any ways for them to know with certainty to whom any specific passage is addressed and to tell their people with authority what God intends them to be and do. That is the root cause of the yawning gap between classroom exegesis and pulpit proclamation" (J. Robertson McQuilkin as cited by Daniel J. Estes, "Audience Analysis and Validity in Application" *Bibliotheca Sacra* 150, no. 598 [April 1993]: 221).

16 William W. Klein, Craig L. Blomberg and Robert L. Hubbard, *Introduction to Biblical Interpretation* (Dallas: Word Publishing, 1993), 403.

CHAPTER 1 UNDERSTAND THE LIFE-CHANGING POWER OF PREACHING

1 Doug Murren, *Baby Boomerang: Catching the Boomer Generation as They Return to Church* (Ventura, Calif.: Gospel Light Publications, 1990), 103.

2 J. I. Packer, *The Preacher and Preaching: Reviving the Art in the Twentieth Century,* ed. Samuel T. Logan (Phillipsburg, N.J.: Presbyterian & Reformed, 1986), 17.

3 D. A. Carson in *The Primacy of Expository Preaching* at The Bethlehem Conference (Trenton, Mich.: Christway Media, 1995), cassette TPLAC001.

4 Edwin Charles Dargan, *A History of Preaching* (Grand Rapids: Baker Book House 1954; reprint), 13.

5 David Eby in his book *Power Preaching for Church Growth: The Role of Preaching in Growing Churches* (Ross-shire, Great Britain: Christian Focus Publications, 1996) does an excellent job demonstrating the connection between preaching and dynamism in the ancient and modern church.

6 William E. Sangster, *The Craft of Sermon Construction* (reprint, Grand Rapids: Baker Book House, 1972), 187.

7 Ibid., 25–26.

8 Kittle's *Theological Dictionary of the New Testament* (Grand Rapids: Eerdmans, 1964) identifies over 30 illustrative words, as does Colin Brown's *New International Dictionary of New Testament Theology* (Grand Rapids: Zondervan, 1967) under various headings.

9 The verb *kerysso* is used 61 times in the Greek New Testament.

10 The cognate *keryx* is used three times in the New Testament (1 Tim. 2:7; 2 Tim. 1:11; 2 Pet. 2:5) to describe the preacher himself as God's royal representative.

11 *Euangelizo* occurs 54 times in the Greek New Testament.

12 *Katangello* occurs 18 times in the Greek New Testament.

13 *Anangello* occurs 14 times in the Greek New Testament.

14 For a helpful catalog of the most descriptive Old and New Testament terms translated "preaching" and "preachers," see tables 4.1 and 4.2 found in Bryan Chapell's *Christ-centered Preaching* (Grand Rapids: Baker Books, 1994), 89–91.

15 Kittel, Gerhard; Friedrich, Gerhard, *The Theological Dictionary of the New Testament* (Grand Rapids: Eerdmans Publishing Company, 1964) 2:474.

16 Walter Bauer, Wilber F. Gingrich and Frederick W. Danker, *A Greek-English Lexicon of the New Testament and Other Early Christian Literature* (Chicago: University of Chicago Press, 1979), 303.

CHAPTER 2 ADOPT A LIFE-CHANGING METHOD OF PREACHING

1 Carson, *Primacy of Expository Preaching*, cassette.

2 John Calvin as cited by Graham Miller in *Calvin's Wisdom* (Carlisle, Pa.: The Banner of Truth Trust, 1992), 252.

3 Dietrich Bonhoeffer, *Worldly Preaching: Lectures on Homiletics,* trans. Clyde E. Fant (Nashville: Thomas Nelson, 1975), 145.

4 James Heflin demonstrates the diversity of opinion regarding the definition of expository preaching in his helpful summary of popular homileticians in *Old Wine in New Wineskins: Doctrinal Preaching in a Changing World,* co-authored by Millard Erickson (Grand Rapids: Baker Books, 1997), 167–82.

5 This is admittedly a minimal definition of expository preaching but it serves the purpose and emphasis of this present work. For other, more comprehensive, definitions of expository preaching see Haddon Robinson's frequently used offering in *Biblical Preaching,* 19–29. Also of help is Bryan Chapell's discussion on expository elements in *Christ-centered Preaching*, 22–25; 35–94. Richard L. Mayhue provides a concise definition of what "expository preaching" is and *is not* in his introductory article in John MacArthur, Jr.'s, *Rediscovering Expository Preaching* (Dallas: Word, 1992), 9–14. Also see Haddon Robinson, "What Is Expository Preaching?" *Bibliotheca Sacra* 131, no. 521 (January-March 1974): 55–60.

6 Sidney Greidanus, *The Modern Preacher and the Ancient Text* (Grand Rapids: Eerdmans Publishing Company, 1988), 13.

7 This is not to say that with additional work other approaches cannot be truly expository. See Irvin A. Busenitz, "Must Expository Preaching Always Be Book Studies? Some Alternatives" *Master's Seminary Journal* vol. 2, no. 2 (Fall 1991): 140–57.

8 Jay Adams, *Preaching with Purpose: The Urgent Task of Homiletics* (Grand Rapids: Zondervan, 1982), 16.

9 For more on the importance of the relationship between exegesis and sermon construction see "Homiletics and Hermeneutics" in *Making a Difference in Preaching,* ed. Scott M. Gibson (Grand Rapids: Baker Books, 1999), 69–84.

10 An excellent resource listing classic interpretive tools for the serious student of Scripture is found in the annotated bibliography of William Klein, Craig Blomber and Robert Hubbard Jr.'s *Introduction to Biblical Interpretation* (Dallas: Word Publishing, 1993), 459–491. Bryan Chapell provides a similar resource in Appendix 9 of his *Christ-centered Preaching*, 351–358. Chapell's list is presented with a concise set of abbreviations to indicate the works' theological stance and technical level.

11 Helpful books that can equip the preacher in this area include William Klein, Craig Blomberg and Robert Hubbard Jr., *Introduction to Biblical Interpretation* (Dallas: Word Publishing, 1993); Grant Osborne, *The Hermeneutical Spiral: A*

Comprehensive Introduction to Biblical Interpretation (Downers Grove: InterVarsity Press, 1991); Walter C. Kaiser and Moises Silva, *An Introduction to Biblical Hermeneutics: The Search for Meaning* (Grand Rapids: Zondervan, 1993); Walter C. Kaiser, Jr., *Toward an Exegetical Theology: Biblical Exegesis for Preaching and Teaching* (Grand Rapids: Baker Book House, 1981); Henry Virkler, *Hermeneutics: Principles and Processes of Interpretation* (Grand Rapids: Baker Book House, 1981); Bernard Ramm, *Protestant Biblical Interpretation: A Textbook of Hermeneutics* 3rd ed. (Grand Rapids: Baker Book House, 1970); Terry S. Milton, *Biblical Hermeneutics* (Grand Rapids: Zondervan, 1974); Gerald Bray, *Biblical Interpretation: Past & Present* (Downers Grove: InterVarsity, 1996); Willem A. VanGemeren ed., *A Guide to Old Testament Theology and Exegesis* (Grand Rapids: Zondervan Publishing House, 1999); Robert B. Chisholm, Jr. *From Exegesis to Exposition: A Practical Guide to Using Biblical Hebrew* (Grand Rapids: Baker Books, 1998).

12 Joseph Parker as cited by Ramm, xiv.

13 Timothy S. Warren, "A Paradigm for Preaching," *Bibliotheca Sacra* 148 (October-December 1991): 473.

14 Sidney Greidanus, *The Modern Preacher and the Ancient Text: Interpreting and Preaching Biblical Literature* (Grand Rapids: Eerdmans, 1988), 308.

15 Edwin Dargan's *A History of Preaching,* 2 vols. (Grand Rapids: Baker Book House, 1954) traces the decline of preaching during this period. The chapter titles describing this period are indicative of his detailed descriptions: "The Decline of Preaching in the Fifth and Sixth Centuries," "The Low Estate of Preaching in the Seventh and Eight Centuries," "Voices in the Night, or Preaching During the Ninth, Tenth and Eleventh Centuries," etc. I am also indebted to the insights of Jay Adams' lecture series, which included a survey of the "Historic Decline of Preaching" during the scholastic period (Westminster Theological Seminary in California lecture notes, January 1998).

16 A. Vos, "Scholasticism," in Sinclair B. Ferguson and David F. Wright, eds. *New Dictionary of Theology* (Downers Grove: InterVarsity Press, 2000), 622.

17 Dargan, vol. 1, 232.

18 Dargan is careful to point out exceptions like Gisbert Voetius who were "scholastic in type and uncompromising in spirit . . . along with his scholasticism and dogmatism he carried a very genuine piety." (Dargan, vol. 2, 79.)

CHAPTER 3 MAKE SURE YOUR LIFE IS CHANGING

1 Calvin Miller, *Market Place Preaching: How to Return the Sermon to Where it Belongs* (Grand Rapids: Baker Books, 1995), 7.

2 Richard Baxter, *The Reformed Pastor* (Edinburgh: Banner of Truth, 1974), 61.

3 Andrew Murray, *Humility* (New Kensington, Pa.: Whitaker House, 1982), 19.

4 Baxter, 53.

5 Benjamin Breckenridge Warfield as cited by David L. Larsen in *The Anatomy of Preaching* (Grand Rapids: Kregel, 1989), 86.

6 Erroll Hulse reflecting on Richard Baxter's description of the high call of preachers in Logan's *The Preacher and Preaching* (Phillipsburg, N.J.: Presbyterian and Reformed, 1986), 68.

7   Richard Newton as cited by E. M. Bounds, *Power Through Prayer* (Grand Rapids: Baker Book House, 1972), 38.

8   Robert Murray McCheyne, *Sermons of Robert Murray M'Cheyne* (Edinburgh: Banner of Truth Trust, 1991), backcover.

Chapter 4 Study Your Passage and Your Audience with Life-change in Mind

1   The importance of the distinction between the work of hermeneutics and the work of application is understood in this statement. The order is also of importance. There is no attempt to blur the lines between the two endeavors. With some rightly concerned about subjective, applicationally driven exegesis and the redefining of hermeneutics (see Brian A. Shealy, "Redrawing the Line Between Hermeneutics and Application" *Master's Seminary Journal* vol. 8 no. 1 [Spring 1997]: 83–107), it is important to note that I endorse the clear distinction, yet understand that application must closely follow on the heels of the work of hermeneutics. Application is the God-ordained extension of hermeneutical work, and many hermeneutic principles and skills will be needed to accurately decipher the applicational intent, the parameters, extent, and transferability of the application of a given passage.

2   The terms "meaning" and "significance" are used by several hermeneutical authors and were popularized by E. D. Hirsch, Jr. in *Validity in Interpretation* (New Haven: Yale University Press, 1967). Though some object to Hirsch's shifting definitions in his *Aims of Application* (Chicago: University of Chicago Press, 1976), I intend to use these terms with the controlling belief that Scripture's unchanging and authoritative meaning is not subject to one's personal perspective or opinion, and that a passage's application is manifold within the parameters of, and as governed by, the interpretation rightly arrived at through the work of exegesis.

3   W. James S. Farris, as cited by Timothy S. Warren, "The Theological Process in Sermon Preparation" *Bibliotheca Sacra* 156, no. 623 (July-September, 1999): 339. This "bridge building" concept is also the idea behind the title of R. W. Stott's homiletical work *Between Two Worlds* (Grand Rapids: Eerdmans, 1982).

4   Harry Emerson Fosdick, "What Is the Matter with Preaching" *Harper's Magazine* 157:2 (July 1928), 135.

5   Douglas Webster summarizes the features of the kind of "liberalism" to which I am referring, by stating: "The 'essence of Christianity' [i.e., our subjective experiences] replaces the authority of Scripture" (Walter A. Elwell, ed., *Evangelical Dictionary of Theology* [Grand Rapids: Baker Books, 1984], 632.). Refer to the classic work by J. Greham Machen, *Liberalism and Christianity* (Grand Rapids: Eerdmans, 1923); see also: William Hordern, *A Layman's Guide to Protestant Theology—Revised Edition* (New York: MacMillan, 1968). For its residual effect on expository preaching see John MacArthur, Jr., "The Mandate of Biblical Inerrancy: Expository Preaching" in *Rediscovering Expository Preaching* (Dallas: Word, 1992), 22–35.

6   Stephen Neil as cited by D. A. Carson, *To Wound and to Heal: Preaching to Real People* (Trenton, Mich.: Christway Media, 1995), TPLDAC 003, audiotape.

7   John F. Bettler in Samuel T. Logan ed., *The Preacher and Preaching* (Phillipsburg, N.J.: Presbyterian and Reformed, 1986), 338. This is also the premise of Jay Adams' approach in his book *Preaching with Purpose* (Grand Rapids: Zondervan, 1982).

8   Haddon Robinson, "The Heresy of Application" *Leadership Journal* vol. 18, no. 4 (Fall 1997), 21.

9   See J. W. Sire, *Scripture Twisting: Twenty Ways the Cults Misread the Bible* (Downers Grove: InterVarsity, 1980).

10 See Sidney Greidanus' list of "Improper Ways of Bridging the Gap" between the "then" and "now" which each demonstrate a kind of preaching that does something less than remain faithful to the original intent of the passage being preached, in *The Modern Preacher and the Ancient Text* (Grand Rapids: Eerdmans, 1988), 159–66.

11 Note that on occasion, participles and infinitives will carry an imperatival force in the New Testament. See Daniel B. Wallace, *Greek Grammar Beyond the Basics: An Exegetical Syntax of the New Testament* (Grand Rapids: Zondervan, 1996), 608, 650–52

12 Other and more extensive offerings that seek to guide the "transferability" of application can be found in William W. Klein, et al. *Introduction to Biblical Interpretation* (Dallas: Word Publishing, 1993), 409–21; J. Robertson McQuilkin, "Problems of Normativeness in Scripture: Cultural Verses Permanent" in Earl D. Radmacher and R. D. Preus et al., eds., *Hermeneutics, Inerrancy, and the Bible* (Grand Rapids: Zondervan, 1994), 222–40.

13 Haddon Robinson, "The Heresy of Application," 25.

14 Chapell, 40–44; 263–67.

15 Robinson, 24.

16 The most important remedy to every aspect of our depravity (i.e., Christ's work on our behalf) must flavor every sermon, not only in evangelism, but in the weekly preaching to redeemed men and women. Much more on this in chapter 9.

17 Klein, 417.

18 With these words Jesus shows us that polygamy was not God's design, though the ramifications of it were tolerated with askance in the Mosaic Law. As R. C. Ortlund, Jr. writes, "[Lamech's polygamy] in striking contrast with the tender monogamy of Eden, casts a shadow upon all subsequent polygamy as having arisen not from God's original design but when the race was tumbling from one level of ignominy to the next." T. Desmond Alexander et al., eds., "Marriage": *New Dictionary of Biblical Theology* (Downers Grove: InterVarsity Press, 2000). Also see Walt Kaiser, Jr., *Toward Old Testament Ethics* (Grand Rapids: Zondervan, 1983), 182–90.

19 Some staunch advocates of a misinformed brand of expository preaching have seen this aspect of preparation as unnecessary or, at best, unimportant. But it will in fact prove to be a key to ensuring that biblical preaching changes lives. As William MacGregor wrote, "It is a teacher's maxim that if with success you are to teach Tommy Latin you must not only know some Latin you must know Tommy.... And here we run at once upon a common obstacle, for many candidates for the ministry are little concerned deeply to know their people." MacGregor, *The Making of a Preacher* (Philadelphia: The Westminster Press, 1946), 50. Calvin Miller adds that effective preachers "must plunge fearlessly into both worlds—ancient and modern, the biblical and the contemporary—and listen to both." Miller, *Marketplace Preaching* (Grand Rapids: Baker Books, 1995), 133.

20 Ramesh P. Richard suggests a more involved analysis in "Methodological Proposals for Scripture Relevance, Part 3: Application Theory in Relation to the New Testament" *Bibliotheca Sacra* 143, no. 571 (July 1998): 206–18.

21 Pitt-Watson as cited by Greidanus, 184–185.

CHAPTER 5 FRAME AN OUTLINE THAT WILL CHANGE YOUR AUDIENCE

1 While David Buttrick, Harold Freeman, Eugene Lowry, Fred Craddock, Thomas Long, David Larsen, Don Wardlaw and many others have written much about the

modern emergence of narrative preaching and its move from "points" to "scenes" or "movements," it is important to note that the highpoints of any truly biblical sermon should emerge as applicational statements. While I recognize that certain homiletical structures may vary from those presented in this chapter, I am hopeful that the guidelines presented in this chapter will help to safeguard any preaching form from missing the life-changing intention of all biblical proclamation.

2   Dr. A. W. Blackwood, "A Young Man at Worship," as cited by John A. Broadus, *On the Preparation and Delivery of Sermons* 4th ed. (San Francisco: Harper Collins Publishers, 1979), 59.

3   A surplus of these kinds of outlines can be found in the 31-volume *Preacher's Homiletic Commentary* (reprint, Grand Rapids: Baker Books, 1996), and the 23-volume *Pulpit Commentary* (reprint, Peabody, Mass.: Hendrickson Publishers, 1985). The present and almost uniform pattern of this kind of outlining can be found in abundance on websites which post outlines from hundreds of different pastors such as *www.sermoncentral.com.*

4   Greidanus, 157.

5   Similarly, William Perkins, in his 1592 primer on preaching, described preaching as: "1. Reading the text clearly from the canonical Scriptures. 2. Explaining the meaning of it, once it has been read, in the light of the Scriptures themselves. 3. Gathering a few profitable points of doctrine from the natural sense of the passage. 4. If the preacher is suitably gifted, applying the doctrines thus explained to the life and practice of the congregation in straightforward, plain speech." *The Art of Prophesying* (reprint, Edinburgh: The Banner of Truth Trust, 1996), 79.

6   Allen C. Guelzo, "When Sermons Reigned," *The American Puritans: Christian History, Issue 41,* 1994, 23–25.

7   Jay Adams, *Truth Applied* (Grand Rapids: Zondervan, 1990), 85.

8   Jay Adams, *Preaching with Purpose,* 54.

9   Adams, 56–57.

10 Bryan Chapell, *Christ-centered Preaching,* 203.

11 Broadus, 45–48.

12 Robinson, *Biblical Preaching,* 37–44.

13 Adams, 21–33.

14 Robinson, 39–41.

15 Joseph M. Stowell III, in Keith Willhite et al., *The Big Idea of Biblical Preaching* (Grand Rapids: Baker Books, 1998), 141.

16 Broadus, 165.

17 Broadus, 59.

18 Martin Luther, as cited by Plass, 1114.

19 Richard Baxter, *The Reformed Pastor* (Edinburgh: Banner of Truth, 1974), 115.

20 Martin Luther was "a highly-trained academic" but insisted on appealing to the common people in the common language, in the most common of formats, and in simplistic terms. Perry Brown, "Preaching from the Print Shop: Martin Luther—The Early Years," *Christian History Magazine, Issue 34,* 1992, 34.

21 Guelzo, 24.

22 John MacArthur, Jr., "Question & Answer Session" at the *Preach the Word Conference* (Riverside, Calif.: Harvest Ministries, 1999), cassette SP994.

23 Adams, 82.

CHAPTER 6   PRAY, PRAY, PRAY FOR A SERMON THAT WILL CHANGES LIVES

1 Philip Schaff, *History of the Christian Church,* 2nd edition (Grand Rapids: Eerdmans Publishing Company, 1981), vol. 7, 111.

2 See Martin Luther's *Large Catechism,* Part 3, "Of Prayer."

3 Bounds, 38–39.

4 Martin Luther as cited in Ewald M. Plass, *What Luther Says* (St. Louis: Concordia Publishing House, 1959), 1117.

5 John Piper, *The Supremacy of God in Preaching* (Grand Rapids: Baker Book House, 1990), 60.

6 David L. Larsen, *The Anatomy of Preaching: Identifying the Issues in Preaching Today* (Grand Rapids: Kregel Publications, 1989), 53.

7 *Peter Wagner. PastorNet. "Pastors' Daily Prayer Habits." http://www.pastornet.net (17 June 2001).*

8 Mary Ann Jeffreys, "Colorful Saying of Colorful Luther," *Martin Luther The Early Years: Christian History, Issue 34,* 1992, 28.

9 See Jay Adams' "Distractions" in *A Consumer's Guide to Preaching* (Wheaton: Victor Books, 1991), 81–88.

10 Jeffreys, 28.

11 John Chrysostom as cited by Adams, 81.

12 Bounds, 40.

CHAPTER 7   COME TO GRIPS WITH THE TIME IT TAKES TO PREPARE
A LIFE-CHANGING SERMON

1 G. Campbell Morgan as cited by Richard L. Mayhue, "Rediscovering Expository Preaching" *The Master's Journal* vol. 1, no. 2 (Fall 1990), 111.

2 Bruce Thieleman as cited by Joseph Stowell, *Shepherding the Church Into the 21st Century* (Wheaton: Victor Books, 1994), 209.

3 John MacArthur, *Question & Answer Session* at the Preach the Word Conference (Riverside, Calif.: Harvest Ministries, 1999), cassette SP994.

4 John Calvin as cited by J. Graham Miller in *Calvin's Wisdom* (Carlisle, Pa.: The Banner of Truth, 1992), 256.

5 Dietrich Bonhoeffer suggested that a sermon should require twelve hours of preparation as a "good general rule," *Worldly Preaching: Lectures on Homiletics* (New York: Crossroad Publishing, 1991), 121.

6 Ibid.

7 Fred B. Craddock, *Preaching* (Nashville: Abingdon Press, 1985), 71.

8 MacArthur, *Question & Answer Session,* cassette.

9   A notable exception is a book written by a bi-vocational pastor that unfortunately is no longer in print: Mark Porter, *The Time of Your Life: How to Accomplish All that God Wants You to Do* (Wheaton: Victor Books, 1983).

10 Craddock, 71.

11 Charles Spurgeon as cited by Bonnie Wheeler, *The Hurrier I Go* (Ventura, Calif.: Regal Books, 1985), 169.

12 Carson, *The Primacy of Expository Preaching*, cassette.

13 Leonard A. Paris as cited in Porter, *Time of Your Life*, 144

14 Martin Luther as cited by Ewald M. Plass in *What Luther Says* (St. Louis: Concordia Publishing House, 1959), 1110.

15 Grant S. Osborn, *The Hermeneutical Spiral: A Comprehensive Introduction to Biblical Interpretation* (Downer's Grove: InterVarsity Press, 1981), 346–47.

16 Charles F. Kemp, *The Preaching Pastor* (St. Louis: The Bethany Press, 1966), 25–26.

17 Haddon Robinson, "What Authority Does a Preacher Have Anymore?" in Bill Hybles et al., *Mastering Contemporary Preaching* (Portland: Multnomah Press, 1989), 18–19.

18 *Geoffrey Godbey. The Academy of Leisure Sciences. "White Paper #8—The Problem of Free Time: It's Not What You Think." http://www.eas.ualberta.ca/elj/als/alswp8.html (17 July 2001).* Godbey writes: "A recent survey found that 47 percent of Americans thought their free time had decreased during the last five years, while only 22 percent reported more free time. Such beliefs, however, don't necessarily reflect what is actually happening in terms of how long we work during a week or the percentage of our lives given to work. In terms of hours worked per week, for example, the findings of the largest national time use studies show that Americans gained almost one hour per day of free time during the period of 1965 to 1985. American males average about 40 hours of free time per week while females average 39—hardly the workaholic country we envision."

19 *National PTA, "TV Violence . . . What the Surveys and Research Say." http://www.pta.org/programs/tvsurveys.htm (17 July 2001).*

20 This pertains to the growing number of people who have Internet access. *Harris Poll Library. "The Harris Poll #18." http://harrisinteractive.com (17 July 2001).*

21 See *Jim Spring. American Demographics. 15:50–53. http://www.halo.ee (17 July 2001).*

22 *Barna Research Group. "Lifestyle Activities" http://www.barna.org/cgi-bin/PageCategory.asp?CategoryID=26 (15 March 2002).*

23 New American Standard Bible (LaHabra, Calif.: The Lockman Foundation, 1977).

24 Donald Guthrie, *The Pastoral Epistles* (London: Tyndale, 1969).

25 New Living Translation, (Wheaton: Tyndale, 1996).

26 This radio quotation from J. Vernon McGee was apparently his own restatement of George Whitfield's response to his concerned doctors: "I'd rather wear out than rust out" (Harry S. Stout, "Heavenly Comet" *Christian George Whitfield: History Magazine,* Issue 38, 1993).

CHAPTER 8   REALIZE THEY WON'T CHANGE WHAT THEY DON'T HEAR AND UNDERSTAND

1   Webb B. Garrison, *The Preacher and His Audience* (Westwood, N.J.: Fleming H. Revell Company, 1954), 64.

2 Bill Hybels, "How to Improve Your Preaching" workshop, *Preaching Today* (Carol Stream, Ill.: Christianity Today, Inc.) cassette tape #202.

3 Mark Galli and Craig Brian Larson, *Preaching that Connects* (Grand Rapids: Zondervan, 1994), 35.

4 Jay Adams refers to this as "occasional preaching." See *Truth Applied,* 67–70.

5 Adams, *Preaching with Purpose*, 65.

6 Robinson, *Biblical Preaching,* 167.

7 Attributed to a variety of preachers and professors. Cited by Haddon Robinson at the Hester Lectures on Preaching (February 27, 1997), Kansas City, Mo.

8 Webster's Encyclopedic Unabridged Dictionary of the English Language, (New York: Random House, 1996), 649.

9 Ibid.

10 Martin Lloyd-Jones, *Preaching and Preachers* (Grand Rapids: Zondervan, 1971), 87.

11 Spurgeon once commented, "To stand and drone out a sermon in a kind of articulate snoring to people who are somewhere between awake and asleep must be wretched work." As cited by Calvin Miller in *Marketplace Preaching,* 13.

12 William Carey as cited by J. D. Douglas and Philip W. Comfort, eds., *Who's Who in Christian History* (Wheaton: Tyndale House Publishers, 1992), 138.

13 J. I. Packer in Dick Lucas, et al., *Preaching the Living Word: Addresses from the Evangelical Ministry Assembly* (Geanies House, Great Britain: Christian Focus Publications, 1999), 32–33.

14 Dietrich Bonhoeffer, translated by Clyde E. Fant, *Worldly Preaching: Lectures on Homiletics* (New York: Crossroad Publishing, 1991), backcover.

15 Richard Baxter, *The Reformed Pastor* (Edinburgh: Banner of Truth, 1974), 121.

16 Robinson, *Biblical Preaching,* 83.

17 Ibid.

18 Gallop polls show people's shift from a high view of Scripture when asked about Americans' confidence in the Bible. The admittedly poor wording of the question "Do you agree that the Bible is the actual word of God and is to be taken literally, word for word?" still reflects a layman's rejection of a belief that the Bible is to be believed as true and authoritative: In 1980, 40 percent agreed; in 1993, 35 percent agreed; in 1998 only 33 percent agreed. Source: George Gallup, Jr. and D. Michael Lindsay, *Surveying the Religious Landscape: Trends in U.S. Beliefs* (Harrisburg, Pa.: Morehouse Publishing, 1999), 35.

19 Miller, *Marketplace Preaching,* 113.

20 Stuart Briscoe, "The Subtle Temptations of Preaching" in Bill Hybles, et al., *Mastering Contemporary Preaching*, 142–51.

21 An entry recorded by Haddon Robinson in his diary at the age of fourteen after hearing Dr. Harry Ironside of the Moody Memorial Church preach as a guest at the First Baptist Church of New York, *Art of the Sermon* produced by John Koessler (Chicago: Moody Bible Institute, 1999), videocassette.

CHAPTER 9   KEEP THE LIFE-CHANGER AT THE CENTER OF YOUR SERMON

1 For a helpful discussion on implications of the modern shift to a man-centered gospel and man-centered evangelism see Will Metzger, *Tell the Truth: The Whole*

Gospel to the Whole Person by Whole People (Downers Grove: InterVarsity Press, 1984) and Walter Chantry, *Today's Gospel: Authentic or Synthetic?* (Carlisle, Pa.: Banner of Truth, 1970).

2 Greidanus, *The Modern Preacher and the Ancient Text,* 163–66.

3 John 13:31–32 concisely describes the Father's intent at and beyond the Cross, "Now the Son of Man is glorified and God is glorified in Him. If God is glorified in Him, God will also glorify Him in Himself, and glorify Him at once."

4 As to the Holy Spirit's glorification of Christ see also 1 Corinthians 12:3; 1 Peter 1:10–12; John 16:7–10; 1 John 5:6.

5 Karl Dijk as cited in Graeme Goldworthy, *Preaching the Whole Bible as Christian Scripture* (Grand Rapids: Eerdmans, 2000), 3.

6 Adams, *Preaching with Purpose,* 147.

7 Dr. John Redman (December 2, 1990) Anaheim, Calif.

8 Charles Haddon Spurgeon, *Lectures to My Students,* 79.

9 Sidney Greidanus, "Preaching from Paul Today" in Gerald F. Hawthorne, Ralph P. Martin, and Daniel G. Reid, eds., *Dictionary of Paul and His Letters* (Downer's Grove: InterVarsity Press, 1993).

10 Carson, *The Primacy of Expository Preaching*, cassette.

11 Edmund P. Clowney, "Preaching Christ from All the Scriptures" in Samuel T. Logan, Jr., ed., *The Preacher and Preaching* (Phillipsburg, N.J.: Presbyterian and Reformed, 1986), 191.

12 See Sidney Greidanus, *Preaching Christ from the Old Testament* (Grand Rapids: Eerdmans, 1999); Graeme Goldsworthy, *Preaching the Whole Bible as Christian Scripture* (Grand Rapids: Eerdmans, 2000); Walter C. Kaiser, *Toward Rediscovering the Old Testament* (Grand Rapids: Zondervan, 1995) and *The Messiah in the Old Testament* (Grand Rapids: Zondervan, 1994); Edmund P. Clowney, *The Unfolding Mystery: Discovering Christ in the Old Testament* (Phillipsburg, N.J.: Presbyterian & Reformed, 1988).

13 Goldworthy, xii.

14 Greidanus, 168.

15 Clowney, 165.

16 Greidanus writes: "Even the most generous reviewers will admit that Spurgeon makes many errors in his interpretation of Scripture." *Preaching Christ,* 160.

17 In a dissertation entitled, *Charles Haddon Spurgeon's Christological Homiletics: A Critical Evaluation of Selected Sermons from Old Testament Texts,* John David Talbert notes of the 532 Old Testament sermons he examined almost 70 percent were preached from one verse or only part of one verse. Greidanus, 161.

18 Compare Spurgeon's sermon no. 2627 "The Best Friend" (February 23, 1882), in Spurgeon's Sermons volume 45: *The Metropolitan Tabernacle Pulpit* (Albany, Ore.: Ages Software, 1998).

19 Chapell, *Christ-centered Preaching,* 271.

20 The phrase *"en Christo,"* occurs 70 times in Paul's epistles. See N. T. Wright's article "Paul" in Ferguson et al., eds., *The New Dictionary of Theology.*

21 Adams, 152.

22 Church growth seminars frequently contend that "people don't want to go to a place that reminds them how bad they are." They warn preachers that "negative preaching attracts negative people who like to be spiritually spanked." The remedy we are often told is to "keep the messages light" and "make sure the sermons remain positive." While at times the charge is rightly leveled that some preachers are long on diagnosis and short on cure, the analogy follows that the cure is irrelevant to the patient if the disease is never convincingly diagnosed.

23 Chapell, 267.

24 Robinson, "The Heresy of Application" 24.

25 See Bryan Chapell's description of "inner-canonical" roads which display Christ's redemptive work in "Expounding the Redemptive Message" in *Christ-centered Preaching,* 272–80.

26 Chapell, 275.

27 Goldworthy, 113.

28 Adams, 147.

28 Chapell, 281.

CHAPTER 10 PREACH CHANGE WITH AUTHORITY

1 Though there is still much debate as to the use of the terms modern and postmodern, most will agree that there has been such a significant epistemological shift in our times that has made biblical preaching an increasingly greater challenge. A number of books have attempted to identify the shifts that have taken place in recent decades: Millard Erickson, *Postmodernizing the Faith: Evangelical Responses to the Challenge of Postmodernism* (Grand Rapids: Baker Books, 1998); D. A. Carson, *The Gagging of God: Christianity Confronts Pluralism.* (Grand Rapids: Zondervan, 1996); David F. Wells, *No Place for Truth: Or Whatever Happened to Evangelical Theology?* (Grand Rapids: Eerdmans, 1993); Gene Edward Veith, Jr., *Postmodern Times: A Christian Guide to Contemporary Thought and Culture.* (Wheaton: Crossway Books, 1994), etc.

2 John Calvin as cited by Graham Miller in *Calvin's Wisdom,* 252.

3 Carson, *The Gagging of God*, 39–40.

4 Carson, *The Primacy of Expository Preaching*, cassette.

5 J. I. Packer, "Some Perspectives on Preaching," Dick Lucas et al., *Preaching the Living Word*, 41.

6 Charles Haddon Spurgeon as cited by Miller in *Marketplace Preaching,* 13.

7 Packer, 31.

8 Haddon Robinson, "What Authority Do We Have Anymore?" *Leadership Journal* 13:2 (Spring 1992): 28.

9 Packer, 32.

10 *William Ernest Henley. "Invictus." www.constitution.org/col/invictus.htm (15 March 2002).*

11 Stott, *Between Two Worlds,* 51.

12 George Barna, *What Americans Believe: An Annual Survey of Values and Religious Views in the United States* (Ventura, Calif.: Regal Books, 1991), 83.

13 George Gallop, Jr., *Surveying the Religious Landscape,* 23.

14 Barna, 201.

15 This has recently been called into question on a popular level by well-known evangelists and prominent pastors. Many works have been written to attempt to specifically address this issue, which include: Ronald Nash, *Is Jesus the Only Savior?* (Grand Rapids: Zondervan, 1994); Paul House and Gregory Thornbury, *Who Will Be Saved? Defending the Biblical Understanding of God, Salvation, & Evangelism* (Wheaton: Crossway, 2000); D. Clendenin, *Many Gods, Many Lords: Christianity Encounters World Religions* (Grand Rapids: Baker Books, 1996); Ravi Zacharias, *Jesus Among Other Gods: The Absolute Claims of the Christian Message* (Nashville: Word, 2000); N. Anderson, *Christianity & World Religions: The Challenge of Pluralism* (Downers Grove: InterVarsity, 1984).

16 Carson, *The Primacy of Expository Preaching*, cassette.

17 Francis J. Beckwith and Gregory Koukl, *Relativism: Feet Firmly Planted in Mid-air.* (Grand Rapids: Baker Books, 1998), 143.

18 Beckwith, 146.

19 G. K. Chesterton as cited by James S. Stewart, *Heralds of God: The Warrack Lectures* (London: Hodder & Stoughton, 1946), 210.

20 Stewart, 212.

21 Greidanus, *The Modern Preacher and the Ancient Text,* 12.

22 Robert Schuller, *Your Church Has a Fantastic Future* (Ventura, Calif.: Regal Books, 1986), 317.

23 George Barna, *Frog in the Kettle* (Ventura, Calif.: Regal Books, 1990), 120.

24 John Charles Ryle, "Only One Way of Salvation" in David Otis Fuller ed., *Valiant for the Truth* (New York: McGraw-Hill, 1961), 371.

25 Robinson, "What Authority Do We Have Anymore?," 28.

26 A classic example of a widely misquoted statistic used in many pulpits is the oft quoted stat that "half of all marriages will end in divorce." This statistic is a distortion, based on the proportion of marriage licenses to divorce decrees granted in a given year. While it is true that there is approximately 1 divorce decree to every 2 marriage licenses issued each year in states like California, it does not follow that half of all marriages will end in divorce. If there are 100 people in a room and 10 people enter the room and 5 people exit it (2 to 1) we would not then conclude that half of the people in the room will end up leaving it. The actual percentage of marriages that will end in divorce is unknown and can only be speculated. Currently estimations range from 12 to 22 percent. See *J. Allen Peterson, Louis Harris, Jeanne Hinds, et al., "50 Percent Statistic Untrue?" http://www.patriot.net/~crouch/adr/50percent.html (1 June 2001).*

27 The differentiated levels of application are adapted from Haddon Robinson as referenced in *The Art of the Sermon*, videocassette.

CHAPTER 11 GIVE THEM MORE THAN THE BOTTOM LINE

1 It can be demonstrated that the common usage of the word "doctrine" today is more narrow than its biblical usage. The words *leqach, shemu'ah,* and *mucar* in the Old Testament, and *didaskalia* and *didache* in the New Testament (all of which are translated "doctrine" in various English translations) represent both abstract propositions

and practical directives. See James Orr, ed., *International Standard Bible Encyclopedia* (Albany, Ore.: Ages Software, Inc., 1999).

2   Upon reviewing the use of the phrase "doctrinal preaching" in a number of articles from respected theological journals, it can be seen that there is no clear consensus as to what is meant by the phrase. At times it is used by authors to represent a form of preaching that stands in contrast to emotionalism. At other times it is used as a synonym for biblical exposition. Still others use it to refer to the systematic or topical presentation of theological truths as a sermon's theme.

3   Lee Eclov, "The Danger of Practical Preaching" in *Preaching Today Journal* (Wheaton: Christianity Today, Inc., 2001), website: www.preachingtoday.com.

4   C. I. Scofield, "Jesus as a Preacher," *Bibliotheca Sacra* vol. 100, no. 400 (October 1943), 549.

5   See Millard Erickson's "The Value and Benefit of Doctrine" in *Old Wine in New Wineskins: Doctrinal Preaching in a Changing World,* 20–38.

6   L. R. Scarbourough as quoted by Henry C. Thessien in his review of *Products of Pentecost* in *Bibliotheca Sacra* vol. 92, no. 365 (January 1935), 123.

7   See Keith Willhite's discussion regarding the bridge from exegetical to theological work, and from theological to homiletical work in *Preaching with Relevance without Dumbing Down* (Grand Rapids: Kregel, 2001), 61–65.

8   David F. Wells sketches the tension between the two models of education and ministry in his chapter, "The New Disablers" in *No Place for Truth; or, Whatever Happened to Evangelical Theology?* (Grand Rapids: Eerdmans, 1993), 218–57.

9   Ibid, 218.

10 See Timothy Warren, "The Theological Process in Sermon Preparation" *Bibliotheca Sacra* vol. 156, no. 623 (July-September, 1999), 336–56.

11 Lloyd-Jones, *Preaching and Preachers,* 137–38.

12 For the biblical concept of the "thinking heart" see Matthew 9:4, Acts 8:22; Matthew 12:34; etc. Also see "Heart" in Leland Ryken, et al., eds., *Dictionary of Biblical Imagery* (Downers Grove: InterVarsity, 1998), 368–69.

13 Charles H. Spurgeon, sermon no. 635, *Spurgeon's Sermons: Volume 11*, electronic ed., Logos Library System; Spurgeon's Sermons (Albany, Ore,: Ages Software, 1998).

CHAPTER 12   PREACH PERIODICALLY ABOUT LIFE-CHANGING PREACHING

1   The exceptions which have not received much attention are Jay Adams, *A Consumer's Guide to Preaching* (Wheaton: Victor Books, 1991); David J. Schlafer, *Surviving the Sermon: A Guide to Preaching for Those Who Have to Listen.* (Boston: Cowley Publications, 1992). A few works include a chapter or two that address this important issue: Richard L. Mayhue, ed., "The Listener's Responsibility" in *Rediscovering Expository Preaching,* (Dallas: Word Publishing, 1992); Richard Baxter, "Directions for Profitable Hearing The Word Preached," *A Christian Directory,* reprint (Morgan, Pa.: Soli Deo Gloria Publications, 1996); Christopher Love, "The Right Hearing of Sermons" in *The Mortified Christian,* reprint (Morgan, Pa.: Soli Deo Gloria Publications, 1998).

2   Note the second person, plural, present, active, imperative of *akouo.*

3   Richard Baxter, *A Christian Director, Volume 1,* (1846; reprint, Morgan, Pa.: Soli Deo Gloria Publications, 1996), 473.

4   John Stott, *Between Two Worlds* (Grand Rapids: Eerdmans, 1982), 113.

5   Ibid.

6   F. W. Boreham, *Faces in the Fire* (New York: Abingdon, 1919), 22 as cited by Jay Adams in *A Consumer's Guide to Preaching* (Wheaton: Victor Books, 1991), 42.

7   This data was compiled as a result of multiple surveys and interviews with 235 church attendees.

8   Charles H. Spurgeon as cited by Tom Carter in *Spurgeon at His Best* (Grand Rapids: Baker Books, 1988), 158.

9   Richard Baxter, "Directions for Profitable Hearing The Word Preached," *A Christian Directory.* (Morgan, Pa.: Soli Deo Gloria Publications, 1996), 472.

10   Spurgeon, sermon no. 420, *Spurgeon's Sermons: Volume 7*, electronic ed.

11   Gardiner Spring, *A Plea to Pray for Pastors* (reprint, Hoschton, Ga.: Shiloh Publications, 2000), 3–4, 7–8.

12   Donald S. Whitney, *Spiritual Disciplines within the Church* (Chicago: Moody, 1996), 69.

13   See Adams' discussion in *A Consumer's Guide to Preaching*, chapter 4, "Your Basic Attitude," 31–37.

14   Ibid., 48.

15   Baxter, *Directory*, 475.

CHAPTER 13   CULTIVATE A CULTURE OF COMMITMENTS AND ACCOUNTABILITY

1   See Haddon Robinson's encouragement in this regard in "Competing with the Communication Kings" in *Making a Difference in Preaching* (Grand Rapids: Baker, 1999), 109–17.

2   See Phillips Brooks, "The Congregation" in *Lectures on Preaching* (New York: E. P. Dutton & Co, 1907), now reprinted and available under the title *The Joy of Preaching* (Grand Rapids: Kregel, 1989).

3   Brooks, *Lectures on Preaching*, 186–87.

4   See Jim Dethmer, "Why Emphasize Membership," *WillowCreek Magazine* (May/June 1991), 30; Dennis Beatty, *Why Should I Join a Church?* (Vineyard Press, 1981); Mark E. Dever, "Why We Disciplined Half of Our Church," *Leadership*, vol. 21, No. 4 (Fall, 2000) : 101–02; Brian Metke, "Sharper Definition," *Leadership*, vol. 21, No. 3 (Summer 2000) : 61–64.

5   See Donald Whitney, "Why Join a Church?" *Spiritual Disciplines Within the Church* (Chicago: Moody Press), 43–57.

6   Alexandar Staunch, "The Interdependence of Local Churches" *The Erasmus Journal*, vol. 6, no. 2 (Winter, 1997), 209.

7   J. Carl Laney, *A Guide to Church Discipline* (Minneapolis: Bethany House, 1985); John MacArthur, Jr., "Matthew 18:15–35" *Matthew 16–23* (Chicago: Moody, 1988); Hezekiah Harvey, "The Church: Its Discipline" *The Church: Its Polity and Ordinances* (Rochester: Backus Books, 1982); "The Tightrope: A Case Study in Church Discipline" *Leadership*, vol. 5, no. 3 (Summer, 1984), 40–48; Jay A. Quine, "Court Involvement in Church Discipline" *Bibliotheca Sacra* vol. 159, nos. 593 & 594 (Jan-Mar 1992; Apr.-Jun. 1992), 61–74; 224–37; Ted G. Kitchens, "Perimeters of Corrective Church Discipline" *Bibliotheca Sacra* vol. 148, no. 590 (Apr.-Jun., 1991),

202–14; Simon J. Kistemaker, "'Deliver This Man to Satan' (1 Cor. 5:5): A Case Study in Church Discipline" *Master's Seminary Journal,* vol. 3, no. 1 (Spring, 1992), 34–47; "'The Sinews of the Body of Christ' Calvin's Concept of Church Discipline" *Westminster Theological Journal,* vol. 59, no. 1 (Spring, 1997), 88–101.

8   C. H. Spurgeon in Tom Carter's *Spurgeon at his Best* (Grand Rapids: Baker, 1988), 160.

9   Joseph Stowell, in Keith Willhite's, *The Big Idea of Biblical Preaching* (Grand Rapids: Baker, 1998), 125.

10   Richard Baxter writes: We must... ever have our people's necessities before our eyes. To remember the 'one thing needful' will take us off gauds and needless ornaments, and unprofitable controversies... I confess I think NECESSITY should be the great disposer of a minister's course of study and labor... [L]ife is short, and we are dull, and eternal things are necessary, and the souls that depend on our teaching are precious. *The Reformed Pastor* (reprint, Carlisle, Pa.: Banner of Truth, 1997), 113.

CHAPTER 14   PROVIDE TOOLS TO HELP YOUR AUDIENCE MAKE SPECIFIC CHANGES

1   Arnell Motz, *Life-Changing Preaching* (unpublished WTSC D. Min. 1991), 150.

2   All statistics about the congregation to which I preach have been gathered through an anonymous survey of over one hundred congregants.

3   For an analysis of the regrettable trends away from reading in our video age, see Neil Postman's *Amusing Ourselves to Death* (New York: Viking Penguin, Inc., 1985).

4   A. W. Tozer, "The Use and Abuse of Books," *The Alliance Weekly* (February 22, 1956), as cited in J. Oswald Sander's *Spiritual Leadership* (Chicago: Moody Press, 1987), 150.

5   Any Christian book distributor can give you their guidelines for acquiring their services as a distributor for your church bookstore. Some of the larger distributors include Spring Arbor Distributors (LaVergne, Tenn.; www.springarbor.com) and Riverside Distributors (Iowa Falls, Ia.; www.riversideworld.com). Dealing directly with publishers is also a way to acquire desirable books for resale.

6   For information on tape duplication equipment, materials and strategies see Quentin Wagenfield, "Get the Word Out" *Your Church Magazine,* vol. 47, No. 6, *50* (Carol Stream, Ill.: Christianity Today, 2001).

7   John Weborg, "Reborn In Order to Renew," *Pietism: A Much-Maligned Movement Re-examined: Christian History, Issue 10,* (Carol Stream, Ill.: Christianity Today, 1997).

CHAPTER 15   PERSONALLY MODEL THE CHANGES FROM LAST WEEK'S SERMON

1   Haddon Robinson, "What Authority Do We Have Anymore?" *Leadership Journal,* vol. 13, no. 2 (Spring 1992), 27.

2   Howard Hendricks, *A Life of Integrity* (Sisters, Ore.: Multnomah Press, 1997), 196.

3   Warren Wiersbe, *The Integrity Crisis* (Nashville: Thomas Nelson, 1988), 17–18.

4   James S. Stewart, *Heralds of God* (London: Hodder & Stoughton, 1946), 190.

5   As cited by David Larsen in *The Anatomy of Preaching* (Grand Rapids: Kregel, 1989), 59.

6   Eugene Peterson, "How Pure Must a Pastor Be?" *Leadership,* vol. 9, no. 2 (Spring, 1988), 13.

7   Richard Baxter, *The Reformed Pastor,* (reprint, Carlisle, Pa.: Banner of Truth, 1997), 133.

8   Hendricks, 200.

9   An example cited by Craig Brian Larsen in "Gaining Respect the Old-Fashioned Way," *Leadership,* vol. 9, no. 2 (Spring, 1988), 121.

10 J. Oswald Sanders, *Spiritual Leadership,* revised edition, (Chicago: Moody Press, 1980), 101.

11 The Greek compound *Philo-xenos* (literally "love-strangers") calls for a tangible, brotherly love to be extended beyond one's inner circle. See *The Theological Dictionary of the New Testament*, vol. 5 (Grand Rapids: Eerdmans, 1964), 16–24.

12 See the Enrichment Journal (www.ag.org/enrichmentjournal) and "Pastor's Profile," *Pastors* on Barna Research Online (www.barna.org).

13 "Survey Provide Profile of Protestant Pastors," *Barna Research Online* Report, January 6, 1998, (www.barna.org).

14 For instance: Kevin Miller, *Secrets of Staying Power* (Waco, Tex.: Word, 1988); Gary D. Preston, *Character Forged from Conflict* (Minneapolis: Bethany House, 1999; Dean Merrill, *Clergy Couples in Crisis* (Waco, Tex.: Word, 1985); Stuart Briscoe, et al., *Measuring Up* (Sisters, Ore.: Multnomah Press, 1993); Marshall Shelly, *Well-Intentioned Dragons* (Minneapolis: Bethany House, 1985); Leith Anderson, et al., *Who's In Charge?* (Sisters, Ore.: Multnomah Press, 1993).

BIBLIOGRAPHY

Adams, Jay E. *A Consumer's Guide to Preaching*. Wheaton: Victor Books, 1991.

———. *How to Help People Change: The Four-Step Biblical Process*. Grand Rapids: Zondervan Publishing House, 1986.

———. *Preaching With Purpose: The Urgent Task of Homiletics*. Grand Rapids: Zondervan Publishing House, 1982.

———. *Truth Applied: Application in Preaching*. Grand Rapids: Zondervan Publishing House, 1990.

Barth, Karl. *Homiletics*. Translated by Geoffrey W. Bromiley and Donald E. Daniels. Louisville: Westminster/John Knox Press. 1991.

Baxter, Richard. "Directions for Profitable Hearing The Word Preached," *A Christian Directory, Volume 1*. 1846. Reprint, Morgan, PA: Soli Deo Gloria Publications, 1996.

———. *The Reformed Pastor*. Edinburgh: Banner of Truth, 1974.

Blackwood, Andrew Watterson. *The Preparation of Sermons*. New York: Abingdon Press, 1948.

Bonhoeffer, Dietrich. *Worldly Preaching: Lectures on Homiletics*. Translated by Clyde E. Fant. New York: Crossroad Publishing, 1991.

Bounds, E. M. *Power Through Prayer*. Grand Rapids: Baker Book House, 1972.

Broadus, John A. *On the Preparation and Delivery of Sermons*, fourth edition—revised by Vernon L. Stanfield. San Francisco: Harper Collins Publishers, 1979.

Brooks, Phillips. *The Joy of Preaching*. Grand Rapids: Kregel Publications, 1989.

———. *Lectures on Preaching: Delivered Before the Divinity School of Yale College*. New York: E. P. Dutton & Co., 1907.

Brown, Steve, Haddon Robinson and William Willimon. *A Voice in the Wilderness: Clear Preaching in a Complicated World*. Sisters, Ore.: Multnomah Press Books, 1993.

Carson, D. A. *The Gagging of God: Christianity Confronts Pluralism*. Grand Rapids: Zondervan, 1996.

Chapell, Bryan. *Christ-Centered Preaching: Redeeming the Expository Sermon*. Grand Rapids: Baker Books, 1994.

———. Haddon Robinson and Joseph Stowell. *Art of the Sermon*. Produced by John Koessler. Chicago: Moody Bible Institute, 1999. Videocassette.

Craddock, Fred B. *As One Without Authority*. Nashville: Abingdon Press, 1971.

———. *Overhearing the Gospel*. Nashville: Abingdon Press, 1978.

———. *Preaching*. Nashville: Abingdon Press, 1985.

Curtis, Gene E. "How to Teach People to Listen More Effectively to the Preaching or Teaching of God's Word." D.Min. project, Gordon-Conwell Theological Seminary, 1999.

Dargan, Edwin Charles. *A History of Preaching*. Grand Rapids: Baker Book House, 1954.

Davis, Ken. *Secrets of Dynamic Communication: Preparing & Delivering Powerful Speeches*. Grand Rapids: Zondervan Publishing House, 1991.

Eby, David. *Power Preaching for Church Growth: The Role of Preaching in Growing Churches.* Ross-shire, Great Britain: Christian Focus Publications, 1996.

Erickson, Millard J. and James L. Heflin. *Old Wine in New Wineskins: Doctrinal Preaching in a Changing World.* Grand Rapids: Baker Books, 1997.

Estes, Daniel J. "Audience Analysis and Validity in Application" *Bibliotheca Sacra* vol.150, no. 598 (April 1993): 219–29.

Galli, Mark and Craig Brian Larson. *Preaching That Connects.* Grand Rapids: Zondervan Publishing House, 1994.

Gallup, George, Jr. and D. Michael Lindsay. *Surveying the Religious Landscape: Trends in US Beliefs.* Harrisburg, Pa.: Morehouse Publishing, 1999.

Garrison, Webb B. *The Preacher and His Audience.* Westwood, N.J.: Fleming H. Revell Company, 1954.

Goldsworthy, Graeme. *Preaching the Whole Bible as Christian Scripture: The Application of Biblical Theology to Expository Preaching.* Grand Rapids: Eerdmans Publishing Company, 2000.

Greidanus, Sidney. *The Modern Preacher and the Ancient Text: Interpreting and Preaching Biblical Literature.* Grand Rapids: Eerdmans Publishing Company, 1988.

———. *Preaching Christ from the Old Testament: A Contemporary Hermeneutical Method.* Grand Rapids: Eerdmans Publishing Company, 1999.

Hendricks, Howard, ed. *A Life of Integrity: 13 Outstanding Leaders Raise the Standard for Today's Christian Men.* Sisters, Ore.: Multnomah Press, 1997.

Hirsch, E. D., Jr. *Validity in Interpretation.* New Haven: Yale University Press, 1967.

Hybels, Bill, Stuart Briscoe and Haddon Robinson. *Mastering Contemporary Preaching.* Portland: Multnomah Press, 1989.

Jenson, Richard A. *Thinking in Story: Preaching in a Post-literate Age.* Lima, Ohio: CSS Publishing Co., Inc., 1995.

Jones, D. Martyn-Lloyd. *Preaching and Preachers.* Grand Rapids: Zondervan Publishing House, 1971.

Kemp, Charles F. *The Preaching Pastor.* St. Louis: The Bethany Press, 1966.

Kemper, Deane A. *Effective Preaching: A Manual for Students and Pastors.* Philadelphia: The Westminster Press, 1985.

Klein, William W., Craig L. Blomberg and Robert L. Hubbard, Jr. *Introduction to Biblical Interpretation.* Dallas: Word Publishing, 1993.

Kraft, Charles H. *Communication Theory for Christian Witness.* Nashville: Abingdon Press, 1983.

Larsen, David L. *The Anatomy of Preaching: Identifying the Issues in Preaching Today.* Grand Rapids: Kregel Publications, 1989.

———. *The Company of Preachers: A History of Biblical Preaching from the Old Testament to the Modern Era.* Grand Rapids: Kregel Publications, 1998.

———. *Telling the Old, Old Story.* Wheaton: Crossway, 1995.

Leder, Arie C., ed. *Reading and Hearing the Word From Text to Sermon: Essays in Honor of John H. Stek.* Grand Rapids: Calvin Theological Seminary and CRC Publications, 1998.

Lewis, Ralph L. and Gregg Lewis. *Inductive Preaching: Helping People Listen.* Westchester: Crossway Books, 1983.

Logan, Samuel T., Jr., ed. *The Preacher and Preaching.* Phillipsburg: Presbyterian and Reformed, 1986.

Lowery, Eugene L. *The Sermon: Dancing the Edge of Mystery.* Nashville: Abingdon Press, 1997.

Lucas, Dick, Alec Motyer, J. I. Packer, et al. *Preaching the Living Word: Addresses from the Evangelical Ministry Assembly.* Geanies House, Great Britain: Christian Focus Publications, 1999.

MacArthur, John, Jr., Richard L. Mayhue, et al. *Rediscovering Expository Preaching.* Dallas: Word Publishing, 1992.

MacGregor, William M. *The Making of a Preacher.* Philadelphia: The Westminster Press, 1946.

Marcel, Pierre Ch. 1963. *The Relevance of Preaching.* Translated by Rob Roy McGregor. Grand Rapids: Baker Book House.

Markquart, Edward F. *Quest for Better Preaching: Resources for Renewal in the Pulpit.* Minneapolis: Augsburg Publishing House, 1985.

McCracken, Robert J. *The Making of the Sermon.* New York: Harper & Brothers, 1956.

McDill, Wayne. *The 12 Essential Skills for Great Preaching.* Nashville: Broadman & Holman Publishers, 1994.

McLaughlin, Raymond W. *Communication for the Church.* Grand Rapids: Zondervan Publishing House, 1968.

Miller, Calvin. *Marketplace Preaching: How to Return the Sermon to Where it Belongs.* Grand Rapids: Baker Books, 1995.

Motz, Arnell. "A Workbook on Life-Changing Preaching." D.Min. project, Westminster Theological Seminary, 1991.

Murray, Andrew. *Humility.* New Kensington, Pa.: Whitaker House, 1982.

Nida, Eugene A. *Message and Mission: The Communication of the Christian Faith.* South Pasadena: William Carey Library, 1960.

Nixon, Leroy. *John Calvin, Expository Preacher.* Grand Rapids: Eerdmans Publishing Company, 1950.

O'Day, Gail R. and Thomas G. Long, eds. *Listening to the Word: Studies in Honor of Fred B. Craddock.* Nashville: Abingdon Press, 1993.

Osborn, Grant R. *The Hermeneutical Spiral: A Comprehensive Introduction to Biblical Interpretation.* Downers Grove: InterVarsity Press, 1991.

Perkins, William. *The Art of Prophesying.* Reprint. Edinburgh: Banner of Truth Trust, 1996.

Perry, Lloyd M. *Biblical Preaching for Today's World.* Chicago: Moody Press, 1973.

Piper, John. *The Supremacy of God in Preaching.* Grand Rapids: Baker Books House, 1990.

Porter, Mark. *The Time of Your Life: How to Accomplish All that God Wants You to Do.* Wheaton: Victor Books, 1983.

Postman, Neil. *Amusing Ourselves to Death.* New York: Viking Penguin, Inc., 1985.

Radmacher, Earl D. and Robert D. Preus eds. *Hermeneutics, Inerrancy, and the Bible: Papers from IBCI Summit II.* Grand Rapids: Zondervan Publishing House, 1984.

Richard, P. Ramesh. "Methodological Proposals for Scripture Relevance, Part 3: Application Theory in Relation to the New Testament." *Bibliotheca Sacra* vol. 143, no. 571 (July 1998): 206–18.

Robinson, Haddon, Professor of Preaching, Gordon-Conwell Theological Seminary. Interview by author, 24 July, 1999, San Clemente. Verbal Interview. Pacific Coast Church, San Clemente.

————. *Biblical Preaching: The Development and Delivery of Expository Messages,* second edition. Grand Rapids: Baker Book House, 2001.

————. *Making a Difference in Preaching: Haddon Robinson on Biblical Preaching.* Edited by Scott M. Gibson. Grand Rapids: Baker Books, 1999.

————. "Scripture and Application." *Leadership Journal* 18:4 (Fall 1997): 20–27.

————. "What Authority Do We Have Anymore?" *Leadership Journal* 13:2 (Spring 1992): 24–29.

Ruhia, Klaas. *The Sermon Under Attack.* Exeter, UK: The Paternoster Press, 1983.

Sanders, Oswald. *Spiritual Leadership,* revised edition. Chicago: Moody Press, 1980.

Sangster, William E. *The Craft of Sermon Construction.* Reprint. Grand Rapids: Baker Book House, 1972.

————. *Power in Preaching.* New York: Abingdon Press, 1958.

Schlafer, David J. *Surviving the Sermon: A Guide to Preaching for Those Who Have to Listen.* Boston: Cowley Publications, 1992.

Schuringa, H. David. "Hearing the Word in a Visual Age: A Practical Theological Consideration of Preaching within the Contemporary Urge to Visualization." Ph.D. diss., Kampen: Theologische Universiteit te Kampen.

Shealy, Brian A. "Redrawing the Line Between Hermeneutics and Application" *Master's Seminary Journal* vol. 8, no. 1 (Spring 1997) : 84–107.

Shelly, Marshall, ed. "Integrity" *Leadership Magazine,* vol. 9, no.2 (Spring, 1988).

Springs, Gardiner. *A Plea to Pray for Pastors.* Reprint, Hoschton, Ga.: Shiloh Publications, 2000.

Spurgeon, Charles Haddon. *Lectures to My Students.* Grand Rapids: Zondervan Publishing House, 1975.

Stanley, Charles. *How to Listen to God.* Nashville: Thomas Nelson Publishers, 1985.

Stewart, James S. *Heralds of God: The Warrack Lectures.* London: Hodder & Stougthton, 1946.

Stott, John R. W. *Between Two Worlds: The Art of Preaching in the Twentieth Century.* Grand Rapids: Eerdmans, 1982.

Stowe, Eugene L., et al. *Go... Preach: The Preaching Event in the 90's.* Kansas City: Nazarene Publishing House, 1992.

Stowell, Joseph M. III. *Shepherding the Church Into the 21st Century.* Wheaton: Victor Books, 1994.

Turner, Timothy A. *Preaching to Programmed People: Effective Communication in a Media-Saturated Society.* Grand Rapids: Kregel Resources, 1995.

Warren, Timothy S. "A Paradigm for Preaching" *Bibliotheca Sacra* vol. 148, no. 592 (October 1991) : 464–87.

————. "The Theological Process in Sermon Preparation" *Bibliotheca Sacra* vol. 156, no. 623 (July-September, 1999): 335–55.

Wells, David, F. *No Place for Truth; or, Whatever Happened to Evangelical Theology?* Grand Rapids: Eerdmans, 1994.

Welsh, Clement. *Preaching in a New Key.* Philadelphia: Pilgrim Press, 1974.

Whitney, Donald S. "How to Make Every Sermon Count: Preparing Your Heart and Mind to Hear God's Word," *Discipleship Journal* no.106 (1998): 86–89.

————. *Spiritual Disciplines Within the Church: Participating Fully in the Body of Christ.* Chicago: Moody Press, 1996.

Wiersbe, Warren. *The Integrity Crisis.* Nashville: Thomas Nelson, 1988.

————. *Living with Giants: The Lives of Great Men of Faith.* Grand Rapids: Baker Books, 1993.

————, comp. *The Best of A. W. Tozer.* Grand Rapids: Baker Book House, 1978.

Wiersbe, Warren and David Wiersbe. *The Elements of Preaching: The Art of Biblical Preaching—Clearly and Simply Presented.* Wheaton: Tyndale House Publishers, Inc., 1986.

Willhite, Keith. *Preaching with Relevance Without Dumbing Down.* Grand Rapids: Kregel, 2001.

Willhite, Keith and Scott M. Gibson, eds. *The Big Idea of Biblical Preaching: Connecting the Bible to People.* Grand Rapids: Baker Books, 1998.

Willimon, William H. and Richard Lischer, eds. *Concise Encyclopedia of Preaching.* Louisville: Westminster John Knox Press, 1995.

Zink-Sawyer, Beverly. "The Word Purely Preached and Heard: The Listeners and the Homiletical Endeavor." *Interpretation* 51, no.4 (1997): 342–57.